# PORTFOLIO
## THE TCS STORY & BEYOND

Born in 1944 into a Brahmin family at Nagpur, Subramaniam Ramadorai is a man steeped in simplicity and discipline. Ramadorai retired as CEO & MD of Tata Consultancy Services in 2009, after serving the company for thirty-nine years; he continues to work with TCS in the capacity of Vice-Chairman, and is actively involved as Chairman/Director of various Tata and non-Tata companies and educational institutions. He took on a public service responsibility when the Indian government appointed him as the Advisor to the Prime Minister in the National Skill Development Council with the rank of a Cabinet minister. Ramadorai was awarded the Padma Bhushan, one of India's highest civilian honours, in 2006 and the CBE in 2009. Among his many interests, Ramadorai is passionate about photography and Indian classical music. His wife Mala is an accomplished musician and an active educator; his son Tarun is a Reader in Finance at the Saïd Business School while his daughter-in-law Purnima is a film producer in the UK, where she runs her own production company. Mala and Ram live in Mumbai.

# THE
# TCS
# STORY
# & BEYOND

## S. RAMADORAI

PORTFOLIO
PENGUIN

PORTFOLIO
Published by the Penguin Group
Penguin Books India Pvt. Ltd, 7th Floor, Infinity Tower C, DLF Cyber City, Gurgaon 122 002, Haryana, India
Penguin Group (USA) Inc., 375 Hudson Street, New York, New York 10014, USA
Penguin Group (Canada), 90 Eglinton Avenue East, Suite 700, Toronto, Ontario, M4P 2Y3, Canada
Penguin Books Ltd, 80 Strand, London WC2R 0RL, England
Penguin Ireland, 25 St Stephen's Green, Dublin 2, Ireland (a division of Penguin Books Ltd)
Penguin Group (Australia), 707 Collins Street, Melbourne, Victoria 3008, Australia
Penguin Group (NZ), 67 Apollo Drive, Rosedale, Auckland 0632, New Zealand
Penguin Books (South Africa) (Pty) Ltd, Block D, Rosebank Office Park, 181 Jan Smuts Avenue, Parktown North, Johannesburg 2193, South Africa

Penguin Books Ltd, Registered Offices: 80 Strand, London WC2R 0RL, England

First published in Portfolio by Penguin Books India 2011
This paperback edition published in 2013

ISBN 9780143419662

Typeset in Scala by SÜRYA, New Delhi
Printed at Replika Press Pvt. Ltd, India

A PENGUIN RANDOM HOUSE COMPANY

*For my wife Mala and son Tarun*

# CONTENTS

# AUTHOR'S NOTE

I WAS AN unlikely candidate for writing a book. Had it not been for the encouragement of my wife Mala, my son Tarun and my close colleagues, my attempt to tell the Tata Consultancy Services (TCS) story would not have been possible. Until now TCS's history has appeared piecemeal, an article here and a write up there. Someone needed to put it together. So I decided to take the plunge, a plunge into the unknown—and with great passion, in my characteristic style, to write about TCS's history and my own journey in a way that readers would enjoy.

In the making of the book, several people have played an important role. Paul Taylor of the *Financial Times*, who flew down from the US to spend long periods with me, interviewed several people from both Tata and non-Tata companies and worked labouriously on transcripts with great passion and enthusiasm. Anita Rajan from my team, with her eye for detailing, who worked on the structure, flow and language, added constructive suggestions and criticisms, checking and rechecking information for accuracy and interfacing with the publishers. Without her the book would not have seen the light of the day. Jayant Pendharkar once again proved beyond doubt that he is the one person you can count on always; he recollected incidents which he was witness to and subsequently helped me in validating the facts, sometimes even testing my patience! S. Mahalingam, a colleague and friend, has been a sounding board, whose opinion I greatly value. My office staff member Radhika Shastri dug through the archives of TCS to pull out photographs for the book, and my faithful secretaries Anita Puthran and Sapna

Hemant scheduled interviews and organized logistics for the team to function efficiently.

I would like to thank all the TCSers who provided information for this book and who are too numerous to name individually. And I would particularly like to thank my colleagues outside TCS whose views and inputs I greatly value; amongst them are Prof. Clayton Christensen, Prof. Pankaj Ghemawat, Prof. Nitin Nohria, Y.P. Sahni, Frank Susino, Max Meth, Admiral Cutler Dawson, Amit Chandra, Dominic Price, Hemandra Kothari, Diju Raha, Pierre Page, Jack Schimdt, Dr Arvind Singh, Ranjit Barthakur, Digvijay Singh, V. Thyagarajan, R. Chandrasekhar, F.C. Kohli, Ratan Tata, Dr M.S. Swaminathan, Dr V. Sumantran, C.B. Bhave, Roger Pereira, S.M. Gupta, Joe Ackerman and Ishaat Hussain.

I would like very specially to thank Udayan Mitra, Publisher of Penguin Portfolio, who patiently guided me—a first-time author—through the publishing process. His expert help has been invaluable in keeping the story tuned to the readers' interest and helping us keep to timelines.

Finally, I am indebted to my extended family and my in-laws for providing their insights and always being an encouraging force.

Whatever I have achieved personally and professionally has been possible because of a lot of support that has been there behind the scenes. I thank my wife Mala for patiently bearing with me and my long absences, for helping me think through difficult moments at TCS, for the positive disruptions in my own functioning including the selection of some wonderful people at my office. I am grateful to my son Tarun, for his support, his critical reasoning at all times and for encouraging me to continue to work on things that I am passionate about and things that interest me.

I function best in the company of people who are hungry for knowledge, have high values, are team players and most importantly have a sense of humour that keeps them going under the intense work pressure they are under most of the time. I have been fortunate to work with many such young people who were part of my immediate office.

One of the first to work for me in the capacity of a secretary was Nina Screwvala. Nina was vivacious and full of life. Although she chose to retire after the arrival of her two sons, she could not stay away from TCS for too long. Today Nina is back with TCS and plays a key role as the Global Head of TCS Maitree.

I was then joined by another bright young secretary, Melanie D'lima, an extremely gentle and quiet girl who was exceptionally good at her work, coming up with almost perfect drafts. She had to leave in 2001, when her family immigrated to New Zealand.

At about the time I became CEO, Chandra became my Executive Assistant. Apart from supporting me, he became deeply involved in the business and suffice it to say that he soon went from strength to strength and of course ultimately took over from me as CEO in 2009 when I retired.

Harish Menon was the next to join me as my Executive Assistant. Harish was smart, a perfectionist and adept at handling difficult situations including making long technical notes readable. He went on to join the Corporate Marketing team.

Mala always criticized me for having created a male-dominated office. But all that changed in 2002 when Anita Rajan joined me as the first woman Executive Assistant on my team. She brought in many 'softer' changes in a male-dominated environment, apart from being able to multitask with ease. She learnt to convert my cryptic ideas conveyed with brevity to elegant prose; her impeccable communication skills and eye for detail make her a person I can count on to 'get the job done'. Anita is the seniormost member of my team and has grown over the last nine years to someone I trust immensely.

Swati Shah was inducted to my team a little after Anita joined. Having moved from the Visual Computing group she brought in unique strengths. She worked well with Anita and helped make the CEO's office an open and welcoming place. She started a family in 2007 and soon moved to New York with her husband.

It was then that we brought in the young and efficient Radhika Shastri, who was previously part of the Internal Branding and Communications team at TCS. She now manages my complicated and highly 'dynamic' schedule in addition to communications at my office. A people's person with a flair for languages who is deeply involved in planning and execution, she is a determined young lady who knows what is required and how to get it done efficiently.

Binaisha Kotwal came on board when Radhika went on maternity leave. Her outgoing and bubbly personality and talent for managing events brought in a new flair to the office. A skill that worked especially well for all of us was that she made exotic desserts to beat stress, which she never ate all by herself.

The administrative work is shared between two very dedicated and competent secretaries, Anita Puthran and Sapna Hemant, both of whom have been with me for over ten years, silently working behind the scenes and managing my day-to-day schedules, meetings, calls and basic correspondence. Highly loyal, sincere and hardworking, they have over the years made my life infinitely easier by taking care of the little things that make all the difference.

Mala helped make the disruptive change and now I have a woman-dominated office—but these talented ladies are all a great asset and speak their minds which helps me to function. They never say 'no' to anyone except me and make me work harder than what I already do. One person who has always been a part of my extended team is Jayant. I trust him implicitly. His wonderful sense of humour is well known but behind this persona lies a sharp mind and a rare talent. He has been more than a friend for over forty years and our families enjoy a close bond.

Another person who is no more but whom I would like to acknowledge is Captain George, who headed administration in TCS till his sad demise. He kept the entire TCS machinery working smoothly and was a great personal help.

I would also like to thank the hardware (IDM) engineers who have fixed all technical problems for me and the administrative staff of TCS who have served me so well over the years.

I am immensely grateful to all my personal staff including my drivers Xavier and Surve.

Finally I would like to thank the TCS Board of Directors and the TCS senior management who have worked with me and my colleagues on various Boards I serve, the government officials I have worked with, and our customers who continue to bet on TCS. And I am immensely grateful to all the TCSers who have worked so hard to bring TCS to where it is today; they are the real winners, the real heroes.

The views and opinions expressed in this book are my own. The description of certain events are based on my recollections and on interviews done by my team with me and with several others. The accuracy of dates and events have been verified to the extent possible.

Royalties earned from this book will go to TCS Maitree's skill initiatives for the physically challenged.

# PROLOGUE

WHEN I RETIRED as TCS Chief Executive in 2009, many friends and colleagues asked me what I was going to do with all the spare time on my hands. I smiled and said I was sure I would find things to keep me busy. As it happens, today my family and friends complain that I am busier than ever before.

Retirement has certainly given me the chance to be reflective. As I look back at the long and winding road I have traversed, it gives me a sense of warmth that I have made so many friends and of course a sense of satisfaction for what I, and others in TCS who shared my vision, have achieved.

As a child I was a regular from a typical Tam Bram (Tamilian Brahmin) family. I am told I was naughty and restless, always disappearing out of sight. We were fortunate to live the city life and yet enjoy the simple pleasures in our family village. I loved the outdoors and would have liked to have spent much of my time playing games and flying kites. I enjoyed watching the brightly coloured paper gliders swaying in the breeze at the end of a string. But much to my dislike, there were more serious and scholarly pursuits to follow, for my traditional upbringing placed great importance on education and religion including chanting Sanskrit slokas or prayer verses each morning.

I was born on 6 October 1945 (my parents pretended I was born a year earlier, in 1944, so I could go to school a year earlier since I was too mischievous to be kept at home). I was the fourth of five children, all born in Nagpur, Maharashtra. Although my mother's family came from south India they settled in Nagpur, typical of quite a few South Indians at that time. My maternal grandfather was in the Posts and Telegraph audit department in Bombay and subsequently retired to Nagpur. My paternal grandfather was born in Sengalipuram (Shivakalipuram as it is known in the shastras), a famous village in Tamil Nadu where he was the village accountant (his name, Kannakupillay, in Tamil means 'a person who keeps track of accounts'). He also owned some land which was used primarily for rice farming and which we cultivated until the 1970s.

My paternal grandfather passed away when he was fifty-two or fifty-three and my father was brought up in the nearby town of Kandur by an aunt and uncle who were very strict. After high school my father went to St. Joseph's College in Trichy where he studied mathematics and eventually became a civil servant working for the office of the Accountant General of India. His job meant we moved from city to city every few years. Most of his career he spent in Delhi and subsequently retired from Madras as the Accountant General of Tamil Nadu.

My father was a great teacher. His love for teaching resulted in his taking a particular interest in our academic studies which included teaching us mathematics. I clearly remember his excellent handwriting. He would prepare well for these study sessions and would sit us down and give us mathematical problems to solve. If for some reason we were not able to solve one, he would give us a clip on the ear, which was most painful—but of course we could not protest. Like in all traditional Tamilian households, my father encouraged us to appreciate the arts and music, though he was more a listener than a performer himself.

After Independence in 1947 my father's work took him to Shimla and then to Delhi but I went to live with my paternal grandmother Mathuratammal in Sengalipuram since my mother was not in the best of health. My elder brother Sukumaran went to live with the same aunt and uncle that my father grew up with. The couple had no children of their own and in those days it was common, if you did not have any children, to adopt a child from your father's family. I think I remember my mother saying it was against her wishes, but it was the father's side that always decided these things, so she had to abide by it.

My brother came back to live with us in Delhi after the tenth grade, and I came back to Delhi when I was six or seven and started studying at the Madrasi Education Association Higher Secondary School (now known as Delhi Tamil Education Association School); later I studied at the Sardar Patel Vidyalaya. I don't remember much from my schooldays except for some stray incidents involving a few teachers who were a source of distress. I did not have too many friends in school, but books were my companions. I liked reading because both my mother and father used to read a lot and so we grew up with a lot of Tamil books and scriptures around us (we also studied Tamil as a subject up to the eighth grade and Sanskrit thereafter at school). Often we went to listen to religious discourses at the temple.

Some of my fondest childhood memories are of family trips to Sengalipuram where my grandfather owned land and did some farming, mainly rice. The difficulty of looking after the land and managing the returns led to the family eventually selling the land off in the 1970s.

As children we used to visit our village every year for a month or two. The entire family including our cousins would travel to the village. Even now I have very pleasant memories of these family gatherings, of experiencing first-hand the hard but gratifying life of farming and agriculture, of sowing grains, tending to them and reaping the produce. It gave me an appreciation of nature, of doing things yourself and seeing the results.

Sengalipuram village is where great saints like Sengalipuram Muthanna and Sri Anantharama Deekshithar, as well as the Tamil writer Thiru, were born. The people from this village are believed to have descended from the Aryan Brahmins who moved from central India (Madhya Bharat). At that time Sengalipuram was known because of our 'dikshadhar' or village priest who was very famous for his religious discourses on Indian mythology, the *Ramayana* and the *Mahabharata*. As children we used to play around the temple and listen to these discourses at the same time. Sometimes the priest and his entourage would come and stay with us in Delhi, so the house was often full of religious talk and seemed to revolve around things spiritual.

In Sengalipuram we used to go to the riverside to bathe but we were not supposed to take a dip in the river, so sometimes we would just sit on the banks and splash our legs in the water, which annoyed the other people there. They called us the 'town children' and would snigger to each other saying, 'The city crowd has come now.'

We played simple rustic games, one of which was a game called pallankuzhi, played with a wooden board and tamarind seeds. We could never defeat the village kids at this game as it called for a lot of dexterity of the fingers; they were better practiced at it and very quick too, so that was another reason for them to tease us city children. Back in Delhi I played cricket or hockey on most evenings after school with my brothers, who claim that I often insisted on being the captain!

Like most men of his generation, my father demanded—and was given—a lot of respect by his family. He was a strict disciplinarian and I was often in trouble at home because of my naughty ways. For him any activity other than studies was unacceptable. He wasn't interested in the least if we were good in sports or extra-curricular activities; all that mattered to him was being extremely good at mathematics or science.

Our misdeeds while he was at work usually became known to him once he reached home from office, and our worst fears would be realized then. Our offences would be rewarded with a spanking and in some extreme cases a cane would suddenly appear and be applied vigorously.

When my cousins came over we were at our mischievous best; egged on by each other we tested how far we could throw stones and the street lights seemed like attractive targets. We must have had a good aim because the stones we threw with our catapults hit their targets often and we broke several street lights. On one occasion I was playing with my cousin in the street and there was a brand new car parked there; for some reason we decided it would be fun to make a small scratch on its shiny new body. My father was very angry when he found out about this. He ran his fingernail sharply across my cheek; when I yelled in pain he told me that's what the car would have felt when it was scratched by me. I learned my lesson very quickly! It was painful but effective.

But my father found it harder to be so strict with my sisters and we soon found we could exploit this. Sometimes we children wanted to go to the movies, but we knew if my brothers or I asked to go my father would simply say 'no' and tell us we had to study. So instead we used to send our sisters on our behalf to ask his permission. He would say, 'This is the last time, do not ask me again,' but he would let us go.

I am not really sure why I was always getting into trouble, but I think it was because I was restless and always had a lot of energy. That high energy has lasted through the years. I still find it difficult to sit still. My mother-in-law observes that the only time she has ever seen me sit still for more than ten minutes at a time are at a music performance or when I am glued to a cricket match on television.

Probably because I was the most hyperactive of the lot I was spanked by my father the most. But I never resented him for that, or lost any respect for him as a person. At the back of my mind I probably felt I had asked for some of it! As you grow up and move through your career you change, you mellow and become more tolerant. As a father myself, I do not remember spanking my son, nor was I strict. I was a vastly different parent from what my father was. Today as I actively engage with young professionals I am more understanding of the impulsiveness and immaturity and give them the extra leeway for their behaviour.

My father always wanted one of his children to become a doctor and for some reason I was singled out to fulfil this dream. I was put in a biology class but I was not very good at laboratory work— my mother used to complain that my shoes and lab coat were full of holes as a result of my spilling acid on them during chemistry lab classes. Any remaining hopes that I would become a doctor were dashed after I was asked to dissect a frog in class. The experience, particularly the smell of chloroform, made me feel sick—and I summoned up all my courage and told my father that medicine was not for me.

Generally I didn't find school very interesting as a child, but I did have several hobbies including collecting stamps and had built up a big collection which unfortunately was lost during one of the family moves.

When I was older I learned to play bridge which I found both interesting and challenging. I also took up photography and processed my own films—I still always travel with a camera. Of course advances in digital cameras ensured that one could not potter around in the darkroom any more.

After finishing high school, I went to Deshbandhu College to do a pre-university course in 1961–62. While I was there, I finally began to take academics seriously, although I still wasn't sure at that stage exactly what I wanted to do. I studied physics, chemistry and mathematics and came in the top two or three positions in the class. That was a turning point for me and from then on I never looked back.

I went to Hans Raj College in Delhi to study for my BSc degree in physics and mathematics. I stayed in the hostel, which still looks the same today; even my room on the ground floor still exists. I graduated from there in 1965 and then attended the Indian Institute of Science (IISc) in Bangalore for a degree in electronics and telecommunications.

My closest friends during this time tended to be hostel roommates rather than my own classmates. I was extremely shy and found it easier to be part of a crowd outside the classroom. In class I was quite timid, constantly scared of the teacher picking on me to ask a question to which I may not know the answer. Even if I knew the answer I did not like being singled out.

That shyness has stayed with me, but over the years, I have become better at hiding it. As I advanced in TCS, work forced me towards more interactions. People would approach me, rather than me having to approach them. I am comfortable with people today— I have come a long long way from those early days.

After Hans Raj College and the IISc, from where I graduated in 1968, I worked at the Physical Research Laboratories (PRL) in Ahmedabad which was established by the great science technocrat Dr Vikram Sarabhai, the father of the Indian space research programme. There I met some of the promising scientists of India. The experience helped me develop a scientific temperament and curiosity and understand the importance of good work ethics. I then decided that I needed to do a doctorate, so I applied and was accepted at the University of California at Los Angeles (UCLA) with a full scholarship to study computer science at the Master's level.

I remember that my mother was very concerned when I told her I was going to the US. Right up to the time we got to the airport she was worried that I would lose my passport and other documents. I think she was also worried that, like many other Indian graduates who went off to the US to continue their studies, I would not come back.

The journey to the US in 1969 was long—from Bombay I flew to Calcutta, and from there to Bangkok, Manila, Saigon, Tokyo, Honolulu and finally Los Angeles—over forty hours of travel in all. At the end of it, all I wanted to do in the so-called land of dreams was to get myself a glass of water, some good food and some sleep.

America then was something of a culture shock for a country bumpkin like me; every day was a learning experience. But my curiosity overcame any concerns I had at the time about venturing into a strange new environment. I wasn't scared even though I was the first from my family to go to America. Rather I was worried about not living up to my family's expectations.

It was a daring thing to do, but the excitement of the challenge overshadowed any apprehension that I may have felt. UCLA certainly broadened my horizons and made be more self-reliant. At college in Los Angeles I enjoyed the classes, because you could choose what courses to take and work at your own pace. I had a job as a lab technician twenty hours a week on campus to earn money. Although my tuition was covered by a scholarship, I did not want to be dependent on my parents to pay for my lodging. I shared an apartment with K.L. Prakash, a student from Bangalore. We became very close since we had similar tastes—we would listen to Indian music on tapes and cook vegetarian Indian food. We continue to be close friends to this day and our families are good friends as well. There were three other Indian students in the apartment next door and out of us all, I was the only one to come back to India soon after I finished my studies.

After graduating from UCLA I started working for National Cash Register (NCR) in Hawthorne, a suburb of Los Angeles, and was earning $12,000 a year—very good money for a young computer science graduate. But a combination of factors was about to draw me back to India. By this time my parents were living in Madras and clinched the deal when they told me they had found a pretty Madras girl for me—even though my mother did insist that the final choice should be mine.

Mahalaxmi (Mala for short) had been born and brought up in south India. We married when she was nineteen and I twenty-six. She was a little younger than most brides, but her father was very traditional and agreed to the arrangement; in those days girls were sometimes married at an even younger age.

Like most marriages involving South Indian Brahmin families, the developments were carefully choreographed. Before we met, Mala's mother Ambujam, who is actually a very broad-minded person, compiled a full dossier on me to make sure I was suitable. She did background checks and took references from my friends who were living with me in America to find out what kind of a person I was. It was like an FBI investigation but it was necessary because by tradition, the bride would only meet a potential husband once, before having to decide.

The one thing Mala's mother was not able to find out was my height. She was concerned about how tall I was because Mala is quite tall for an Indian woman. So the first thing she asked me when we met was, 'How tall are you?' She seemed satisfied with my reply.

Anyway, I came back from the US on a visit and we had a kind of a 'seeing ceremony' with both families present. Mala and I were not allowed to talk to each other and we could only look at each other with shy sidelong glances.

My father interviewed Mala because, although he knew the answers to his questions, he wanted to know how well-spoken she was. He also asked Mala to sing but she initially refused to sing alone. She said she was 'not going to put on a show for me', but her aunt said she would sing with her, so she eventually agreed.

Mala had been brought up in the South where it was traditional for girls to be exposed from an early age to dance and music. She had been taught dance for three years before her teacher told her parents, 'She can be lazy but she knows all the songs and sings everything, so why don't you teach her music instead?' So from the age of eight she had singing lessons two or three times a week and began learning classical Carnatic music. Carnatic songs are mostly prayers so at our first meeting she sang the first raga-based song she had learned: *Om sharvana bhava*, which has remained a favourite of mine ever since. It is, if you like, 'our song'.

Later I discovered that long before I first met Mala, her mother had had a dream about a boy for Mala who liked pastel-coloured shirts, particularly light green ones. In her dream it was the Diwali festival and the boy was sitting in the courtyard of her house with a light green shirt on. Ambujam told Mala when she woke up that the man she dreamt of had a long nose and was wearing spectacles and that although she had been asking for a person much taller than her (Mala), he was not too tall. As she recounted her dream, Mala's father, who was an artist, made an impromptu sketch of the man.

Well, it so happened that when I arrived for the meeting with the family I was wearing a shirt that wasn't green by any stretch of the imagination. But I did buy a light green shirt for the first Diwali after we were married, and Mala's father's sketch looked quite a bit like me. It was a strange coincidence.

Mala could of course have turned me down if she had taken a violent dislike to me. In fact before the meeting she had asked her mother what would happen if she did not like me. Her mother had told her not to worry about it—the family would simply have made up a plausible excuse about some 'superstitions'. For example, they might have said something untoward had happened, so they didn't think they should go ahead.

But anyway, after the first meeting my family was quite keen on the match and so when we did not hear anything from Mala's family we approached her granduncle to ask what had happened. It turned out that Mala was insistent that I should come back from the US and take up a job in India before she agreed to the wedding.

I think she was worried I might have a girlfriend or wife in the US that no one knew about. At the time there had been a series of incidents like this where boys were scared to tell their families that they had got married while in America.

She joked later that TCS was my first marriage, so in a way I was married before anyway!

Although the family meeting had gone well, she also had some other concerns and was not immediately convinced that I was the right person. Her family members were quite liberal—her mother was a lawyer and her father an artist and an entrepreneur—and she was worried that I was too conservative and perhaps a bit orthodox.

Anyhow I decided to accept a job offer from TCS in part because I really wanted to contribute something to India and working with the Tata Group appealed very much to me.

When I got back to India I decided to write to Mala. The letter arrived while she was staying with her aunt for a couple of days in Madras. Mala's mother phoned her and said, 'You know what, you've got a letter and I think it's from him.'

At the time it was rather unusual to send letters to a prospective bride, but I think Mala liked the letters. We corresponded for some time and finally she agreed to marry me. It was a very traditional kind of wedding, a very big glittering ceremony which the Governor of Tamil Nadu attended.

Actually I felt quite uncomfortable at my wedding because Mala's aunts and cousin sisters were loud and boisterous—there was much laughter and bantering when they were around. I was not used to such informality and felt quite out of place.

Mala had grown up in a big house with a retinue of servants and chauffeur-driven cars and I don't think it ever occurred to her that we would be starting our married life without such creature comforts. When we got back to Bombay, we found a small one-bedroom apartment. It was nice, but I think for Mala it was very small and rather modest compared to what she was used to.

We didn't have any furniture so for our wedding present, some of the TCS staff got together and gave us a dining table and chairs. We didn't have anything else, just a dining table and chairs. We didn't even have a bed.

Initially of course there were a lot of adjustments we had to make because Mala didn't know how to cook or run a household, something which she says she had to learn. We didn't have a vehicle either, so for the first time in her life Mala had to travel by public transport to visit her grandparents.

I spent a lot of time at work, sometimes sleeping on the couch in the office at the end of a long day, so my wife had to find things to do to occupy herself. I think the only holiday I took was when Mala was pregnant two years after we got married and she insisted I take some time off.

She told me, 'I'm not going to have the baby just by myself, you have to be there and you'll have to stay from the time I have the baby for at least a month.' That was the only time I took a one-month-long holiday in my life.

Family has always been very important to me but inevitably TCS took up much of my time and I think my wife sacrificed a lot, especially in the early days of our marriage and after our son Tarun was born. Mala's younger sister, Padma, was just two years old when we got married, so she was the other child around. I would buy her all the things she wanted: cherries, a pink raincoat and a huge doll from Italy. On one occasion I remember showing her a big poster of computer artwork—it was a horse's head made up of zeroes and ones printed out on a dot matrix computer. I told her, 'Look, the machine made this.' I think she was quite fascinated. Padma was four when Tarun was born so for him it was like having an older sister. She came to stay with us for three months when we lived in New York and she remembers how fascinated she was by New York, particularly the Manhattan skyline. Today Padma is an author with several published books to her name and lives in the US.

New York was a very challenging experience for both Mala and me, but it was also quite different from working in Bombay. Mala has always described me as being 'not just passionate about work, but really devoted to it'. I used to spend so many hours at work in our Bombay offices that sometimes Mala would bring Tarun to the office in the evening to wait for me. The tenth floor of the Air-India building, where TCS was headquartered at the time, was completely empty except for a big computer in one corner, so there was a huge empty space for Tarun to run around in while they waited for me. If it got too late Mala used to put two chairs together to make a makeshift bed and Tarun would sleep on it. My being at work must have played on Tarun's mind for on one occasion when he was still a child, he confronted my boss Kohli and asked him why he made me work so hard.

I also used to travel a lot at that time and would often spend three months in the US and then one month back in India. We moved to New York in 1979 and lived in a small rented apartment in Queens which, at the time, wasn't the best neighbourhood. On one occasion when Tarun was very ill and at home with Mala she became very frightened when someone tried to break into our apartment. I think incidents like this and her frustration with being stuck at home while I was at work were some of the reasons why she later urged me to set up the Maitree group for employee engagement within TCS.

Mala didn't want to send Tarun to the local public school which was quite rough, so he went to a Catholic school. But Tarun was a very active and impatient child and the nuns were not very forgiving. He could grasp things very quickly and so he used to be very disruptive in the class; he always wanted to give all the answers. I have always been an early riser and after we returned to India, I used to trick Tarun into waking up early in the morning so we could spend some time together before I went to work and he went to school. In the late 1980s we felt that Tarun was beginning to get disinterested in mathematics. We reached out for help to Mala's uncle Dr Naranan who was a scientist at Mumbai's Tata Institute of Fundamental Research. Dr Naranan's enthusiasm proved infectious and Tarun soon began to appreciate science and in particular mathematics. In many ways he was Tarun's mentor and guide. He later shared that although he had no experience in tutoring high school students, he essentially taught Tarun to systematically follow the rules of algebra and proceed step by step in solving problems; but most of the time, he spent talking to Tarun about the pleasures of science—physics, astronomy and mathematics and some of their beautiful discoveries

After he finished his schooling, Tarun did not want to become an engineer or a doctor and applied to Williams College in Massachusetts for a liberal arts degree. Mala was upset because he was just seventeen years old and it meant he would be leaving home for the first time, but I thought that it was the right thing for him to do and would help him find his own way in the world. Tarun went on to study at Oxford and Harvard and chose the field of Business Economics, in which he earned a PhD. Both Mala and I are proud that our son opted to be an 'academic' and I would attribute Tarun's choice to the influences of both Mala and Dr Naranan.

I have become a firm believer that most people rise to new challenges. This was something I learned from Kohli, my mentor. He challenged me throughout my years with him by presenting me with new opportunities.

I had the opportunity to go to the Massachusetts Institute of Technology (MIT) in 1993 to do a senior management course that changed my perspective radically. MIT introduced me to the concept of case studies and I found the mixture of classwork, group work and class visits including a trip to Washington—during the Clinton healthcare debate—exhilarating.

MIT reinforced my belief in the importance of bringing multiple disciplines to bear in order to solve a problem. For example, an appreciation of the poetry of the Bhagavad Gita can illuminate other aspects of one's life. Similarly, there can be interactions between IT and vastly different disciplines, say life sciences or literature. Exposure to multiple disciplines broadens one's outlook and reduces the risk of developing tunnel vision.

At MIT I struck new friendships with people from different walks of life including US Vice Admiral Cutler Dawson and Kurt Woetzel, a Munich-based banker. Admiral Dawson fuelled a new interest of mine in large ships.

After MIT I approached things in TCS differently. I became convinced that in order to succeed, TCS needed to expand and become a truly global company that embraced a multidisciplinary approach towards problem solving and was willing to take risks in order to reap bigger rewards. The visit to MIT reinforced my belief that information technology was going to have a huge impact on almost all aspects of our lives, and that innovation was a key driver of change.

MIT also boosted my confidence that I could organize events and make a difference. On the last day of the nine-week MIT course, the course participants put on a show highlighting some aspect of their home countries. I organized a Bharatanatyam dance performance and managed to invite a famous Indian classical dancer to come to MIT and perform.

Symbolic perhaps of the personality change I felt, I wore a churidar pyjama for the first time instead of the white shirt that I usually wore. Until then, beige was probably the brightest colour I had ever worn because of my self-consciousness.

To my surprise, when I got back to India and subsequently wore coloured shirts, people said they looked good on me. People noticed the change and one day when I wore an orange shirt, even Kohli's wife said she wished her husband would be more bold.

Of course my family has had a tremendous influence on my life. I have always had a relatively modest lifestyle unaffected by the trappings of wealth and success. But among the fine things Tarun has introduced me to are ties and today I have a fine collection acquired from all over the world.

Mala meanwhile has been my best friend, confidante and trusted adviser, and has helped enrich my life in many ways. For example, she was always an avid reader and encouraged me to read more. Now she jokes that I read more than her. Typically I will have two or more books 'on the go' at the same time. I mostly read business books, biographies and books on science.

Mala also fuelled my existing interest in classical Indian music which is what I now listen to, especially when I am being driven to and from meetings. Unfortunately my parents thought it was more important for boys to concentrate on studies rather than music, so while my sisters were trained in music by a teacher, I was not. Nevertheless I grew up with music around me and learned to identify ragas. Indian music became especially important to me when I went to college in the US because it provided me with memories of home and was a common interest I shared with my friends. We used to listen to tapes of Indian music all the time.

Most importantly perhaps, Mala has always been a sounding board for me when I faced problems that I needed to talk through with someone. I found her liberal arts background complementary to my background in science and engineering in formulating a more comprehensive perspective on the world at large. My mother-in-law tells me that my influence and academic bent of mind made Mala more serious about pursuing her studies and music; she did in fact do several postgraduate courses after marriage. As a teacher, Mala is a very good observer and often picks up on things I might have missed. She is a good listener too. Even though she is also a private person, she has helped me become less shy. I think the natural instinct for both of us at a party is to hang around at the back. But she has encouraged me to be more outgoing and talk to people.

I learned from her to always put myself in the other person's shoes. If I write a letter, I now consider how the recipient will read it. I learned that if I was angry with somebody, the last thing I should do is to shoot off an e-mail. If a problem was really bothering me I should 'park' the problem and sleep over it. Often I found that when I got up at 2 a.m. I would come up with a good solution.

Mala also taught me that the best way to help others is to give them room to say what it is that you can help them with. Only then can you provide effective assistance.

Mala understands me better than anyone else. She knows that there are very, very few things that make me angry and that except for one or two notable occasions, I am generally level-headed and do not lose my temper. In fact most people have never heard me raise my voice or even get into an argument. I am not confrontational, but nevertheless people say I usually get my way. I would rather persuade people to my point of view and show them the way I would like something to be done than get into a verbal battle.

I consider myself a patriot and get upset if India is criticized unreasonably, perhaps because in many ways I have been a cultural ambassador for the country since I was first posted to the US and had to introduce an often sceptical audience to the capabilities of my country. Conversely, while religion is important to me, I have deliberately steered away from trying to impose my beliefs on anyone else, including my son.

One of the two occasions when Mala has seen me lose my temper was when someone I knew quite well spoke ill of TCS. Mala says I tend to take such criticism personally, perhaps because TCS has been my life and many of the initiatives I put in place have now become reality.

The other occasion was when I was in a car on the Mumbai–Pune expressway with Mala and Tarun and a drunk truck driver with a load of metal rods rammed into the back of our car, sending some of the rods crashing through the back window. It was extremely dangerous and we were lucky that no one was injured. I jumped out of the car and was so angry that although the truck driver was a big chap, I grabbed him by the collar, pulled him out of the cab and smacked him around a couple of times.

Actually my own driving skills—or the lack of them—has become something of a joke with my family and friends. When we lived in New York, Mala became so concerned about my erratic driving that she wisely decided to get a US driving licence and take over the wheel. When we came back to India it was a similar story, so after some close escapes Mala and my friend Jayant plotted that I was not to drive and that Jayant would drive me to office during the week and on the weekends Mala would take over. Fortunately when I became CEO in 1996 I was entitled to a chauffeur-driven car and everyone could breathe more easily.

Jayant has been more than a friend. He was always much more outgoing and communicative than me and being with him taught me how to diffuse difficult or uncomfortable situations with clients and others using humour.

I learned the importance of time management from Nani Palkhivala. While I was general manager he used to come to the US for one week a year and pack in an enormous number of customer visits into that time. I adopted his policy of replying to any memos he received within twenty-four hours. As chief executive, I made a point of getting up each morning at 4 a.m. or 5 a.m. to reply to e-mails I had received, something that always surprised colleagues, particularly those on the opposite side of the world.

Overall, it has been a remarkable journey for me thus far—a journey that I hope you will enjoy reading about in the pages that follow.

But first I would like to thank some very special people whose influences have inspired, challenged and encouraged me to reach this stage in my life.

I'd like to thank my mentor F.C. Kohli for challenging me and trusting me to deliver; Max Meth and Frank Susino, my first US clients, for placing implicit trust in me; Nani Palkhivala, an inspiring role model from whom I learnt time management and precision; Naval Mody, my mentor in the US, who had a wonderful sense of humour; D.N. Maluste, a phenomenal coach who helped me understand government functioning and dealings; and Ratan Tata who always helped focus on the big picture and big dreams even if it meant taking risks.

I would also like to thank my wonderful friends: Ranjana and Jayant, a trusted friend who has always been there to help whenever I have needed it (he's never managed to get me to play tennis though); and Rama and Maha, whose entire family I know so well; and my office colleagues who have provided their unstinting support to me always.

And above all my wife and son who have given up much so that I could give to TCS, my parents and my in-laws and the extended families. My son Tarun's marriage to Purnima has brought a whole new dimension to our lives; they are a great source of joy to both Mala and me.

By the way, now that I am older and wiser I know the hidden message my kite had for me. I have learned never to be afraid of opposition, by keeping in mind that a kite rises *against*, and not *with* the wind.

# 1

# AN AUDACIOUS VISION
## 'TOP 10 BY 2010'

AS A YOUNG boy I was fascinated by kites. Back in my village, I loved to see the colourful flying objects soar high up in the air until they were barely a speck in the sky. Spool in hand, a pull here and a tug there, a release of string and they would go even higher if you had the skill to play the wind and ride the stills. You had to be wary in this battle for the skies, for other kites could slyly cut the string sending your kite floating away wherever the breeze took it. Several decades later I still recall the thrill and excitement of those moments.

For some reason my thoughts went back to the soaring kites when I looked up at the clear sky that cool February morning in Bangalore, as I made my way through the manicured lawns of the Indian Institute of Science (IISc), Bangalore and towards the conference room where I had summoned a meeting of the top forty managers of team TCS.

The scene that greeted me only firmed my own resolve further. This was my team, the team that I must inspire to seek greater heights, ride the breeze blowing our way, and fly high and higher still, just like the kites did. I was intensely aware that a lot depended on me, the buck stopped with me now. The thought quickly brought me back to the reality in the room.

The cold February air had done little to keep the senior team from warming up to each other. The swing in their gait, the relaxed air and the back-slapping camaraderie signalled the mood: upbeat and positive. Why shouldn't they be? The year was 1998, business was good and TCS was growing quickly. The future looked bright.

But it soon became apparent to most of them that I had called the meeting not to celebrate the achievements of TCS, important though they were, but as a kind of corporate reality check for my colleagues.

The choice of Bangalore, the South Indian city that is most closely identified with the astonishing growth of the Indian IT industry, was no accident. Tata Consultancy Services Limited (TCS) is headquartered in Mumbai, the business capital of India and the home of the Tata family to whose vision TCS owes its existence. However, prohibitive real estate costs drove many of TCS's early competitors to base themselves in Bangalore.

Equally significantly, the IISc was conceived by the founder of the Tata Group, Jamsetji Nusserwanji Tata, who sought to create an institution which would conduct advanced research in multidisciplinary areas—a mission that TCS has also embraced.

In the late 1990s the Y2K software 'bug' was shining an international spotlight on Indian software companies. TCS was making good profits for our corporate parent, Tata Sons, but as a series of PowerPoint slides demonstrated, we were still a minnow in an industry dominated by giants like International Business Machines (IBM), Accenture and EDS (now part of Hewlett-Packard). Also, while we were focused on managing growth internally, younger competitors had emerged and by 1999, it was impossible to ignore the growing competition any longer.

I felt it was time to pause and take stock. Bangalore and the Institute were a natural for a meeting designed to both reinforce our achievements and point up the challenges ahead.

I had become TCS's Chief Executive two years earlier when I took over from my predecessor, Faqir Chand Kohli, often called the architect of India's IT industry. The Bangalore summit highlighted the radical difference in management styles between myself and Kohli, differences that were to become even more apparent in 2000 when Kohli stepped down as Deputy Chairman.

Whereas Kohli often appeared rather autocratic to those around him, I wanted to build a management culture of inclusion, one that embraced discussion and nurtured new ideas. Instead of TCS being driven by one individual, I wanted to build a team atmosphere at the helm and I needed a core group of trusted senior executives around me who would help me map out the future strategy for TCS, and then execute that strategy.

This team was made up of hardcore operational personnel. This was entirely intentional; many of them had been with TCS since its inception and understood it well. It was apparent to me that TCS could no longer function as a start-up where everyone knew everyone else and people handled multiple functions. Running a company that employs tens or even hundreds of thousands of people had to be differently carved.

We were by then successfully establishing our credibility in the western markets we wanted to operate in. Alongside finding clients in the West, we had begun to construct the ecosystem that was needed for this fledgling industry to survive, supporting the Indian Institutes of Technology (IITs) to teach more computer science classes, working with engineering schools to develop curricula, importing computers to build technology skills and sending people abroad to gain experience. The foundations were being laid. The cumulative passion, drive and risk-taking ability of many excellent individuals over the years was helping TCS rise to its feet.

For anyone who doubted our grand vision as being too ambitious, peeping into the future as we stood at the brink of the twentieth century was enough to convince them of the potential opportunities waiting to be taken up. If the first wave was one of building credibility, the second wave would surely be about achieving scale—expanding into new geographies and investing in internal capacity- and capability-building.

That was what we were at the IISc to discuss, to brainstorm on the TCS we wanted to build for the future.

How do you scale up even as you are growing so fast? To reach our full potential we needed to restructure the company quickly, put in place the systems and protocols that would ensure that our internal operations supported our business model and did not hinder our efforts to serve our customers better. We desperately needed to automate our internal systems and I needed a system—

a management dashboard if you will—that would provide me with real-time information about the operations and performance of the company. We also needed to rebrand the company, but that would come later.

The Bangalore management meeting marked the start of a strategic rethink for TCS that would eventually crystallize into a bold new mission statement in 2003 and pave the way for the company to go public in a 2004 Initial Public Offering (IPO) that was the biggest on record in India at the time.

In the wake of the Bangalore summit, I set up a corporate 'think tank' comprising six or seven people. We used to meet at least once a week at my home (in Worli Seaface), often on a Saturday or Sunday morning, or in the evenings. That is where we did most of our thinking—friends sitting round discussing the world in an informal atmosphere.

The home setting was important because I wanted ideas to be shared openly, with no hierarchy in place, no officious strings attached, just a simple, warm, family atmosphere. The aroma of South Indian filter coffee would fill the air and Mala, my wife, would often join in serving fruits or South Indian sweets. Sometimes she would come up with her own creative suggestions. Some of the best ideas came out of these free-for-all discussions which also helped forge the collegiate management style that I was seeking and which was to become a hallmark of TCS.

The only outsider privy to these discussions was Pankaj Ghemawat, a Harvard Business School professor, who we took on as our adviser on strategic planning. I chose him because I wanted a completely new insight into strategy-making, a view from the outside.

In these think tank sessions I kept pushing everyone to think about what we needed to do next to move the company forward. I wanted to set a new vision, a goal which would rally the TCS workforce towards doing something audacious, something big.

So we scanned the numbers, the competition, the market and the opportunity. We realized that we were in an industry where the technology spend was continuously growing, but the segment of that spending which we could address was very limited.

If we were to achieve my vision of transforming TCS from a relatively small IT service business into a global giant and continue our growth trajectory, we not only had to capture more market share, but also expand the services we offered and therefore our market.

In 2003 about 90 per cent of our revenues were derived from IT services. So we rolled up our sleeves and began with what we had. On a PowerPoint slide one of us drew a single bubble and added the text 'IT Solutions and Services'. How do we expand the market, we asked ourselves. Which are the other areas where we might be doing work on a smaller scale today but which had good market potential? Some collective crystal gazing and animated discussions later, we were convinced of the potential in developing a suite of related businesses alongside IT services. Five more bubbles followed on the PowerPoint slide: Global Consulting, Engineering and Industrial Services, Asset-based Offerings, Infrastructure Services and IT-enabled Services (or BPO).

There we were with six neat bubbles on a PowerPoint slide. We declared we would grow each of these into a $1 billion plus business.

Since Pankaj was based in Boston, we held one of the early think tank sessions at the Charles Hotel there. Pankaj had been looking at the economics of the industry and had what he describes as his 'Eureka moment'. He had worked out that even though revenue per employee was substantially higher at our western competitors, the profit per employee at TCS was comparable or higher than that of its rivals. The core business of TCS was, he said, 'a thing of beauty and not the kind of thing that you find anywhere else'.

It was an important message because in the rush to redefine our strategy, it would have been easy to overlook the value we were creating with our existing business model.

We also looked closely at the number of global Fortune 2000 customers we had, but we could not construct a consistent matrix for this because our competitors did not generally publish details of their customers. Overall, the figures we looked at really just highlighted the fragmented nature of the industry.

One of our first ideas was that we should aim to do Rs 2,000 crore (about $430 million) in revenues by 2000 because it was achievable and had a nice rhyming kind of sound to it. But we soon decided that this was too limited a target.

We also looked at the turnover numbers implied by a McKinsey study of the Indian IT sector published that year. In 1998 our revenues were about $290 million and represented about 12 per cent of the Indian industry. The McKinsey study forecast that the Indian industry would reach $50 billion by 2008. Based on our market share, the forecast implied that TCS would have revenues in the range of $6 billion or $7 billion by 2008 and perhaps $10 billion by the end of the decade.

While benchmarking ourselves against other companies, we discovered something rather interesting. Revenue and profit were the most commonly used parameters but we decided to do it differently. We looked at other companies in the sector from multiple parameters, in terms of revenue and profits, market capitalization, number of employees, revenue per customer, and profit per customer. We did not worry about market cap at that time because we were not listed. But ultimately we decided that rather than target a specific metric, we should just aim for a global position which mattered.

I am not sure exactly who actually came up with the words (everyone claims credit), but what emerged was a new rallying point for the company: we would aim to become a top ten IT software and services company by 2010.

If we had set a qualitative vision, for example to be the best in the industry, it would have been very difficult and hard to sell. But 'Top 10 by 2010' was simple and clear and very catchy. The more we looked at it, the more we liked the sound of it.

This simple message would be the driving force behind TCS and the motivator for each of its employees. While we embraced this vision internally, we had not yet announced it publicly. But the media had got wind of it and we got our first taste of the ways of journalists and their love for headlines (by then we were public). They chose to interpret '10 x 10' as $10 billion by 2010, an inaccuracy that we had to quickly correct.

With a new vision for the company, the sense of unrest I had felt in Bangalore had given way to a clear path ahead. We had something very focused to work towards. We decided to push this simple message and keep aligning people through consistent communication so that everybody started working towards the same goal. The commonality of purpose, commonality of understanding and directional setting was now clear.

In reality, the path to achieve this goal was not yet thought of. The feeling was: let's set ourselves a lofty goal and just go after it. Our collective confidence in our abilities would help us design the steps to get there. Of course we ran the risk of failing, for we had set ourselves a clear deadline, failing which 'Top 10 by 2010' would be purely a dream.

The magnitude of the challenge stood before us as we mobilized forces and helped them understand what they needed to do in their own teams to make this happen. We created presentations because we were still a relatively small company; we went around doing town hall meetings. Every part of the organization started out by deciding what 'Top 10' meant to them; picking those things first would make sense.

In fact the 'open houses' we held to discuss the slogan helped us define it. We wanted people to contribute by articulating what this meant to them, to feel a sense of ownership, to understand their individual role in the grand vision. Among the questions that were asked repeatedly in open houses by the employees were: What is the applicability of 'Top 10 by 2010' to me? What does it mean to me as an individual and what is my contribution to align to this as an individual or as a business unit? The meetings helped us define four key 'Top 10 by 2010' parameters: revenue, profitability, number of people, and market capitalization as proxies for our success in meeting our goals.

This in turn paved the way for perhaps the most dynamic period in TCS's history. In 2003 we had become India's first $1 billion-a-year IT services company. The 'Top 10 by 2010' vision we set for ourselves energized all of us to set in motion a series of landmark changes and the launching of new initiatives to build excellence in quality, delivery and collaboration.

Only six years later, in 2009, we had grown to $6 billion and had achieved our target of becoming a Top 10 player in the global IT software and services industry. We had done it and done it in style, a year ahead of what we had allowed ourselves, and for me personally, well before my retirement as CEO of TCS.

We had ridden the wave of 'establishing credibility', pulled up the gears to ride the wave of 'establishing scale' and moved confidently to face the next wave of 'establishing leadership'. It had been an exciting and incredible journey.

This is the story of the birth of IT software and services in India, the birth of TCS, the shaky start, the struggle and the joy of it all. In many ways it is the story of my journey too, the people I have met, the friends I have made, but most importantly my experiences at the helm of the company, as my team and I aspired to turn TCS into the global IT software and services giant it is today, a company that is confident of pushing the envelop further and further for both the Indian and global industry.

# 2

# 1968–96: BUILDING TCS

## THE EARLY DAYS

THE 1960S WERE a turbulent time for India: food shortages, trade deficits and socialist government controls on the economy coupled with two wars, one with China in 1962 and the other with Pakistan in 1965, sapped national resources.

The economy grew at an average rate of about 3.1 per cent a year in constant prices, or at an annual rate of 1.0 per cent per capita. Governance became synonymous with the 'licence raj' with its elaborate system of licences, regulations and red tape.

It was in this restrictive environment that J.R.D. Tata, Chairman of the Tata Group whose interests spanned from steel and automobiles to power and chemicals, took a fateful decision. Like his forefathers who pioneered basic infrastructure in the country, JRD too had a keen business sense. So when his brother-in-law, aide and confidant Colonel Sawhney suggested pooling together the Group's needs for data processing in a single business unit, he readily agreed.

In terms of technology, India was a backwater at the time and computers in particular were looked on with some suspicion because of their potential to replace labour. But as companies in the West began to invest in commercial mainframes to streamline operations

26

like inventory control and payroll, J.R.D. Tata decided to go ahead with the project and set up an in-house data processing unit.

At this time the Tata Iron and Steel Company (TISCO, now Tata Steel) had the largest data processing requirement followed by Tata Engineering and Locomotives Works (TELCO, now Tata Motors). The new team that was assembled comprised mostly people from Tata Administrative Service (TAS) who were to be trained. Yash Sahni, who had a statistical background and was with National Council of Applied Economic Research (NCAER) at that time, was brought in as the team supervisor in 1962.

Recounting those days, Sahni remembers that talks were held with IBM to acquire their 'Unit Record Machines'; the acquisition would be on a lease basis as at that time IBM never sold their computers, but only provided them on lease.

Sahni and his team moved from the Tata headquarters in Bombay House to the Army Navy building and then finally to a place specially created for them in Ballard Estate, a business district in south Bombay. The team still did not have a name and was referred to as a division of Tata Sons with a mandate to set up a data processing unit to service all Tata group companies. The total investment by Tata Sons was about Rs 50 lakh ($110,000).

But there was a problem. Most individual Tata companies did not want to hand over their data processing work to this new unit, preferring instead to keep the work (and the expertise) in-house. At best they were willing to allow the new unit to do their shareholder accounting work, which was actually quite cumbersome for them and involved obtaining legal clearances.

The only exception was Tata Electric which, perhaps because it was staffed mostly by engineers, gave the fledgling data processing unit more sophisticated work. Unfortunately Colonel Sawhney, who had come up with the idea, died soon after, so the team was left without anyone inside Tata Sons to champion its cause.

In order to meet its rising costs, the unit desperately sought work from outside the Tata Group, but realized that it would need access to a mainframe computer if it were to succeed. One well-respected British company wanted to charge a consultancy fee of £10,000 merely to advise what machine to purchase. Not surprisingly, the proposal was turned down.

In any case, in 1964 there was not much choice. It was either IBM or ICL (International Computers Ltd.), a leading British computer company which was second to IBM in the Indian market. But ICL was considered old technology, and several Tata Sons companies including Tata Motors and Tata Steel already had IBM machines so the general inclination was towards IBM. Ultimately, however, the team started buying time from an IBM data centre on their IBM 1401 computer. As hardware was scarce this was then a very lucrative business for IBM.

At the same time, there was a move to recruit more qualified and knowledgeable people to the team. People like Ashok Malhotra and Nitin Patel, both from MIT, joined the team. This was later augmented with people like Lalit Kanodia, Pravin Gandhi and of course Yash Sahni who had a strong quantitative methods background and were young, innovative and aggressive to boot. Collectively they brought together expertise in areas such as engineering, computer science and operations research. Such a high-powered group from top universities would have been rare to find in any company at that time. One of the early customers was Tata Institute of Social Sciences (TISS) which was planning a major study and needed advice on sampling, design of questionnaires, data collection and analysis.

There was still no work from private industries, but the unit managed to make enough money to pay its own bills right from the beginning. The team, however, had a dispersed structure and many of the staff were still on the payrolls of different Tata companies.

In 1966, the whole unit was brought under Tata Services and moved to the Nirmal building at Nariman Point—then a developing area reclaimed from the sea in south Bombay which was later to become one of the most expensive business districts in the world. The prestigious Nirmal building was the first skyscraper in India and the embryonic TCS unit was its first tenant. By now the unit had earned a good reputation amongst customers for whom it did share accounting and registry work on the data processing machines; as a result TCS was able to win customers away from IBM which provided similar services in their own data centres.

By 1968 TCS had two IBM 1401s on lease and one ICL 1903 which was purchased. All these were housed on the eighth floor of

Nirmal building and nicknamed Able-Baker-Charlie. This space was christened the Tata Computer Centre. The management and consultancy staff were housed on the ninth floor of the same building. For its time the ambience was modern and the envy of many other offices. At the time the company had a small capital so both floors were rented; later these were acquired and became the first home of TCS.

The management's faith in the fledgling company was demonstrated in the acquisition two years later of two floors in the neighbouring Air-India building which for many years was the most sought after business address in India. These two floors added another 20,000 sq. ft of office capacity, at that time raising many doubts and eyebrows among the finance moguls at Bombay House, the Tata headquarters.

The creation of the Tata Computer Centre ushered in a period of aggressive selling and business began to look up. Beginning in 1968 the unit undertook a lot of banking work, mostly reconciling inter-branch accounts, payroll accounting and head office accounting. The volume of banking work was so large that by the mid-1970s there were 500 professionals in Delhi and other places where the Tata Computer Centre had IBM/ICL machines.

Up until this point Tata Sons had very small holdings in Tata group companies, and their earnings were mainly dependent on dividends paid by these companies. To enhance income, the Tatas decided in 1968 to restructure some of the units as operating divisions.

Four separate divisions were born at one go: Tata Consulting Engineers, Tata Economic Consultancy Services, Tata Financial Services and Tata Consultancy Services. The Tata Computer Centre became a part of TCS and P.M. Agarwala, Managing Director of Tata Electric Companies, took over as 'Director in Charge' of TCS in addition to his other responsibilities. PMA as he was often referred to was one of India's earliest telecom/electronics engineers from Roorkee University (now IIT Roorkee) and was a technical member of the Government of India's Posts and Telegraph and Telephone Board before joining Tata Electric.

The young, highly talented team of TCS was often more like a rowdy, boisterous bunch from the Wild West. Every new order created euphoria and each invoice was celebrated with a beer party on the terrace of Nirmal building. Winning a contract warranted a movie in the afternoon at one of the nearby theatres. Spirits were running high but the same could not be said about the cash flow. Agarwala was quickly seized of the situation and realized that he needed a strong hand at the top—a 'headmaster' figure—to bring in order.

He chose Faqir Chand Kohli, a brilliant technocrat who was Deputy General Manager at Tata Electric. His role as Chief Load Despatch meant that he controlled the power grid for the city of Bombay. Agarwala perhaps felt that if Kohli controlled the power to the entire city surely he could control the unruly lot at Nirmal building. Kohli was also knowledgeable about computers and that too would have been an influence on his choice. There was just one problem. Kohli did not want to leave Tata Electric and viewed a move to TCS as a diversion from his ambition to ultimately head Tata Electric which at that time was a prestigious post.

But Agarwala prevailed and despite his reservations Kohli was coerced into joining TCS as General Manager in 1969: a post that was specially created for him. The adjustment to the new environment took him six months. He would pore over technical manuals at home to acquaint himself with technology, thereby earning the respect of his juniors. This held an important lesson for me that as a leader one must have a strong working knowledge of the technical environment that one is managing.

Finally Kohli began to integrate with his new team and a new selling strategy started to emerge. Since neither the government nor private companies were interested in data processing, the TCS team decided to position the company as management consultants. This new positioning opened the doors to new business: once the client was engaged they were encouraged to take on automation and electronic data processing work as a way towards more efficient management. This was a convoluted route to data processing work but was necessary since, manual systems being prevalent, automation at that time was not very well understood. So ironically while TCS began with data processing and moved to management consulting, western management consulting companies on the other hand were diversifying into IT services.

Once he had settled into his new role at TCS, Kohli set about shaping the young company armed with the conviction that in order to use computers, India needed bright young people with good education—something India had in abundance. Kohli had a good relationship with the IITs where he used to teach often. He capitalized on this to recruit the best and the brightest young engineering graduates.

When TCS was formed in 1968 there were no separate IT departments in Indian universities and Indian electrical and electronic engineering graduates with an interest in IT typically went overseas to undertake their graduate studies in computer science. Under Kohli, TCS recruited most of the first batch of students who had completed their Master's in computer science at IIT Kanpur, one of India's premier technology institutes and also the first to introduce computer science doctoral studies—although at that stage it was still under the electrical engineering department. Other early IIT Kanpur graduates went on to set up many of India's other IT industry start-ups.

In those early days it was as though TCS was a Silicon Valley start-up. Here was a group of India's brightest people with no dictated agenda and because we were a division of Tata Sons, there was no requirement to produce a balance sheet.

Management consultancy was becoming big for TCS. It involved working with government organizations like Hindustan Aeronautics Limited (HAL), providing major production planning and control systems for light combat aircraft. These were very complex systems and spoke of the strong expertise TCS had. A major system engineering and cybernetics activity was set up with the help of George Mason University who helped with the training. The training was on the simulation systems used in the US for war games; TCS's interest was in using these very applications with changed variables, to solve societal problems. Later a centre in Hyderabad was set up for these services. One of the earliest organizations TCS worked for was the Delhi Development Authority (DDA), helping them in their corporatization with a focus on societal benefit. Similar work was done for the Government of India's Department of Atomic Energy around the time that the Nuclear Power

Corporation of India was being formed as a public sector company. TCS also worked with the north-eastern states to try and figure out why government aid was not reaching down to the people.

The management consulting work established our intellectual leadership and helped position TCS as a thought leader.

In 1974 when Kohli was still General Manager Agarwala took ill and began to operate from home. Unfortunately he did not recover and succumbed to his illness a few months later. Kohli took over as TCS Director in Charge the same year. He reported to the TCS Consultancy Committee whose members were Tata Sons Directors: A.B. Billimoria, Freddie Mehta and Nani Palkhivala, who was also chairman of the committee.

For the first time Kohli was now in a position to drive TCS's vision. From General Manager to Director in Charge was a big jump. In the normal course of things, had Agarwala lived through his term, Kohli may well have returned to Tata Electric.

However, despite his initial reluctance, directing, influencing and shaping a new company in an emerging field was a compelling challenge for Kohli. Automation and computerization had growing business potential and this leadership opportunity may well have influenced Kohli's decision to stay with TCS rather than return to Tata Electric.

Armed with an electrical engineering degree from the Massachusetts Institute of Technology (MIT), Kohli had already earned a reputation as a visionary man. His early contributions at Tata Power included the use of control system methodologies to provide a stable power supply system for Bombay. At Tata Electric he introduced advanced engineering and management techniques and made significant use of digital computers for power system design and control. In 1968, ahead of all but four utilities in the US, Tata Electric installed a Westinghouse computer to control the operations of its power grid which comprised three hydro stations, thermal units and energy supplies from the Tarapore atomic energy and Koyna hydroelectric stations of the Maharashtra State Electricity Board.

What Kohli realized was that monitoring and controlling were critical to the provision of a reliable power supply. He clearly understood the power of technology.

Kohli always wanted India to be part of the computer revolution that was beginning in the West. His electrical engineering degree and MIT training coupled with his voracious appetite for books on technology gave him the confidence to try new things in India and to create value.

I often wonder what might have happened if Kohli had stayed at Tata Electric. Perhaps he would have enabled great transformations in the power sector with his zeal and enthusiasm for applying new technologies to the generation and transmission of power.

All that he gave to the IT industry would have gone instead to the power sector. Perhaps he would have built up a huge talent base that would have met the Indian government's mission of power for all by 2012. Unfortunately today, sectors such as these face a huge shortfall of good people and leaders to drive the agenda aggressively.

## Joining TCS

I was one of those lucky enough to go to America to do my Master's in computer science at UCLA in 1969. After I completed my Master's, I joined NCR in 1970 as a diagnostic programmer.

From a learning perspective I enjoyed the job. I was based in Los Angeles while my office was in Hawthorne, so I used to get up in the wee hours of the morning in order to get to the office early and get computer time to run diagnostic routines.

Soon, however, I was faced with a difficult choice between a career in the US and going back to India. Compelling reasons on both the professional and personal front made me decide to return to India after a few years, unlike many of my contemporaries who stayed on in the US. I had been the first in the family to get an American education. I was also the first to have decided to come back to India, leaving a lucrative career behind.

On the personal front, my parents had found me a pretty young bride, while on the professional front I had the opportunity to join TCS, a division of Tata Sons, perhaps the most prestigious industrial group in India at that time. It was a difficult decision to make, but back in those days an opportunity with the Tatas was considered a better option than a job in the US.

At the time, America was the destination of choice for quality education. Politically, however, in the post-Independence years India had leaned more towards the USSR which was considered an ally. Political relationships with the US were still rather nebulous, probably because of underlying suspicions in the West about Jawaharlal Nehru's liking for the Soviet socialist model. Ironically, however, with the US leading the first mainframe and then the mini-computer revolutions, relations between the business communities of both nations had begun to warm.

America was the land of innovation and I was fortunate to have received the best education in one of its best institutions. This I felt would be a great asset back in India, where I would have the chance to create my own future. Whatever I did in India would never have been done before. The idea of treading an unknown path and applying the knowledge I had learned in the West excited me. A job with the Tatas was the icing on the cake.

I joined TCS as an assistant systems programmer and analyst in March 1972. It proved to be a pivotal decision in both my professional and personal life. At the princely salary of Rs 1,000 a month (about $1,600 a year at the exchange rate in 1972 which was about Rs 7.60 to a dollar)—it was a big drop from the $12,000-a-year salary I was earning with NCR at the time.

Like other early TCS recruits, I saw the TCS job as an opportunity to train our own people on new technologies and one day make these available to Indian markets when they were ready for it. The 'big idea' was to create something for the future, and that was very much in the Tata tradition.

When I look at the history of TCS and what the original founders stood for, I see it as being directly aligned with the 138-year-old vision of the Tata Group where being ahead of the curve, investing in the future and building excellence around people have always been central themes.

Way back in 1874, Jamsetji Nusserwanji Tata set up the Central India Spinning, Weaving and Manufacturing Company marking the Group's entry into textiles. From 1874 to 1904 Jamsetji Tata made forays into steel, power and hotels. As a nationalist, he believed that for India to be truly independent, it needed a strong industrial base.

At the same time the Tatas pioneered many industrial practices that have since become standards such as an eight-hour workday, free medical aid, schooling facilities for children, leave with pay and workers' provident fund schemes.

Since its inception TCS has been a company staffed by highly qualified professionals. Enhancing learning and the professional well-being of its people was the company's core strength and indeed its raison d'être. Technology was the new frontier and we sensed even then that an entry into this area would have as far-reaching an impact as the forays into steel and power had earlier.

Joining TCS was still a big gamble for me, especially since I had such lucrative alternatives in the US. I was taking a risk professionally but risk-taking was set to become a recurrent theme in my life. In fact I have always believed that it is important to move when the time is right, when things are going well and not when one is a spent force. I believe the timing is important and it is better to face up to a new challenge than to avoid stepping outside your personal comfort zone.

Historically, if you look at what TCS has done as a pioneer of the IT industry in this country, you will find transitions, right from the beginning until now, that have always been based on this core concept. TCS charted a completely new path by importing the necessary state-of-the-art technology, and then making an impact in the West at a time when those in the West either knew nothing or very little about India's and TCS's capabilities.

## Working with Kohli

When I joined TCS I got to know my mentor F.C. Kohli for the first time. At that time Kohli was actively involved in recruitment and used to meet every new recruit.

Most young entry-level engineers were afraid to speak to or approach Kohli because of his reputation as a stern taskmaster. But our initial trepidation began to go away as we started to learn a little more about Kohli and realized that he was a man who was very direct and very quick to grasp issues.

He would tell us quite bluntly what was the right thing to do, and what was not. If, however, you were sure you were right you could challenge him, and he would respect that. One of my colleagues wondered how I could deal with his formidable personality. One even described him as 'a benevolent dictator . . . or perhaps not so benevolent'. Kohli was certainly not known for his patience and he was tough, but as I learned later, he also had a soft heart.

Perhaps most importantly, he taught me the importance of under-promising and over-delivering to clients. I also found that he was always willing to help you succeed if you were willing to put in the work. I remember days when I worked from 4.30 a.m. to 11.30 p.m. in order to meet a customer deadline. Times like these helped us establish a comfortable relationship based on mutual respect.

When Kohli spoke, you listened, which taught me the importance of being a good listener; but he was also a man of few words and his instructions were often quite minimal, which trained me to anticipate what was required to be delivered.

Today, it is quite common to have a full and frank discussion between a subordinate and a boss but in those days, companies were quite hierarchical and it was difficult for a relative junior to communicate with a senior without appearing to question or challenge them. Holding an open discussion with a boss was against the ethos of the time and against the upbringing I had had.

As a result, I often found myself communicating with Kohli by writing memos to ensure that I had understood what he wanted and correcting it if I had got it wrong. More importantly, it provided me with the opportunity to disagree in a non-confrontational way. As I discovered, if you believe in something there is always a way to communicate it. Being intimidated by your boss is no reason to not express yourself.

In retrospect, Kohli knew that challenging people was one way to bring out the best in them. So he threw us challenge after challenge, stretching all of us towards continuous improvement while at the same time allowing us broad latitude for experimentation. The assignments were tough and sometimes we even resented having to go through the pain, but the taste of success always made it worthwhile. It was an important lesson in leadership for me that challenging subordinates to step out of their own comfort zones was one of the best ways to develop their skills and discover what they were capable of.

Just as importantly, Kohli's 'can do' attitude was passed on to us.

In India we had no previous models really to learn from, no reference points. Everything we did was for the first time—and this gave us a bit of a cavalier attitude. We used to joke that it was like being thrown into water—even when you did not know how to swim, you just had to figure it out. Kohli was a tough taskmaster, but I was hungry to learn, so although a part of me wanted to just walk away, I stuck with it and faced each challenge head on. I learned to embrace change in much the same way that as a young boy I learned to adapt to new environments when my family moved cities.

My father was with the Indian Audit and Accounts Service and his regular transfers moved us out of the comfort zone of Madras to Nagpur and then into the whole new culture of Delhi. Here I learnt to speak Hindi with ease, which helped me years later when as CEO I could give media interviews in the national language. I was quite proud of that.

The early days at TCS were tough but also came with benefits. I made some of my best friends among the early recruits at TCS. Some of these were Jayant Pendharkar, Sainath Iyer, Dushyant Lal, S. Ramakrishnan, Anil Dixit and S. Mahalingam. Although we were not in the same team, having been allocated between management consulting and the data centre group of TCS and had differing roles ranging from sales to software to hardware, yet we were a close-knit team. We worked together in a friendly, almost family-like atmosphere, helping each other beyond the call of duty. It helped that we were mostly of the same age, had similar values and were very family-oriented. We lunched together and spent our evenings together with each other's families. The home and office were extensions of each other, and if I worked late Mala, my wife, and my son, Tarun, then one year old, would come to the office regularly.

Back in the summer of 1978, we often discussed interesting things to do in the office to keep our minds engaged. Jayant mentioned that IBM ran a quiz for its entire factory which had become quite popular. We decided to replicate this in TCS as well. After all, the best brains in the country were already at work in TCS and we felt that they might be interested in participating. Some doubts were expressed about participating after office hours since people had long distances to travel from Nariman Point to their homes. But we went ahead and announced that a team quiz round would be held on Wednesday evenings for an hour. We invited people to form teams of three to compete. The format followed was that of the popular BBC quiz show *University Challenge*.

To our surprise, nearly twenty teams turned up on the first night, and more amazingly, there was even an audience who stayed back to watch and participate in the proceedings. They turned up for every single round. The desks on the eleventh floor of the Air-India building which had since become our headquarters were cleared to accommodate the crowd. During one of the quiz evenings Kohli became curious and stopped by. I am sure he was also surprised to see so many people staying back on a working day to participate in a quiz. He was gracious enough to come for the finals and give away the prizes to the winners and runners-up. The warmth and comfort of being a part of such a team convinced me later that team building happens not so much by working in a project together, but more by being together outside of it.

Amongst my close friends was Maha (S. Mahalingam, now TCS's finance chief) who joined the company in 1970 when TCS had about 250 people in a card punching department and about twenty-five engineers mostly working on consultancy projects for Tata group companies including TISCO, a forerunner of Tata Steel.

Maha says that he saw me as 'intense, knowledgeable and highly focused' at the time, and 'a real engineer', and I suppose I was. But although I had been trained as a hardware engineer, I actually did some programming in those early days such as writing billing routines for utilities companies like BEST (Bombay Electricity Supply and Transport) and examination paper processing applications. These were written on the two mainframes—an IBM 1401 and a 1903—which we had on the eighth floor of Nirmal building.

We used to program in assembly language so my software experience really was from the lowest level of the value chain. I still believe that rolling up one's sleeves and getting down to basics is the most empowering form of learning and that one realizes the value of this when one reaches the very top. Despite our relative youth, we were fully empowered and had all the support we needed. As young engineers we thought we could do almost anything and that was important because in the early 1970s, we were not sure how the IT market would develop and TCS was still casting around for work.

Our initial strategy was to leverage the extended network of the Tata Group, and Tata Electric in particular. So one of the first external contracts we undertook was for a power company in Iran. The Shah of Iran was in power then and India was a friendly partner. Power companies were being set up in Iran as part of an infrastructure building programme and TCS won projects to build inventory and stock control systems for these power stations.

But not all projects went according to plan. We tried to get into data entry with a partner in the UK but the partner went bankrupt. So it was a slow and difficult beginning, but things began to change dramatically in 1973.

## Days of the licence raj

In 1973, Indira Gandhi's government, was facing a severe dual problem of fiscal deficit and foreign exchange shortage. Therefore it passed the Foreign Exchange Regulations Act (FERA). This act imposed strict restrictions on use of foreign exchange and had direct bearings on imports, and any import would require an import licence which would be granted only after detailed scrutiny by several ministries. Foreign travel was restricted, only engineering and medical students with very good grades would get the most meagre foreign exchange, for studies abroad. Here I might add that the software industry played a sterling role in earning valuable foreign exchange for the country. FERA was later repealed when the foreign exchange situation improved. It was replaced by Foreign Exchange Management Act (FEMA) which made foreign remittances that much easier and import restrictions were reduced. Import tariffs at that time were as high as 100 per cent and sometimes higher for computers. Software was not considered an industry, so exporters could not avail of bank finance and had to rely on internally generated funds. Only computer imports could be financed by banks as it was hardware. Even opening an overseas sales office was not allowed until 1979. Under FERA, a foreign multinational could only operate in India through a joint venture (JV) with a domestic partner and foreign ownership was restricted to a maximum of 40 per cent.

Many foreign multinationals eventually decided to withdraw from India and closed down their Indian operations. These included Coca-Cola and IBM which left India in 1978 citing concerns about the protection of their intellectual property based on dilution of their equity.

But IBM was not the only mainframe maker and Kohli, who was head of one of the Institute of Electrical and Electronics Engineers (IEEE) regions (Region 10), had been developing a close relationship with some senior managers in Burroughs. It was during these IEEE meetings that the idea of a partnership with Burroughs first germinated.

Burroughs, one of the big-three mainframe computer makers, had originally approached Tata Sons in 1973 about the possibility of setting up a JV in India. Under the plan, the JV would have sold Burroughs systems in India and developed software to run on the systems. It also planned to manufacture Burroughs hardware for the domestic Indian market.

TCS was to acquire the necessary permits and licences required for the joint venture but in the meantime we signed a distribution agreement with Burroughs under which we began to sell Burroughs systems in India and provide maintenance and support.

Burroughs, which was on a sales surge buoyed by the introduction of a new family of mainframes, needed the Tata partnership in part because of the restrictions imposed by FERA and it suited TCS which gained access to advanced technology. As a distributor for Burroughs in India, TCS imported state-of-the-art machines and handled all the government procedures and the inherent difficulties that went with the import of high-tech equipment.

Doing business in India during the licence raj was a challenge and importing even more difficult. Many in business preferred to limit their growth rather than deal with the government's red tape. But we persisted and in 1974 we imported a Burroughs B1728, their latest series mainframe computer with very advanced architecture for that time. The machine cost about $300,000 with an equivalent amount of duty. It was at that time a very large outlay. TCS also had to give an export commitment of twice the import cost over the next five years. We hoped to recover these costs by using the machine to provide software development services to Burroughs and help them migrate their older generation of software onto this new platform.

Importantly, this also provided the opportunity for us to send our people overseas to implement similar changes at client locations. Burroughs asked TCS to send programmers to the US to install system software and help some of its new US and European customers to migrate software running on IBM and other rival systems to its own hardware platform.

The strategy of doing part of the development work in India and then working at client locations on implementation was, looking back, the beginning of the Indian outsourcing model. It was the first IT software and services 'outsourcing' contract and the springboard that we had been waiting for.

Over the next few years we began serving international customers with a combination of deputing people at customer locations abroad and working on our machines in India. It is worth remembering perhaps that the offshore projects we talk so much about today have their roots in concepts that originated way back during 1974–76 in TCS.

Today of course code is sent over high speed communications links, but back in those days we saved code onto tapes and disks which were then flown to our programmers and engineers in the US, a process which took several days. There was no Internet, no mobiles and even land phone services were erratic.

Our partnership with Burroughs lasted for four years and was important because Burroughs was one of the top three companies in the world in terms of fundamental concepts in micro-programming and software architecture, as well as the software engineering of operating systems. Our expertise was built by training batches of engineers in these technologies, building a valuable in-house experience. We also used the Burroughs system we acquired for domestic applications including payroll and bank inter-branch reconciliation. At the time we were running a data centre for domestic customers like Pune University, secondary school results processing, Bombay telephone billing and directory printing, municipal corporation water billing, electricity billing and inventory accounting for Bharat Heavy Electricals Limited (BHEL). So we were already proving that there was a need for building a data processing capacity in India.

As the distributor of Burroughs equipment in India TCS also provided maintenance and support services and we soon discovered that we needed to expand the TCS team. Under the guidance of Dr Chandrasekhar Iyer who was in charge of the Burroughs initiative, TCS recruited a new batch of electronic engineers including B. Gopal, Frederick Mony and Sunder Kumar. Two teams were sent to Canada and the US for training. One team comprising Haridas, S. Dhanabal and R.C. Goel focused on systems software while I was sent along with M.K. Sellappan and M.V. Mantri (from Tata Electric) to several facilities in USA and Canada to train on small, medium and large systems and all the peripherals such as line printers, card readers and the different types of tape drives.

After completing the fourteen-week-long training, I was appointed as a Systems Engineering Manager and was put in charge of the hardware unit in TCS, responsible for hardware maintenance of Burroughs computers in India.

The job was not only challenging from a technical point of view but as a field engineer I had to work with my hands using screwdrivers, pliers and yes, sometimes sticky tape, to fix the equipment and keep it running. We could have simply bought new machines instead, but the 'do it yourself' approach saved precious foreign exchange and forced us to learn about system software and the support of hardware.

This theme of self-reliance from the cost and capability perspective was never forgotten and is till today the hallmark of Indian IT. We are able to learn, unlearn and relearn quickly. I believe when you are building an organization, self-sufficiency is important. Too many external dependencies mean you run the risk of the rug being pulled from under you.

They were interesting times. We worked closely with the sales and marketing team comprising Jayant Pendharkar, Adi Cooper, Anil Dixit and Sainath Iyer (sadly both Sainath and Anil died a premature death). Amongst these colleagues, Jayant and I got to know each other well. We were very different personalities. He was an extrovert and quite social while I was shy. But both of us hit it off and so began a friendship that lasts to this day. The differences in our personalities and the ease with which we related created a bond between us. Each of us brought strengths to the relationship and we had no hesitation in learning from each other. After all, teams are all about building upon the strengths of the members, and we did that well.

Burroughs was a competitor to IBM in the mainframe market, and like IBM, supplied its customers with a full range of equipment, peripherals and supplies. Its machines had performed well, but were not rugged and were susceptible to changes in the environment that could not be strictly controlled. For instance, we discovered that a fluctuating external power supply—common in India at the time—caused read/write errors in the disk cartridge drives.

Electromechanical parts like disk drives, tape drives, line printers and card readers in particular failed regularly. This truly taxed my ingenuity and that of the other hardware engineers. These failures at odd hours severely interrupted the little time I had with the family. At that time we were living in a rented apartment in Chembur, a long way off from Nariman Point. Often, just as I reached home I was called back to the office because there was a problem. The parts always seemed to fail at night or over weekends and I would have to take the train back to Nariman Point. I was hardly ever at home and the task of bringing up our son, Tarun, fell squarely on my wife Mala. She often teases me today that I was married to TCS.

At that time, about 90 per cent of project costs quoted to the client were hardware costs while software and people costs were about 5 per cent each. The opposite is true today. Hardware costs are only 5 per cent now while people costs are highest at 50 per cent and software costs are about 45 per cent. This is an indication of the enormous technological progress we have made, as well as the importance of intellectual capital.

One effect of the prohibitive hardware costs at the time was that there was a big focus on its efficient management, and because I was in charge of hardware, this was an initiative that I championed. Getting replacement parts, however, was always a big challenge and I had to fix these technical problems, and motivate my team while looking for ways to save costs. It helped that in India frugality and doing more with less were accepted and practiced personal values for all of us. Frugal innovation may be a modern term but the practice of it at TCS has been around for a long time.

If a part failed we naturally tried to get a replacement at the lowest cost possible. In addition to sourcing parts from the original suppliers to Burroughs, we also had our own repair facility and used creative means to extend the life cycle of parts, often using Araldite glue to quick-fix a broken part so that we could get a machine going again.

The Burroughs printer itself cost $20,000 or so which was a huge sum in those days. Today you would not probably think twice about it but back then it was a big expense, so we scanned all the technical journals extensively and found the company in California that was selling these printers to Burroughs.

In this process we discovered a company, Data Products, which made printers which were cheaper (costing perhaps $12,000 or so), had a better duty cycle and had lower operating costs but had to be adapted to work with the Burroughs machines. Fortunately we also came across Charles Wallace, a World War II veteran who had served in India in 1943 and who had started his own company to make cheaper printing solutions amongst other things. Charles's company called Combur (**Com**patible with **Bur**rroughs) sold an interface to connect the Data Products printer to the Burroughs machine, saving almost 50 per cent of the costs of buying a new Burroughs printer.

Perhaps it was our 'developing nation attitude' that led to our being enormously creative when it came to finding hardware solutions and replacement parts. We extracted every ounce of utility from whatever we paid for, vastly different from the 'use and throw' approach of today's generation. Today when I hear of washing machines being used to churn lassi and diesel engines from water pumps to create vehicles for transporting people and farm produce in India, it reminds me of the old days. Kudos to the 'can do' attitude, the experimentation and ingenuity of the Indian mind.

## The first overseas work

The first real 'outsourcing' contract we did for Burroughs was pretty small. It was for $24,000 and involved converting a hospital accounting package called the Hospital Information System, written in Burroughs medium systems COBOL to Burroughs small systems COBOL.

TCS engineers in Detroit got the software manuals and source code for both systems and sent them to the TCS team in Bombay, but instead of doing one program at a time, we made the process more efficient by writing a convertor or filter program—an assembly language program that ran on an ICL 1903 machine. The filter accepted the source code of the Burroughs medium systems machine and spat out the source code for the Burroughs small systems computer. In those days programs were written at your desk on paper and then converted into punch cards. However, first drafts always had errors and so to avoid a first cut program being run on expensive computer time, filters were written to correct simple things like syntax errors etc.

Interestingly, TCS had acquired this unused ICL machine from the Calcutta-based Life Insurance Corporation (LIC) some years earlier when LIC's communist unions had blocked its use. The mindset against automation and computers was driven by the perceived threat that they would replace human effort and thus cause a loss of jobs. Reportedly the machine sat unused in its crates before the Tata Group agreed to take it off LIC's hands for a fraction of its purchase price.

The impetus for the next big leap for TCS, and the first step towards becoming a future multinational, actually came from an external event.

In 1977 the industrial licence we had applied for that would have enabled the manufacture of Burroughs equipment in India finally came through. But after all the effort involved in getting it, Tata Sons decided the risk of entering the computer manufacturing business was too high.

Instead, in 1978 Tata Sons formed a formal joint venture with Burroughs called Tata Burroughs that sold and maintained Burroughs equipment in India. For a while the Tata Burroughs JV also made dot matrix printers in India but exited that business after a few years.

I sometimes wonder if this was a missed opportunity for Tata and for India. If we had taken up the manufacturing licence we could have manufactured a wide range of IT equipment for the Indian market and perhaps exported it as well. Instead of being left behind by the IT hardware revolution, India could have been at the centre of it in terms of manufacturing capabilities and hardware credentials.

As it turned out, the only real loser from the deal was TCS. Burroughs got the foothold in India that it wanted and Tata Sons could look forward to receiving an annual dividend check from the new JV.

But it left TCS in a very awkward position. It could either be folded into Tata Burroughs—an option favoured by some Tata executives—or it could continue to exist as a separate entity undertaking non-Burroughs business. If we continued to function as a separate entity, then we had the situation of TCS and Tata Burroughs competing for business, which again seemed undesirable. The situation was a serious threat to TCS's very existence with a strong likelihood of our being forced to fold up before we even had a chance to prove ourselves.

After a somewhat tense period between F.C. Kohli and Minoo Modi, the Chief Executive of Tata Sons, it was decided that TCS would continue as a separate entity, but it was agreed that TCS would transfer around twenty-five people to Tata Burroughs. Jayant Pendharkar and I were the first to be offered positions in Tata Burroughs, but Kohli clearly wanted us to stay with TCS. In our minds the choice was between a start-up and an established multinational organization. We agreed with Kohli because TCS offered greater freedom, flexibility and the potential to grow without being reliant on the whims of a foreign partner.

But staying with TCS was also a risky option. Suddenly we found ourselves in a virtually unknown company with no business to call its own and no 'godfather' looking out for us in the Tata hierarchy. We were an independent software house that was allowed to seek non-Burroughs business in a Burroughs-dominant environment! All business brought in directly or through Burroughs's customers had now to be funneled to Tata Burroughs, effectively closing the Burroughs sales pipeline for TCS.

In contrast, Tata Burroughs was a multinational which had instant sales that would add to the Tata revenue stream. We quickly realized that no one at Tatas was going to nurture us, so in that sense TCS was no different from a start-up. In fact we were handicapped because we could not compete with Burroughs. We needed a new source of revenue if we were to grow and flourish and we had to create it ourselves.

Until then TCS had largely hung on to Burroughs's coat tails. We were not known as an independent entity so sales and marketing became vital. Unfortunately no one in the team had any real sales experience. We also knew that our real market was overseas because that was where the action was.

Reflecting back, I believe that cutting the umbilical cord from Burroughs was the best thing that happened to us because it made TCS into a great entrepreneurial company.

At that time, India's domestic IT market was not yet ready and TCS became the first Indian IT software and services company to obtain permission to set up an overseas unit in New York. Kohli asked me to go to New York in 1979 as the first TCS Resident Manager to build a new revenue stream.

Why did Kohli choose me? I asked him much later and he said, 'There was no one else I could trust.' He wanted someone who was willing to take up this immense challenge. He felt I fitted the bill.

It was another big gamble for both me and him. I had no sales background at all, but I knew the hardware we had in India well and I believed we were smart enough to learn to fix anything. It was the kind of confidence that accompanies youth. Armed with a modest 'sales kit' of projects we had done for Burroughs and its customers, I set off to conquer the 'Wild West'.

Together with Mala and my son, Tarun, we packed up in Bombay and headed to New York where we found a relatively inexpensive apartment in Long Island City in Queens.

## The American experience

Arriving in New York was a pretty daunting experience. One person who was more than a little sceptical about my mission was Naval

Mody, President of Tata Inc., the US subsidiary of Tata Sons and the Tata man in the US. Naval had an accountant's mindset. He saw my presence as an unnecessary expense. Besides, while he understood trading, sales was a concept totally foreign to him, so he did not see any value in my role.

Perhaps he also viewed me as a threat because he told me quite clearly that there was no way I could set up a business in the US for an Indian company like TCS, and that I should just take the next flight home. Certainly it was not very encouraging for someone just setting up shop. There I was, caught between two bosses: Kohli who had all the confidence in me and Mody who saw no value whatsoever in my presence.

But Mody's words proved to have the opposite effect on me from what he must have desired. Everything we had done thus far had been a challenge. Nothing of what we learnt in books was of any real use in the environment we were in. We were thinking on our feet and devising our own solutions. This reinforced my conviction that determination and a will to learn can make all the difference. I had also become used to looking at every challenge as an opportunity, so I was even more determined to succeed. Fortunately it didn't take long to bring Mody around.

In 1980 there was a subway strike in New York, the first since 1966. Thirty-four thousand members of the transport workers' union walked off their jobs on 1 April 1980 in a strike aimed at increasing the wage for contracted workers. The city lost an approximate $2 million a day in taxes and another $1 million a day in overtime expenses for city employees.

Many people used the strike as a reason to stay at home. I, however, had a meeting with clients on 1 April, a commitment that I was determined to meet. From Long Island City I could see the Manhattan skyline, so I figured it could not be that far. I decided to walk from my Queens apartment over the East River to Manhattan. Of course it was much further than I thought and the trek took one and a half hours. My legs felt cramped at the end of it, but at least I made it to the meeting. (Unlike me other New Yorkers used more creative options like skateboards and bicycles.)

Unknowingly my long trek was significant in more ways than one. I would like to believe that Mody saw me in a different light after that day. Perhaps I went up more than a few notches in his estimation and it led to a turning point in our relationship. We did later become good friends with a mutual respect for each other. I still remember being invited to his home for dinner and having the chance to meet and exchange views with J.R.D. Tata. I got to know him in an informal setting for the first time.

My early experience in New York was like being a one-man start-up. I typed letters, sent faxes and sometimes I was even the delivery boy. Money was tight, foreign exchange regulations back home ensured that we were perennially short on cash. The basic rule imposed by Kohli and reinforced by Mody was that we had to earn before we spent.

In those days, an Indian selling software services to the Americans was a matter to be laughed at. Just imagine an Indian country bumpkin negotiating Manhattan, its streets and subways (there was no luxury of a car). I walked around armed with a simple sales portfolio on the way to meet clients who were likely to slam the door on me. With the ongoing battles on the Mody front, you needed more than talent to survive this onslaught.

I felt I was not just selling India and TCS, but managing Mody (with a little help from Kohli and Maluste, an adviser to TCS). I was communicating with my bosses in India, handling administration of the office, writing proposals, making cold calls across the US and mentoring colleagues. I spent the little time that was left with Mala and Tarun. One family trip to Disneyland and a visit to New Orleans was all that I could carve out for ourselves in the two years we spent in New York.

I continued to knock at doors and set up meetings hoping for the lucky break. For a one-person team, it was a huge country to cover. With the Burroughs umbilical cord cut, I forged new relationships with IBM, Tandem, Hewlett Packard (HP) and other hardware vendors. It was important to keep in touch with everyone, because they might just provide an introduction or know of a business opportunity. Globally Tata Sons were not very big; the Group's presence mostly comprised offices that acted mainly as purchasing agencies so their connections with overseas companies were not at very high levels, unlike today. We therefore had to make our own efforts to win customers and build TCS as a brand.

We had begun to establish ourselves with IBM systems and had worked onsite quite a lot, so there was some recognition of our capabilities. Even so, winning just one client was a big thing. It was very tough, but somewhere deep down I believed that we were not building a mere business but a new industry for India, and that was a dream worth working towards. During those trying times the support of Mala was invaluable to keep me going.

## The first big break

Fortunately in 1978 TCS had already begun doing some work for the Institutional Group Information Corporation (IGIC) through Mody's contacts. In the mid-1960s the New York-based Union Dime Savings Bank had set up an information processing division called the Union Dime Service Corporation. But computing power was very expensive in those days so Union Dime looked for ways to share the costs and decided to spin off its IT division as a separate company, IGIC.

IGIC quickly became a pioneer in the provision of online banking services which was just an evolving technology in the 1970s. At the height of its operations it provided online real time banking services to fourteen savings banks and handled over 2 million customer accounts. Frank Susino, IGIC's senior vice-president in charge of technical services, and his boss, Max Meth, deserve much of the credit for this remarkable success. In the early 1970s IGIC acquired a Burroughs 6700 mainframe to support its expanding portfolio of online banking services. The B6700 enabled the bank branches (tellers and front office) to be connected to the main branch through a front end machine, a DC140. This posed a challenge because the programming on the DC140 could only be done in Assembly language which was more difficult. Also, testing the code to verify correctness meant taking user inputs from the teller terminal and the application on the mainframe (B6700). The support of the DC140 was therefore very tricky but we managed it, which earned us the respect of the IGIC team.

IGIC, like other Burroughs customers, faced a shortage of technicians and programmers because, at least in the US, everybody wanted to be trained on IBM equipment. If they were available at all, programmers with Burroughs experience in the US tended to be expensive and not so experienced. But IGIC learned through Mody that the Tata Group had access to highly qualified technicians and programmers in India. The relationship was a very casual one initially, but when I arrived in New York in 1979 I negotiated a three-year contract with Frank Susino.

At that time neither TCS nor IGIC had legal departments which made doing business and structuring contracts much easier compared to the complicated ways of today. We drew up a simple contract that basically said: 'We will supply programmers as you need them and this will be the rate'. At that time, because we trusted each other, we worked on what was known as a 'best endeavour clause'. This meant if there was a problem TCS would try its best to fix it using all the resources at its disposal. The same applied to IGIC.

I drew up the contract with Frank Susino and then ran it past Mody, who I am sure must have anxiously puffed through over twenty cigarettes while he scanned the document.

Initially, we sent two programmers over to IGIC at a time for a six-month stint; then the number was increased to three. Once the three-year contract was in place it became an open-ended commitment to provide as many programmers as IGIC needed. At the peak we had thirty-six programmers working round the clock.

When Burroughs began to lose market share to IBM, we developed a competency in conversion work, converting clients' existing Burroughs software applications to work on IBM hardware. Then, in 1982, IGIC converted to an IBM system—and that is when our relationship really took off.

TCS supplied about one-third of the software conversion team effort which took about two years. At one point we had over fifty technicians helping IGIC with the conversion which included writing conversion filters and some new code skills we were able to put to use elsewhere later.

It was during this period that we introduced the concept of offshore/onshore working. I realized that the time difference between Bombay and New York could be used to our advantage, so I suggested to IGIC that TCS engineers in India work on the software code while the US was asleep and then send the results over to New York, so it was ready first thing in the morning New York time.

The system worked very well. I am not sure how many millions of lines of code we actually ran. Given the state of communications links, it was a slow process, but we benefited from the time difference between India and the United States. Effectively IGIC ended up with a twenty-four-hour-a-day operation. At the time, I don't think anyone else was doing this.

Max Meth says that some of his people resented the fact that, as they saw it, IGIC was exporting all this work to India while there was a demand for people in the US. They felt that they were being short-changed by the management's decision to enter into this arrangement with TCS. 'My biggest problem was getting support of the Board of Directors,' Max told me later. 'They felt that there was something not proper about this.'

But he confronted the issue head on. He told the Board, 'Either we can move ahead without me being able to commit to a date when the project will be finished, or you can accept this arrangement.' Eventually the Board backed Max Meth and Frank Susino.

I had told IGIC that we would do whatever it took to make sure the arrangement worked and that if at any time they were not pleased with the services we were providing, or the people we sent to them, we would send our people back to India. But I made sure they never had any reason to be dissatisfied. In fact Frank told me that TCS people were more dedicated, loyal and hard-working than his own staff.

The TCS people working on the project did not watch the clock. They arrived early and stayed late—essentially, they stayed until whatever they were working on was finished. They were incredibly loyal to TCS and to the customer. That was just the way we were.

As a result, the relationship blossomed and over a ten-year period between 300 and 400 TCS associates worked with IGIC. Many of them went onto other key projects for TCS in the US and elsewhere.

The IGIC relationship was also of particular importance to me. I became friends with both Frank and Max and we used to go out to lunch and dinner from time to time with our families. The Jewel of India restaurant on 44th Street in New York was a favourite of ours. Sometimes Mody would be there too and Kohli would join us if he was in town. Mody, who had a great sense of humour, would often take a jibe at the 'best endeavour clause' or on particularly mischievous days would remind the IGIC executives that they had not paid the latest bill. Sometimes he would manage to embarrass either Frank or Max so much that they would produce a cheque right there and then.

On one occasion Kohli was visiting and was staying at the Pennsylvania Hotel across Madison Square Garden. One night as the guests rested, the fire alarm went off. A frantic Kohli came out into the street in his nightrobe saying, 'Well I guess we made it out alive.' It became a bit of an inside joke that we were now risking our lives to set up business in the US.

The success of the relationship I developed with IGIC and subsequently with other early US customers including American Express helped build Kohli's confidence in me. It also helped me to appreciate the importance of building relationships with people as an element of building a business. The IGIC arrangement of supplying software professionals was an unconventional one and it taught me the need for flexibility in an organization and the need to be constantly evolving new skills to meet customer requirements. Our challenge at IGIC and then American Express was how to build skills in a non-Burroughs environment: we had to be in a learning mode right from the start.

I was also getting lessons on managing a team. I found myself playing coach and mentor to my younger colleagues and sometimes to those older than me. Apart from professional advice it became apparent that they needed help on other fronts as well. The frugal Indian mentality and the need to save the dollars led to some very amusing moments.

When we won our first contract I decided to introduce the entire local TCS team to the client so that the client had the opportunity to meet the people behind the work that would be done. With great enthusiasm and pride I introduced the team who had even put on their best suits for the occasion. This was all very well, except for the fact that, to my great embarrassment, one of them seemed to be outfitted for the 'future'. In typical Indian fashion, the suit he wore was of a size that he expected to grow into many years later; so, when he raised an arm for a handshake, all that was offered was a coat sleeve instead. To my horror, there was no 'hand' at all in the handshake.

Perhaps there was a sale going on on extra-long and larger sizes because I later noticed some of the team had folded their shirt sleeves and one particular gentleman wore trousers too long and used sticky tape to hold up a folded hem. Unfortunately, a walk in the snow soon undid the tape and all of a sudden he developed a trailing trouser leg. All of this produced some very awkward moments and I hoped that this apparent lack of spit and polish did not get in the way of the customer's regard for TCSers, because behind this apparent lack of sophistication lay real talent. Our tag line then of 'Beyond the Obvious' aptly described the TCSer as well!

Such incidents are amusing to reflect on now, but they should also be seen in the light of a cultural shift that was beginning to take place within TCS as we became more exposed to an international market. Thankfully the young TCSer of today is more likely to invest in an expensive, well-fitted suit than we were back then. Today's TCSer would also have the benefit of a cultural adaptation programme as part of his or her training, something that none of us had back then.

Apart from IGIC, the American Express contract was another milestone. Mike Abrams and Carl Brown from American Express were our initial supporters. Like many other customer relationships, it began with a small 'trial' project to test our capabilities but eventually evolved into a very significant partnership. We ended up working for American Express in a wide range of places including Arizona, Florida, Argentina, the UK, Australia and Yugoslavia where American Express had a development centre. It was also the time when we pioneered the concept of the customer relationship manager (CRM), then known as account manager, when we sent a dedicated person—Jayaramakrishnan—to the American Express office in Phoenix, Arizona.

While we were struggling with coming to terms with being in America it was apparent that the Americans were dealing with some challenges of their own. To begin with our names were a mouthful and difficult to pronounce, let alone remember. Cliff apparently took one look at Jayaramakrishnan's name when he showed up for his first staff presentation and said, 'I do not think anybody is going to get your name right, so let me make it simpler.' From then on he was known simply as JRK.

Like IGIC before it, American Express became a key reference customer for us. It helped us win deals with other clients and prove that the offshore/onshore delivery model which we pioneered could work and that we had the internal skills and competencies to go far beyond basic maintenance and conversion projects.

Anyhow, by the time I left the US in 1981 and handed over to Maha our US revenues had grown to about $700,000 a year. Maha continued to expand our US operations adding customers like Tandem, Young and Rubicam (the advertising agency), Smith and Wesson (the revolver company) and a Fresno-based cotton company. Our US revenues grew to $2.5 million in 1983 when Maha completed his tenure. Even though I returned to India, I visited the US regularly perhaps eight times a year, often with Kohli.

During Maha's time in the US, Tandem in particular were keen to build a presence in India. They were known for manufacturing fault tolerant computer systems, best suited for transaction processing customers who used them for ATMs, banks and stock exchanges. Their architecture was branded 'Non Stop'.

Tandem wanted to sell their equipment in India and for us it was an opportunity to develop our business and platform expertise. I recall Maha set up a big meeting in Cupertino, California with Tandem's president Bob Marshall that I and Kohli flew out to attend. Coincidentally that very day the Wall Steet Journal had carried a profile piece on the front page about J.R.D. Tata which was a big help because no one really knew much about TCS or India at that time.

Actually we very nearly did not make it to that meeting because we were in Los Angeles the day before for another meeting and all of us were staying with friends and acquaintances that night in Orange County. Between the three of us we had agreed that I was the best driver, so, early in the morning of the Tandem meeting I hired a car with Maha to pick up Kohli and drive to the airport to catch our flight to San Francisco. Unknowingly though, I took a wrong turn somewhere and got a bit lost, so when we arrived at the airport there wasn't very much time before the flight. So much for my driving skills! Maha suggested that Kohli and I go ahead while he returned the hired car and took care of the two big suitcases we had with us. Maha managed to take the next flight but to complicate matters, my suitcase went missing. Maha stayed back to sort out the missing luggage; by the time it was found there had been a considerable delay and Maha managed to get to the Tandem meeting only close to lunchtime. Fortunately, however, the meeting had gone well so his latecoming did not matter.

By the early 1980s it was clear that TCS had come a long way in its journey that had begun somewhat shakily in the 1960s. Circumstances had put TCS on a global journey. The early struggle with selling data processing on the back of management consulting was clearly over. There was a pronounced need now for higher-level work and TCS was the company of choice for the most talented and qualified Indians. I returned to India with a big agenda to reinforce our offshoring base in India as we entered the next decade.

## BIG WINS IN FINANCIAL SERVICES

ANY START-UP NEEDS a couple of good breaks to get going. Most would not think of TCS as a start-up but in many ways it was. The world was our market, and we had no credentials other than the Tata name backing us. The projects that catapulted us to a noticeable position were won by sheer grit, determination to succeed and sometimes a cheeky sense of overconfidence. Each project, however, helped build TCS's reputation and represented an important milestone in our journey.

Throughout the 1970s, '80s and '90s the technology market was predominantly outside of India. Not only were these overseas markets a lot more exciting for TCS, but we really had nowhere else to go because there was no domestic market to speak of. Throughout my career one of my greatest desires has been that TCS can and should make a difference to India. So TCS participated in the global market, developed it further and brought back what we learned from overseas engagements to India.

During much of this period, India and its political leadership had other more pressing issues to deal with, such as floods and food shortages. Information technology was relegated to an afterthought. But that began to change in the 1990s with the opening up of the economy and a growing political awareness in India of the role IT was playing in powering transformation in other countries.

Even through the 'dark ages' of IT in India, TCS's fundamental approach to India always was to ensure that the domestic market got as much attention, if not more, than our overseas operations. For us it was only a matter of time before IT became as critical for India's development as it already was in other nations. We felt it was important for TCS to prepare for that time.

Globally, the financial services sector has always been an early adopter of technology. It was therefore strategically important for TCS to secure some early contract wins in this space in order to gain experience and domain knowledge. But we had to build this from scratch.

The key global financial markets were in Switzerland (which was the most advanced) followed by the US, the UK and, closer to home, Singapore and Hong Kong. The financial and banking business is highly sensitive to security, to zero fault tolerance and a stringent delivery schedule. We not only had no credentials, but there was a negative perception to be dealt with. After all, we were an Indian company from nowhere, attempting to enter a sophisticated market.

TCS started as a bureau organization but we also developed experience in the banking and financial sectors. For example, right from 1968 we operated as registrars and transfer agents both for Tata companies and others. By 1977 we were handling dividends and transfer deeds for sixty-five companies and by 1988 we were doing custody systems for the Stock Holding Corporation of India (SHCIL).

Our early banking experience was built through a turnkey project we won in 1981 for Western Trust and Savings Limited (WTSL), a fifty-year-old British retail bank from Plymouth with a network of twenty-eight branches. WTSL subsequently became a wholly owned retail financial services subsidiary of the Royal Bank of Canada.

TCS developed an innovative retail banking system for WTSL from scratch, a project that took over 135 person-years to complete. The system was fully implemented by the end of 1986 and met with all information technology requirements including all aspects of electronic banking.

It was an integrated system designed to aid the management of customer relationships in personal financial services. It supported activities such as strategic planning, marketing campaigns, account opening, relationship management and bad debt management as well as functional products ranging from savings and deposit accounts to loans and checking accounts.

As the system met the functional needs of modern retail financial services organizations, it was subsequently marketed by Software Sciences (a UK-based firm) as a readymade product called the TAMAR Retail Financial Services System and was subsequently successfully implemented at six or seven UK-based retail banks and building societies between 1988 and 1993.

WTSL was a complex turnkey project that involved building an end-to-end advanced system from scratch and integrating multiple technologies. The project helped TCS build deep domain knowledge in the retail banking sector and master the then latest technological advances such as automated teller machines and point of sale terminals, and also gain experience managing large projects. This experience was very useful for TCS when we began development of a branch banking software product known as Integrated Standard Banking Software (ISBS) for banks in India. This was later superseded by core banking software. As telecom infrastructure in India improved and became more reliable, banks increasingly opted for the core banking solution, thereby making the standalone banking software obsolete.

The project, which was undertaken at the TCS facility within the Santacruz Electronic Export Processing Zone (SEEPZ) in Bombay with twenty-nine people on site, represented 9 per cent of TCS's revenue in 1986. Today hardly any project represents that proportion of revenue, and it is unimaginable that a project would run for over six years.

But at the time, the scale and complexity of the WTSL project enabled TCS to develop crucial knowledge and helped the early TCSers gain valuable mainframe experience. As a result they became banking experts as well as mainframe experts and learned how to manage and deliver projects. Unfortunately TCS did not retain the intellectual property rights for the project—we had yet to learn the importance of owning the IPR.

## Swiss National Bank

One of TCS's early banking experiences was in Switzerland which was one of the most advanced financial markets in the world at the time. TCS already had a footprint in Switzerland because of a 1984–85 collaboration with Teknosoft (TKS), founded by the Swiss entrepreneur Pierre Page. We had implemented a few successful projects in Switzerland including the largest, a project for the Swiss National Bank (SNB). In 1983, that was the first offshore project done by TCS Delhi. Until then Bombay (SEEPZ) had been our only offshoring destination.

At the time the SNB had 326 employees including a very competent thirteen-member IT team, many of whom held PhDs. TCS sent Jagdish Bhandari to meet with the bank's IT team to help plan the project but ended up being grilled for six hours by the IT team who questioned him about every detail of TCS's approach. Thankfully at the end of this gruelling exercise the IT team felt confident enough about TCS's capabilities to approve us for the project.

But our happiness was short-lived because we soon received a summons from the chairman of the bank. As it turned out, the forty-five-minute meeting with the chairman was really only to satisfy his curiosity because he could not believe that an Indian company was going to do a project for SNB. He wanted to satisfy himself that this was a wise decision, especially since part of the work was to be done remotely from India, an unheard-of concept back then.

Working with the Swiss presented us with our first experience of working with a demanding customer. Milestones for both sides were set, but there was no pressure on TCS to complete the project by a predetermined 'go live' date. Instead the bank trusted us as experts to define the schedule, after which they held us to it stringently. We knew the bank was serious because, based on TCS's schedule, the bank changed all contracts with other service providers, including Burroughs.

We were told repeatedly that no changes were to be made to the user interface and that customers must not be inconvenienced at all. Given the nature of the work, some minor changes to the interface were inevitable but the bank insisted that even these needed to be flagged up in advance so that users could be pre-warned.

For TCS, these experiences were defining moments that helped shape our corporate culture and established benchmarks. The key lessons we learned from this contract included the importance of displaying a sensitivity towards the end user, customer focus, the emphasis on quality, the importance of planning a schedule and sticking to deadlines. We also learned never to give vague estimates: in fact our estimates were 95 per cent accurate. They were all lessons that would serve us well in later years.

## SegaInterSettle (SEGA)

Associations such as the one with the Swiss National Bank served as a strong local reference and helped us get the opportunity to bid for yet another important project: SEGA. In 1989 TCS was presented with an opportunity that helped catapult the company into the big league. SegaInterSettle (SIS), also known as SEGA, wanted to create a real-time securities settlement system or Settlement Communication System (Secom). SEGA already had a depository which it had been using for the past twenty years, but now it wanted a second generation system. Therefore, the fixed price project involved a mixture of migration work and new software development. TCS bid for and won the SEGA project in conjunction with our Swiss partner, TKS-Teknosoft, and we won it against competition from Andersen Consulting (later renamed Accenture).

TCS had no experience in clearing settlements while Andersen Consulting had undertaken many depositories and was an established leader in this field. So how did we do it? First of all, a team of young, eager and bright TCSers was dispatched to study the SEGA requirements. They spent about three months talking to the customer in order to understand what they required. We proposed that we would do the entire development in India whereas Andersen Consulting said they would do it in Manila. I think Andersen took it for granted that they would win the bid and that SEGA would never award it to a company from India. This overconfidence perhaps showed in the way they projected themselves.

In comparison, we were the underdogs. We wanted the contract badly and we saw it as a game changing opportunity. We had the passion and inclination to go the extra mile so we worked as though we were possessed. Although the bid pricing was quite similar, the major difference was in our approach and our commitment. We gave a timeline which was more realistic and produced a technical proposal that was very detailed and comprehensive.

Ultimately I think we won the contract because of two factors. First, the Settlement Communication System was going to be deployed on an IBM mainframe and we had built up considerable IBM mainframe expertise after acquiring an IBM mainframe in 1987 and undertaking the WTSL project. Second, we had domain knowledge from a project we had undertaken earlier for SHCIL, India's largest custodian and depository participant.

SEGA was a 300 person-year turnkey project undertaken over a period of three years. It was the largest project in the Swiss market and a crucial part of the infrastructure of the country. It involved offshoring major components from India and unlike today, there were no contingency clauses built into the contract. The cost of any delays or overruns would have been hard to absorb on TCS's balance sheet. The stakes were high because we were putting our reputation on the line and risking our future in the Swiss market.

Creation of the second generation SEGA system involved enormous developmental work, some of which had to be undertaken from scratch. Because of the sheer size and complexity of the project TCS set up a dedicated offshore development centre in Madras for the first time.

Gathering together the global and local requirements for the project itself took months and involved meeting several different communities. In the Swiss market, the clearing and settlement system is used to settle every instrument in the country, be it bonds or equity. This required a single central interface that was connected to the Swiss stock exchange, to the Swiss National Bank for payments, and to several other agencies. Any failure in this interconnected system could cause the capital market to collapse. Although this was a hugely challenging task, we were motivated by the fact that we were creating a model system that others would aspire to.

The core of our proposal was the repository or the software which supports storage and access to digital content, or storage system, for the project. We already had a Burroughs-based repository from the early days, called ADDICT, and another repository we had built for IBM machines called CasePac. Using these, we built the SEGA repository. Without these tools, we would not have been able to do the SEGA project. These tools also helped us convince the client that we had made significant investments in the right technologies and that therefore we could deliver.

The Settlement Communication System went live as planned in October 1993 and handled 4.6 million transactions in its first year of operations. It was a pace-setting and visionary project for the industry. Today, almost twenty years later, it continues to run flawlessly and remains one of the most sophisticated systems in the world in terms of technology, functionality and its architecture which was way ahead of its time.

It is a system that both TCS and SEGA are extremely proud of. In fact many countries in the world still look at it as a model system. But perhaps most importantly it proved that an Indian company could work in one of the most mature markets in the world and deliver an extremely complex project on time and on budget.

The project helped establish TCS as a world-class systems integrator in the financial services industry. It was an invaluable training ground in Swiss programme management, enabling us to groom a number of professional managers, project leaders and team members who went on to work on other key projects in India like those for the National Stock Exchange (NSE) and the National Securities and Depositories Limited (NSDL).

## National Stock Exchange

Back in India, the financial and economic liberalization of the 1990s was beginning to have an impact. The Harshad Mehta scam in the 1990s revealed the lacunae in the trading system and highlighted the need to introduce international standards into the Indian stock market trading system.

On the basis of the recommendations of the high-powered Pherwani Committee, the National Stock Exchange was incorporated in 1992 by the Industrial Development Bank of India (IDBI), the Industrial Credit and Investment Corporation of India (ICICI), the Industrial Finance Corporation of India (IFCI), insurance corporations, select commercial banks and others.

Stock exchanges, however, had been in existence in India since 1875 when India's first stock exchange was set up in Bombay. The Native Share and Stock Brokers' Association, also known as the Bombay Stock Exchange (BSE), was formed in the wake of the rapid development of commercial enterprise in Bombay from the 1850s onwards. The Ahmedabad and Calcutta exchanges were quick to follow and by the early 1990s over twenty exchanges existed across India.

TCS's experience with stock exchanges until now had been minimal. We had had some exposure to the Hong Kong and Taiwan exchanges and to Singapore's screen-based trading. A few brochures had been collected during TCS visits and a contact with a Hong Kong-based consulting company had been established.

But when IDBI announced that the NSE was to be set up, TCS seized the opportunity and expressed a keenness to partner on the project. We started by meeting an IDBI team led by Dr R.H. Patil and Ravi Narain in order to understand what their plans were. High on confidence and fresh from the success of SEGA, we shared with them our experience in the Swiss market and with SEGA in particular.

From the start the IDBI/NSE team wanted to keep the project consultant and solutions service provider aspects of the contract separate. So they selected a Hong Kong-based company called International Securities Consultants (ICS) to act as a consultant to the exchange and to draw up the overall business plan and model for the stock exchange.

The NSE team comprised some of India's most respected leaders and the international request for proposal (RFP) was faultless—the finest we had seen. The detailing was impressive and included the software platform, hardware, networking and even the air-conditioning. Everything was very well-detailed and was part of the job package.

From the TCS point of view, this was the first system integration project that we had looked at, and the first time we had tackled a trading platform. So even responding to the RFP was extremely challenging for us. We assembled the most experienced team we could, including several veterans of the SEGA team.

Until then, our mindset had been always to develop software solutions because they offered the greatest opportunity to learn and build in-house expertise. The idea of using a third-party solution was alien to us. Nevertheless, after our initial meetings with the NSE team we realized that a readymade solution was required. So we signed an MoU with a US-based company called TCam to work together. TCam had built a trading system and had implemented it at a handful of smaller exchanges including Vancouver and Istanbul.

The NSE RFP was extremely clear that a single party would be responsible for hardware, software and networking; TCam insisted that we should be the lead integrator on the project. This arrangement of working with a third party on a systems integration (SI) project proved to be a whole new learning experience for TCS.

Typically SI projects involve multiple players and create dependencies but still require seamless functioning to ensure smooth delivery. We had never worked like this before; we were used to being in small close-knit teams of like-minded people. We also had to learn quickly about the technical risk TCS would have to shoulder. This was particularly true in the field of communications networking which was extremely difficult in India. Ericsson, the telecommunications company that provided the switches we needed for the project, did not even have a presence in India at the time.

But we knew the real challenge for us was that we had never done this type of trading system. We did not have the domain expertise, so I hired a room for two days and arranged for somebody from the Reserve Bank of India who knew about electronic trading to come and teach about thirty TCS rookies the basics. That is how the team got their induction into stock trading; they were smart and learned the ropes very quickly.

The team worked for two or three months on the proposal and I myself worked on the financial aspects of it full time for two weeks. Not wanting to be distracted from this critical task, I even told my secretary not to forward any telephone calls to me at all during this time.

We needed to understand the risks involved in this type of proposal, because it involved mostly third-party components. There were challenges internally too. Resources were limited and we literally had only one PC and one person—Dharmiya—who was trained to use WordPerfect which was needed to write up the proposal. We all prayed that Dharmiya did not fall sick.

When our proposal was finally ready it was in six volumes, each copy weighing about 6.5 kg. We had to submit two copies of the proposal to three places simultaneously—Hong Kong, the UK and Bombay—so we flew people all the way to Hong Kong and the UK to ensure it was delivered in person and on time. Once again we were bidding against some of the biggest and most respected names in the industry including IBM, Digital Equipment and Wipro which had tied up with a Paris-based company called ISM.

We realized that the NSE was a demanding customer but we had the Switzerland experience behind us and knew we had to deliver nothing short of excellence. In spite of the fact that the NSE project itself was the first major systems integration engagement in India, and the first electronic trading system that we had undertaken, we felt truly driven and confident.

We realized the significance of this initiative for the country's capital markets and we wanted to create a customer experience that would be magnificent. I am convinced that the fact that TCS had no previous SI knowledge made the team work that much harder. No one ever went home before 10 p.m. during the first year of the project. The unspoken rule was that work must be completed and promises kept irrespective of the time it took.

As we had anticipated, the networking part of the project was very challenging because the infrastructure in India was very rudimentary and the plan called for providing access to the exchange from across India. We needed to connect 500 cities so we looked at various technologies including landlines, but they were unreliable.

During the evaluation process, the NSE decided that it might not be the best strategy to have a single vendor for the whole project, so the wide area networking (WAN) part was awarded to an Israeli company and HCL was given that part of the contract. In hindsight it was also a good risk management strategy undertaken by the NSE.

On the software side, when the decision time came there were two consortia left in the race, one led by TCS and the other by Wipro. The trading system was to run on fault-tolerant Stratus hardware and although we did not have much experience with Stratus, we gained on-the-job experience and were able to leverage our experience with other hardware.

After what I believe was a most professional and transparent evaluation, we were exhilarated to learn from Dr R.H. Patil, the Chairman of the NSE, that TCS would be awarded the project. TCS finally had the chance to work on a game changing opportunity in India.

We had sixty people involved in the project and one of our objectives from the outset was to implement the TCam system in the shortest possible time because having their consultants in India was costing us a lot and we did not want to rely too much on TCam. We had planned for 500 days of consulting support from TCam but eventually we managed with only 100 days which reduced our costs. From the execution point of view it was extremely successful. Interestingly, when we started work on the project, the NSE office was actually being built around us—there was not even any air conditioning. That, however, was no deterrent to our singleminded focus.

The sixty TCSers worked very closely with six people from the NSE—it was like one single team. In fact, when the advertising agency employed by the NSE produced the first brochure and asked the NSE which people they should photograph, the NSE management was quick to tell them, 'Everybody here is NSE, we don't distinguish between TCS and NSE.' Looking back I believe that business is as much about building relationships as it is about technical capabilities. There was a comfort level, a sense of trust and confidence that TCS had earned; and the NSE must have known that TCS would never take a chance on such a critical project and would give this their best. After all, the name Tata and trust were synonymous.

Under the terms of the NSE contract there were to be no extensions to the 'go live' date and it was decided that India's finance minister would inaugurate the system on a particular date. So we could do whatever we wanted, but we had to get the system up and running on that day. We did of course meet the deadline and the exchange was inaugurated in the Nehru Planetarium hall by Dr Manmohan Singh, then India's finance minister, in June 1994.

We learned a lot from the NSE project, particularly about performance engineering. For example, we had to work out how to benchmark the performance of live applications, what monitoring systems were needed and what were the best techniques for maintaining performance as a system scales. Of course we also learned a lot about mission critical issues and about complex fault tolerant systems because the impact on the whole market of the system going down even for five minutes could be enormous.

Most importantly for TCS it was the first time we had used third-party systems and this broke us out of the 'developing from scratch' mindset. Another important aspect of the NSE project was that although TCam retained ownership of the source code and held on to the intellectual property rights, TCS had the right to modify the source code the way we wanted. In return we paid TCam licence fees and this enabled knowledge transfer. TCS had full control of the NSE system and has maintained and upgraded it ever since, enabling it to perform without hiccups for the last seventeen years.

Unlike most world exchanges, the NSE uses a satellite communication system that connects traders from 345 Indian cities and the advanced technologies enable up to 6 million trades to be operated daily.

There is no doubt that the creation of the NSE was an inflection point in India's capital markets. The NSE experiment and experience was a great success and it became the number one stock exchange in the nation within one year of beginning operation, overtaking most of the other twenty-three stock exchanges in the country, some of them over a hundred years old.

The NSE also changed the way capital markets worked in India by bringing in best practices. Later in 2004, when TCS went public, the NSE openly acknowledged the contribution to its success by TCS as its IT partner.

Today the NSE is the third largest stock exchange in the world and one of the few trading all types of securities on a single platform. Its operations are divided into three segments: wholesale debt market (WDM), capital market (CM) and futures and options market (F&O). Each segment experienced significant growth within a few years of its launch. The success of the NSE also resulted in the entry of foreign institutional investors into India, highlighting the reduced risk and enhanced efficiency in settlements.

## National Securities and Depositories Limited

The initial success of the NSE was however limited by the fact that India still relied on a paper-based system for settlement of trades which inevitably resulted in problems of bad delivery and delayed transfer of title. Even when everything worked, the paper-based system meant that it often took two or three months for investors to obtain the share certificates.

Even though the system was designed to provide a trading platform access across India, when it went live in October 1994 it could only offer a physical share certificate delivery in Mumbai and there were no readymade software packages that could provide clearing and settlement services across the nation.

Clearing and settlement services are country specific and subject to local requirements. So we had to develop a clearing and settlement system that could work in a distributed manner at a national level, with deliveries not just in Mumbai but also in Chennai, Calcutta and Delhi.

The enactment of the Depositories Act in August 1996 enabled the NSE together with the Unit Trust of India (UTI) and IDBI to establish the National Securities and Depositories Limited (NSDL), the first depository in India. NSDL handles most of the securities held and settled in dematerialized—that is, paperless—form in the Indian capital market.

The RFP for the NSDL project specified a solution based on the Unix open system. But at the time there were only three products to choose from: an IBM-developed product in Belgium which ran on a Digital system, a TCam product in Australia running on a Unix-based system and the SEGA system that we had developed which ran on an IBM mainframe.

Bidding with TCam with whom we had worked earlier and whose system was based on Unix would have been a natural choice. However, Kohli had a different point of view. He felt that TCS should build its own expertise and should therefore use the SEGA experience which was our unique selling proposition. SEGA, however, was a mainframe option and not in line with the RFP. Kohli's comment would later prove to be very strategic because it charted a new, though difficult, path, when most would have taken up the obvious choice. Of course, we went with Kohli's view and offered a solution based on the SEGA mainframe migrated to an open system.

In our hearts we knew that India needed an accounting, not a settlement system, and we were convinced that for India this application should run on mainframe. So we worked on convincing others, especially NSDL, that the software should run on a mainframe machine rather than a Unix system. Arguing this position took a great deal of courage from the TCS team led by Jagdish Bhandari and B. Gopal, because we knew it was not in line with the RFP. But during the evaluation process we felt confident that we knew the subject better than any others and could pull it off.

It was a Saturday when NSDL finally announced that TCS had been selected. They were magnanimous enough to tell us that if we felt squeezed they were open to us revising the bid. An elated Jagdish and Gopal went to Kohli's room with a box of sweets. On hearing that TCS had won the NSDL deal, Kohli was visibly moved; he sat Jagdish and Gopal down and immediately dashed off a note to Ratan Tata.

From the time TCS won the project in June 1996 to the system going live with the NSDL inauguration on 8 November 1996, it was the fastest implementation of a depository anywhere in the world. The Indian government introduced dematerialization of securities scrip by scrip. By June 2000, just three and a half years after the system went live, 98 per cent of settlements on Indian stock exchanges were done in demat (digital, paperless) form and over 2.5 million demat accounts had been opened in the NSDL system.

C.B. Bhave, the managing director of NSDL, was an excellent but tough customer. The schedule was very tight and we had to get it right the first time. We had no time to draw up specifications in advance for the project, so we were collecting requirements and developing the system at the same time. Despite this, it was the fastest implementation for a project of this nature and took just two years from start to finish. We later used this experience overseas, modifying the depository system and implementing it in Johannesburg, South Africa.

In addition to NSDL, TCS also implemented the Tax Information Network (TIN) system that enabled corporate and business organizations to submit details of their income tax deductions.

In April 2004, the Indian government decided to end the policy of providing lifelong pensions and replace them with assured returns for new state and Central government employees. A Pensions Regulatory Authority was set up which recommended replacing the old system with a new scheme where both the employee and the government contributed to a pension fund whose investments could be selected by the employee. NSDL was given the function of a central record keeping organization.

TCS implemented this project which went on to be known internally as the Pensions project. When the Pensions project went live, C.B. Bhave had just moved to the Securities and Exchange Board of India (SEBI) as chairman and R.H. Patil had taken over as chairman of NSDL. Nobody gave more credit to TCS than Dr Patil in his inaugural speech. 'In the building of the exchange and its success, and in institution building of India, the only thing common in all of these was TCS, so all credit goes to TCS,' he said. The then finance minister P. Chidambaram also acknowledged TCS in his opening remarks, even though it is not customary for ministers to publicly acknowledge the work of private companies.

For TCS there was an immense sense of pride when this happened; for us it was always about building the TCS brand and the creation of vital infrastructure for the country, the value and profitability of the project was often secondary.

## Standard Chartered Bank

TCS was quickly gaining experience in the creation of complex systems for financial markets in India and overseas, but one global market where we were finding the going a bit of a challenge was Singapore. In 1994, close on the heels of the success of the NSE project, Yashpal Sahni, TCS's president, heard that Standard Chartered Bank in Singapore needed an off-the-shelf custody system.

He was very keen for TCS to bid even though we had no expertise and no product in this area. The idea behind bidding was not so much to win the project, but to register TCS in the minds of Standard Chartered, a giant in banking. The project was also significant because that year there were only one or two projects that were worth $5 million or more and this was one of them; we thought it could give us an entry into the big arena. So the TCS team was encouraged to put in a really good bid.

In 1993, TCS along with TKS-Teknosoft in Switzerland embarked on an initiative called Project B that was aimed at creating a modern banking platform for small- and medium-sized banks in Europe, with an initial focus on Switzerland. The base concept for such a product was acquired from NCR Corporation in Switzerland. Project B later created the Quartz banking product. In 1995, TCS extended its product portfolio, leveraging the knowledge base of the Project B initiative to create a regional securities processing platform. This initiative called the NCS programme was realized with Standard Chartered Bank as the partner bank and the first taker of the solution. By now we understood the value of IPR and the power that it gave you, so in the Standard Chartered proposal we clearly mentioned that the IPR would rest with TCS.

For the Standard Chartered project, each contender had to make presentations over two days. But we were warned that we could be sent packing in two hours if we failed to impress. What happened was that after two days of presentations we were shortlisted and a fifteen-person team from Standard Chartered came to Delhi to take the discussions further. We had indicated that we had 80 per cent of the product completed although David Awcock, Standard Chartered's head of IT, sensed that TCS was not quite ready. But he also realized that our solution would be more forward looking, so he was ready to take the risk. The bid was certainly attractive, the cost was competitive and the bank was open to TCS owning the IPR.

Ultimately we won the Standard Chartered bid, got an entry into Singapore, and the bank was able to offer custodial services to its customers in thirty nations. This project was our first major turnkey project in a major market with a big name. It was truly a great learning experience.

We had put in our bid knowing that the chances of our winning were slim, but in the end we ended up winning. Perhaps the customer saw our passion and our readiness to go the extra mile and was ready to encourage it. There are so many intangibles that work under the surface but in business interactions, at many times it's just about good vibes and a gut feel.

The Indian financial market had provided TCS with ample challenges and opportunities to learn and build in-depth expertise through the greenfield projects we got to do. Many of these were a first for TCS, both from the technology and applications perspectives. TCS mastered the art of quickly building up the requisite domain knowledge and expertise through training. This gave us the confidence to go after projects in areas which were completely new to us.

If you look at the millions of transactions that the NSE system does every day, its screen-based trading which touches investors in all parts of the country; or the dematerialization of paper scrips in the NSDL and the clearance and settlement that take place; the creation of the major stock exchanges of this country; or the contribution of the Computer Maintenance Corporation (CMC)—which we acquired—to the Railways, to ports, to the BSE, and to Central Depository Services Limited (CDSL), all of these are based on a commitment made to research and its application to address the challenges in India.

Collectively these systems revolutionized the Indian financial markets and have stood the test of time. Today the Indian market is one of the most sophisticated global securities and capital markets. TCS proved that Indian managerial talent is on par with the rest of the world. We have taken some of the cutting-edge solutions we designed for India to our international customers. It has been a two-way process.

Even though India may lag behind in a few areas even today, our financial and banking systems are world class. This is because we embraced IT early enough in the game. I cannot resist imagining what India's progress might have been had we applied technology solutions with equal enthusiasm early enough to other areas such as health, education and employment. Could India have made similar leaps in these sectors as well?

## TRAVERSING THE IMPORT REGIME

THE SUCCESS OF America's Silicon Valley can be attributed to several factors but one that is irrefutable is a supportive ecosystem that encourages creativity, innovation and entrepreneurship.

In contrast, in the India of the 1970s when TCS had just started up, an ecosystem was non-existent, and as a matter of fact the regulatory environment was not even pro-business.

When TCS went public in 2004, we were into our thirty-sixth year of existence. Often people would ask me where TCS had been all this while, and I would tell them that our first twenty years were spent building the foundations of the IT industry, clearing the hurdles with the government, and catalysing the regulatory framework which till then had never catered to importing computers or exporting software. We consciously made investments of time, money and expertise in academic partnerships with a view to building a talent base in the nation, and we did this quietly and without fanfare. Too quietly perhaps did we wear the mantle of a pioneer, something for which we paid a price in later years. Let us not forget that for all other companies that followed, TCS's initial investment created a springboard to take off from.

Four decades ago, there were many challenges for a private sector company in dealing with the Indian government. Indira Gandhi was the prime minister and was determined to carry on the Nehruvian socialist model. Jawaharlal Nehru's education at Trinity College, Cambridge had been influenced by the Fabian socialist movement and he had come to believe that in a poor and populous country like India, the public sector should occupy the commanding heights of industry.

Indira Gandhi fervently followed the same path, creating a centrally controlled economy based on the Soviet model. Under her rule the banking and insurance sectors were nationalized and India adopted a policy of five-year national plans. Everything that the private sector did required permission from the government in the form of a licence. The list of licences was almost endless: private sector companies needed industrial licences, capital goods licences and import licences to name just a few; this eventually led to this period being known as the licence raj.

The government strategy was driven in part by the lack of foreign reserves in our coffers. Precious foreign exchange had to be used to create food reserves, fund oil imports and pay for defence equipment etc. It was to be used sparingly for other purposes.

This had a direct impact on TCS because we wanted to bring mainframe computers and state-of-the-art technology into the country and use it to train our people, just like we had been trained in the US. Obviously, we needed foreign exchange to pay for these purchases.

The second factor working against us was a view that computers were labour-saving devices. As a result there was an inherent resistance to computerization, particularly in bigger public sector corporations and the government sector which had very strong, entrenched unions which felt that automation would take away jobs.

There was also a widespread feeling that the government looked at profit-making with suspicion. Clearly we were on a path that was tangential to the Indian government.

The Indian private sector and foreign companies that were present in the Indian market felt a great sense of constraint. At the time the government had the power, through licences, to dictate to businesses when and where they could increase capacity and what products they could make. No company could expand annual revenues beyond Rs 20 crore without specific clearance under the Monopolies and Restrictive Trade Practices (MRTP) Act.

In fact, many large industrial groups felt that the government's restrictive policies prevented them from serving the country and enriching its economy to the full extent of their capacity and will. An exchange between P.N. Haksar and J.R.D. Tata provides a good insight of the frustration felt at that time by industrialists.

Haksar was a brilliant lawyer who after two decades of outstanding diplomatic service was recalled to serve as secretary, and later as principal secretary to Prime Minister Indira Gandhi. He was a big influence on the shaping of India's domestic and foreign policies.

On JRD's eightieth birthday, Haksar wrote him a congratulatory note and urged him to reflect constructively and creatively on the state of the country. JRD, who probably saw this comment as salt on his wounds, could not resist responding with an unabashed forthrightness.

He wrote:

In the 100 years prior to Independence, opportunities created by the Industrial Revolution were denied to Indian merchants, financiers and affluent members of the bourgeoisie. The advent of Independence brought about a dramatic change in the situation which would normally have provided the same vital base as in other countries for great projects, ventures and adventures by Indians.

An essential pre-requisite however would have been a freedom of choice, of investment and of action which it took no time at all for our politicians and our burgeoning bureaucracy to block or stifle in the process of concentrating of all economic power in the government.

Instead of releasing energies and enterprise, the system of licenses and all pervasive controls imposed on the private sector in the country combined with confiscatory personal taxation, not only discouraged and penalized honest free enterprise, but encouraged and brought success and wealth to a new breed of bribers, tax evaders and black marketers.

In a single generation, great fortunes largely transferred abroad were built at a time when personal incomes of Rs 1 lakh per year were taxed at 98 per cent. The nationalization, on expropriatory terms, of insurance and banks, conveniently created a virtual monopoly of investible and lendable funds while fiscal policies combined with the use made of the Companies Act, the Industries Development & Regulations Act, the Monopolies and Restrictive Trade Practices Act and innumerable other enactments, regulations and administrative decisions, effectively concentrated all real economic power in the hands of politicians in power and bureaucracy. Under such conditions efforts at promoting and bringing to fruition large projects however desirable became a nightmarish and time consuming one or ended in outright rejection.

JRD's words were to echo strongly later with TCS. We too felt extremely constrained. While we saw how the West was leveraging mainframe computers and information technology to achieve efficiency through bulk data processing in sectors such as defence and banking, India was missing out on the IT revolution.

But we were persistent. In just the same way that the Tatas had been pioneers in steel, energy and engines, we believed that TCS could be a pioneer in IT. We had confidence that if we could bring these new technologies into India, they could change the course of the nation and some day be a very important parameter for growth.

To serve an overseas market, we needed the latest learning, the latest generation of computers to be imported and we needed to explore top-of-the-line partnerships. So the first task was to find a way to import the equipment into India. This meant crossing swords with the government and the mighty licence raj.

At that time every industry had an administrative ministry in the Central government. We came under the Department of Electronics (DoE) which was headed by Professor M.G.K. Menon. Prof. Menon was also the Chairman of the Electronics Commission, the Secretary of the Department of Electronics, and the Scientific Adviser to the Government on Defence.

As a scientific department, the DoE reported directly to the prime minister, and unfortunately the department was very wary of our intentions. In addition, since TCS was a division of Tata Sons and the Tata Group was listed under MRTP as a dominant company because of its size and market share, any expansion which resulted in a capacity increase of 25 per cent or more required approval from the Monopolies and Restrictive Trade Practices Commission (MRTPC). In practice this meant another round of bureaucratic torture.

The process for importing a computer was mind-bogglingly complex and every stage had its own challenges, mostly because this was all being done for the very first time in India and the existing laws were open to interpretation by government officials who were unfamiliar with computers.

The process went something like this:

1. First we had to submit an application for an import licence to the DoE. This included an application for import of capital goods as well. As part of this process we had to justify what we wanted to do with the computer. Towards this we would produce a letter of intent from Burroughs placing an order for software services from TCS. Also included was the proforma invoice with model numbers of the machines; sometimes technical literature was also sent.

2. Eleven copies were required as copies would be sent to various ministries including finance, commerce and industries. The DoE would then obtain the capital goods permission.

3. Next we had to obtain approval from the MRTPC as we belonged to a 'large' business house.

4. Then we had to navigate the complicated import tariffs and estimate the customs duty, which as it turned out was more than the cost of the machine itself.

5. We also had to get approval for free foreign exchange (to pay in US dollars for the import) from the government.

6. We had to justify the import by undertaking an export obligation to export twice the import cost (CIF) over a five-year period after the import. Failure to do so would involve confiscation of the machine in addition to severe financial penalties.

7. We also had to obtain an export licence from the US Department of Commerce and provide an 'end user certificate'. This was a problem when we had an order for a defence laboratory. Even so, the exporting nation had the right to monitor the use of the machine and confiscate it and begin criminal proceedings against us should there be any misuse.

8. Once we had secured all the above licences and approvals we had to arrange for the shipment of the equipment which

weighed several tons; for large systems we had to charter a B707 freighter!

9. When the equipment arrived in India we had to clear it through the stringent custom procedures.

10. Finally we had to transport the bulky yet delicate equipment to the data centre and install it. This posed other problems as roads could be bumpy, underpasses not high enough to allow trucks with tall tape drives to pass under without getting jammed, lifts not large enough, false floor tiles not strong enough to take the load without buckling etc. etc.

Once we decided to import our first mainframe, we quickly found ourselves caught in the maze of government departments and their regulations. It is no exaggeration to say that TCS was faced with a totally unprecedented situation.

In the early 1970s Burroughs, then the second largest computer manufacturer after IBM, saw India as a potential market and was willing to share its technology. In 1973 TCS signed an agreement with Burroughs. We agreed to distribute and sell Burroughs computers in India and they agreed to sell us a new Burroughs B1728 'small system' computer.

Though advanced for its day, the B1728 would not be categorized as a mainframe today because it had only 128 KB of memory and 8 MB of disk space to start with. The memory sticks in our pockets today have larger storage capacities.

Our strategy was to import the machine, train ourselves to program and write software applications for it, and then to sell these services to markets outside India in order to earn foreign exchange. But we had not anticipated just how difficult it would be to import a new mainframe into India.

At that time, nobody in the private sector had imported a brand new mainframe. There were about 300 mainframe computers in the country that had been imported by university research departments, government agencies or the Ministry of Defence, but none of them had to pay import duty. Similarly there was also no precedent for customs duty computation for import of new systems in private sector, because till then no one in private sector had imported a brand new computer. The practice till then was that

IBM and ICL used sub systems and parts, which they refurbished in their factories in India before making them available to Indian customers. These imports were treated as "project" imports which had a different duty computation. So when TCS imported a new mainframe it was a whole new matter.

The Indian government said it would give us permission to import a new mainframe, but only if we exported twice its value over a five-year period. It was a bold step for TCS to make this commitment at that stage because we hardly had any export revenue to speak of.

That is how the Indian software industry was born, not by any grand design but by an accident of history because India was short of foreign exchange and we had to earn foreign exchange to pay for the importation of a new Burroughs mainframe.

The government's foreign exchange was reserved exclusively for defence and other government projects. Others seeking foreign exchange were referred to two institutional banks, IDBI and ICICI. Both institutional banks had access to foreign exchange through the World Bank and could provide this to Indian companies in the form of loans. But our owners, the Tatas, did not want to go down this route because the loans came with a convertibility clause that meant if the borrower defaulted, the bank would have an option to convert their money into equity. Tata Sons was a privately held limited company with charitable trusts as the owners, and the trusts did not want any outsiders to have a stake in the company.

So instead of tapping the institutional banks when we wanted to purchase the Burroughs mainframe in 1973, we approached Citibank. The US bank agreed to provide us with a loan in New York at 1 per cent over the London Interbank Rate (Libor) so the interest rate was about 3 or 4 per cent compared to the 8 or 9 per cent we would have had to pay in India.

We planned to service the loan through Tata Inc. in New York using the foreign exchange we earned in the US. Tata Inc. was a company originally set up to procure spare parts for Air-India, but later it became an arm of Tata Steel. The arrangement with the Tatas was that when any Tata group company purchased material from the US, it was routed through Tata Inc. which in turn received a commission for handling the paperwork.

It was a perfectly good idea, but the Indian government rejected it because the bureaucrats said: 'We do not allow Indian companies to borrow abroad.' We enlisted the support of the Secretary of Economic Affairs because he was the contemporary of the father of a TCS colleague when they had been at the Reserve Bank. The Secretary agreed it was a good idea, but the department director had serious reservations. Ultimately I think the bureaucrats were suspicious of any new ideas and it was perhaps easier to say 'no'. Whatever the case, at that time the bureaucrats had the power to block initiatives, and they chose to do just that.

As a result, we had to borrow in rupees, which was more expensive, and then convert the loan into foreign exchange. We obtained the loan from Citibank in Bombay, issued a letter of credit to Tata Inc. in New York who purchased the machine and then exported it to us. But we incurred extra costs all the way. We also had to enter into a forward contract to protect ourselves against a devaluation of the rupee during the five-year term of the bank loan. It was the most inefficient way of doing things, but the government insisted we do it that way if we wanted the import licence.

It fell to Jayant to make all these applications. He had to learn things which nobody knew. The most complicated problem he faced was that nobody knew what the import duty on a new computer should be. Under India's import customs tariff nomenclature there was no mention of 'computers'. Oddly enough it did not come under 'machines' either, even though a computer was formally called an electronic data processing (EDP) machine.

Instead computers came under Section 76 which was for 'electronic appliances and apparatus not specified elsewhere'. That meant a gigantic mainframe computer that required a room to house it and air conditioning to keep it from overheating was lumped together with mixer-grinders, toasters and electric razors. Since it was classified as an apparatus, it also attracted a higher rate of duty. An apparatus was considered to be a non-essential luxury item and attracted a 60 per cent import tax rather than the 40 per cent that applied to machines which were meant to be used for industrial purposes.

Ironically there was a different nomenclature in place for excise duty. Excise duty was charged by the Central government on the value of equipment manufactured in India, before sales tax. When something was imported, in order to protect the domestic industry, the government added the equivalent of excise duty which was called countervailing duty (CVD) to the import tax. To figure out the correct CVD rate we had to refer to the excise manual which followed the Brussels nomenclature and classified computers as machines. So a computer was a machine for CVD purposes and an apparatus for the purposes of import duty.

Over and above this, there were cascading duties as well: if the import duty was less than 40 per cent, the importer paid auxiliary duty at a 2 per cent rate; over 40 per cent the auxiliary duty was 5 per cent. Then you had to add the CVD of 15 per cent. We added all the numbers up and thought the total duty would be about 75 per cent.

But when we went to the customs and excise department at the airport to verify the calculations we were told that the CVD was applied on the ad valorem amount after the import duty and auxiliary duty were calculated, which meant the total duty payable on an imported mainframe computer was 101.25 per cent—although this was not actually written down anywhere.

This new and shocking development had to be communicated to Kohli so Jayant drove to a public phone booth outside the airport and called him. Jayant got through to Kohli's assistant and gave him the news but the assistant said, 'You had better tell him yourself in person.' No one wanted to be the harbinger of bad news.

The drive from Santa Cruz up north to the Air-India building in south Mumbai was the longest ever for Jayant who was chosen to deliver this bit of news. So what would have been a hot drive in a non-air-conditioned car became an even hotter one. In his inimitable style though, Jayant stood through Kohli's dressing-down on why the calculations were so off track.

The system itself cost $340,000 but we ended up paying more than twice that, and losing out on the exchange rate too.

Burroughs also needed a licence to export equipment from the US because the mainframe was considered a strategic item and it needed approval from the US defence department. So we had to provide a statement about what we would do with the computer.

The whole process took between nine months and a year. We started in 1973 and we finally imported the computer in 1974. Later on, it sometimes took two years because the process became even more complicated when the government decided that we were a Monopoly Restricted Trade Practice and our licence applications had to be approved by multiple committees.

The complicated processes, which often defied reason, forced us to become very creative in finding ways to work around the challenges. For example, we found out that we could import the equipment under a special customs bond that enabled us to move it from the airport and open it for inspection by customs at our own offices rather than at the airport warehouse where equipment damage was more likely.

We managed to persuade the customs authorities to agree to a bond which involved the customs officers at the airport wrapping each of the equipment boxes with wire and putting a lead seal on them. Then the boxes were loaded onto two or three trucks which came in a convoy escorted by customs officers to our offices in the Air-India building in Bombay.

When we got to our office at the Air-India building and offloaded the trucks the customs officials decided they were tired so we took them to the Taj for dinner, served copious quantities of beer and gave them taxi fare to get home. They said they would return early the next morning to clear the equipment.

Next day we arrived at the office very early to make sure the documentation was in order. To our horror we discovered that the electrician, in his eagerness to help, had removed the seals, 'so the boxes could be opened easily'!

I was with Jayant and a couple of field engineers and we asked ourselves what we should do now. We found all the seals and the wires which were in a dustbin, wrapped all the boxes up again with the wire and threaded the seals onto the end and bent the wire so it looked as though it had not been tampered with. We didn't know what would happen but we were concerned that the customs officials might say we had broken the bond and would therefore confiscate the equipment. We had visions of ourselves languishing in jail.

The customs people turned up soon. As soon as they arrived we said, 'See, here are the seals,' and quickly broke the seals in front of them before they could inspect them too closely. Luckily the strategy worked beautifully.

Our agony was not over. We still had the task of verifying the list of items on the import licence with the invoice—nothing tallied because we had all the model numbers from the marketing literature, the engineering guys had their own part numbers and the finance department which made out the invoice had yet another set of numbers.

For example, the import licence was for a B1728 computer but the invoice said 'B Series' and somewhere else it said 'CPU 1728' and also '1700 range'. The customs officers asked us, 'But where does it say B1728?' Suddenly one of us saw there was a table on the underside of the box, scrambled under and quickly scribbled 'B1728' in one of the columns. We then called the officers over and showed them the legend. They said 'Okay'. Really all they wanted to do was to tick off something that said 'B1728'.

Next time around, in 1976, when we imported a much bigger Burroughs 6748 machine that cost over $1 million, we told the Burroughs guys to make sure the invoice looked just like the sales material and matched the numbers on the equipment.

Each cabinet in that machine weighed over a ton and the dimensions were larger than the inside of the elevator in the Air-India building. So we actually considered hoisting the cabinets up, slung from a hook on the underside of the elevator. In the end, however, we removed the internal elevator car railings and then somehow managed to slide the cabinets diagonally into the elevator car.

At our offices in the Air-India building we had to create a data centre which involved creating a raised floor so cabling could run underneath. Traditionally the void below would be created like a grid, with slotted angles much like those found in a child's Mecano set. This grid would then be covered with tiles to create the raised floor.

In the case of the B6700, the mainframe also required a cold chamber under it and fans under the computer cabinets which would suck the cold air in to cool the machines. Kohli decided to try out an innovation and suggested that we use 9 in x 9 in x 9 in bricks made of coal ash, a byproduct of electricity generation at Tata Electric, as fillers.

Columns of these would form the grid and tiles would be placed above. However the column distances necessitated larger tiles, so they had to be specially ordered and when we moved the cabinets across the room to position them, the larger tiles sagged much more than the smaller ones, causing them to crack. So the attempted innovation turned out to be more of an irritant. Even so, the attempt to recycle waste material was a cause worth trying out and I am sure it would have met the appreciation of 'green' advocators.

Our frustration was far from over. The day after we installed the new mainframe in the Air-India building, the government's annual finance budget was announced and the duty on computers was reduced from the 101.25 per cent we had paid to a total of 60 per cent.

In those days it was hard to predict what the policy changes would be in forthcoming budgets and Kohli had been expediting the import because of concerns about the possible devaluation of the rupee. But at least we stood to benefit in the future.

We had fought with the government for a rationalization of duties and appealed to the tax administrators on the basis that the mainframe had been wrongly classified. But at every stage we lost because the administrators said a complex electronic circuit board could not be defined as a machine because it had no moving parts. So eventually we decided to take the issue to the civil courts.

Finally, in 1980, four years after we launched the first appeal, I went with Jayant to the Bombay High Court and our case was heard. After listening to arguments from both sides the judge ruled that the government had no case and that the computers we had imported had been wrongly classified as 'appliance and apparatus' rather than EDP machines. He ordered a full refund of customs and excise duties, so we got a refund of Rs 65 lakh in 1980. For all our efforts Jayant and I treated ourselves to lunch.

It was an important ruling not just because of the refund, but because it forced the government to create a specific classification for computers. Not only did we help create a policy to import computers, but we helped create the software export industry and we got computers correctly classified for customs duties too.

In the early 1980s we started working with Britain's WTSL on a project that involved developing code on an IBM mainframe. After WTSL offered to sell us one of their mainframes, the Indian government agreed to give us a licence to import a second-hand IBM mainframe computer from the US.

We bought it for about $110,000 and installed it in the SEEPZ free trade zone in Bombay which was where we undertook the whole offshore project for WTSL. But we had a huge problem getting the software licence from IBM, who had quit India in 1978. At that time IBM sold hardware but their software was leased necessitating the payment of licence fees, leading to a tax liability. IBM imposed all kinds of riders and conditions before they would give us the licence.

Their contention was that since we were using their operating system we should pay for the software licence; the sale did not automatically give us the right to use the software. We found help in the form of Dan Gupta, a US-based senior executive in IBM who was eventually able to arrange the licences we needed and we went ahead with the purchase. That was the first instance of getting a system specifically for an overseas project.

Five years later, in 1987, we began the process of importing our first new IBM mainframe, an IBM 3090-150E. We eventually installed the machine in Madras a year later, in 1988. The process actually took longer than it had back in 1974 with the B1728. We later upgraded to a 3090-250J, making it the largest mainframe site in the country for several years. It was one of the first water-cooled machines in the country, a major technological feature at that time. Water-cooled machines were larger and more powerful than the earlier generation of air-cooled machines. Ironically, air-cooled machines became more effective in the mid-1990s, and all our later (larger) machines were air-cooled; the 3090-250J was the last water-cooled machine in TCS.

The gross block (the total value of the asset) of the 3090

computer was higher than the total gross block of assets of TCS itself at that time and therefore the investment decision was almost like betting the company's future. We had to enhance our business substantially to get a return on what looked like a 'massive' investment at the time.

Once again, the challenge in acquiring the machine lay not in the technology, but in overcoming the bureaucracy and in figuring out the customs tariffs. This time the duties totalled 170 per cent, so the $4 million cost instantly became $10 million.

In fact it took so long to work our way through the approvals process which involved three separate ministries—finance, commerce and defence—that by the time we got the import licence, the model number had changed and there was a newer machine available. TCS always insisted on buying the latest machines because we believed it differentiated us at a time when many saw India as a dumping ground for second-hand technology. So we had to submit a new application and begin the process all over again, which is why it took over two years.

The entire system had to be loaded on a chartered flight and weighed 17 tons—for a machine with the power of a PC today. There were about seventy-five boxes in all. The whole consignment landed in Madras airport, and we were there at the airport to make sure they brought in all the boxes.

We completed customs clearance at the airport and commissioned the machine over two or three days in our office, with the help of an IBMer who flew in specially from Australia for the purpose.

For the next five years after installation, we were busy fulfilling the export obligations. The $10 million purchase price was big money at that time and with trained people in place, IBM laboratories began to give us work; this in turn spurred us on to introduce a process for software development—a key advantage for us in subsequent years.

By the time we imported the IBM mainframe, we had undergone the process of importing computers many times over. Each one proved to be a learning experience. We developed an almost infinite sense of patience in dealing with the government, for whom the 'rule book' was a Bible. We stood through the grilling and questioning of our intentions and most importantly we learnt that focusing on the outcome can keep you going through it all. Working with a 'difficult' government in a challenging environment was a free lesson in being customer-centric without getting frustrated.

Installing each of these mainframes was only the beginning of the journey. Each of us needed to be trained, some on hardware and others on software. My hardware training took me to Toronto and Montreal at the Burroughs labs and to Goleta and Irvine in California at the Burroughs factories and training centres.

On reflection I believe these experiences shaped TCS and all of us in more ways than one. Doing more with less became part of our DNA. Our technical competency was tested because, with both memory and disk capacity in short supply, we had to build applications in the most optimal way with what we had.

At the same time our export obligations meant that quality could not be compromised. This in turn forced us to rely on each other's creativity and talent which brought us together as a team and positively reinforced an attitude of 'can do'. The greatest learning happens in difficult situations.

Today there is much talk about the need for occupational standards benchmarking with global standards, but for the IT industry back then, our standards were set at the very outset by our global customers. They would state their requirements clearly and reject work that did not meet these standards. We had no option but to ensure our people, processes, technologies and solutions met global standards. It did not stop at that. With increasing competition we even had to prove that our value addition to the customer was far greater than others'; this meant that striving for excellence was a way of life and that 'excellence' itself was always a moving target.

# 3

# 1996–2002: THE LATER YEARS

## CHANGE OF GUARD

BY THE MID-1990S, TCS had entered a new phase in its development and was beginning to expand its reach. Within the organization a change of guard was imminent and there was more than one contender for the top job. Kohli had built a senior management team that included myself and a few others like Dr Nirmal Jain and Y.P. Sahni. So, contrary to popular belief, there were several people in the fray for the top job.

Since I had joined TCS, I had been given multiple roles and moved from role to new role and challenge to new challenge on a regular basis. I had moved from hardware to software and from sales to marketing and then spent time fine-tuning my delivery capabilities before joining the Manpower Allocation Task Committee.

It was Kohli's style to throw a problem at you. The more problems you solved, the more were thrown at you. This thorough grounding gave people the confidence to sometimes even take on new challenges on their own. As a result, I felt ready for any responsibility and challenge in the company.

I believe that you need to acquire this inherent strength to build yourself through experience. TCS always welcomed anyone willing to take responsibility beyond their own sandboxed role in the organization. If you showed enthusiasm and the ability to innovate, the organization would provide the opportunities for you to reach your full potential and achieve your dreams. This remains a key feature of the TCS culture even today.

Kohli was passionate about turning us into world-class professionals. He would mentor people in his own unique style which was more critical than complimentary: it was usually a one-way communication rather than a dialogue and certainly not the collaborative process that is prevalent today.

He observed people closely and would not hesitate to redirect them if he felt they were straying from their priorities. I remember an incident narrated to me by an ex-TCSer who was very fond of cricket. Kohli found him missing for too long for his liking so he marched up to him and told him that while he knew he liked working for TCS, he also knew he loved cricket. 'I have nothing against that, but I want you to choose between TCS and TSC,' Kohli said. After a puzzled moment my colleague realized that TSC stood for the Tata Sports Club. That was Kohli's way of communicating that nothing could be more important than the institution you worked for, and that you should never lose that focus.

TCS inherited a strong performance management system from Kohli. He was a great believer in it and had devised the TCS system based on what he saw at Tata Electric. That meant that I as an appraiser was responsible for those working for me. Like others, I took part in the self-appraisal process which involved the appraiser discussing both qualitative and quantitative measures with each team member. If you disagreed with your appraiser's comments, you could go to a higher authority. It was called the spider web assessment. Kohli ensured everyone got a chance and to his credit he was more than fair.

People often ask me whether I was scared of Kohli. My own family felt he was very stern. But because I spent so much time with him, I could see him as the thorough professional that he really was. By then I had devised my own way to get my points across, using the might of the pen, since no one could match Kohli in a verbal exchange. Based on my own experience, I always advise young professionals to find smart ways to deal with difficult bosses. 'Otherwise,' I tell them, 'you have only yourself to blame.'

Kohli's style worked for him and worked for the TCS of that time. Perhaps a strong, bold and visionary leader was what TCS needed at the start, given the challenge we had ahead of building something from scratch. Kohli was a real visionary and although his decisions often seemed questionable initially, in the long run they turned out to be good for the company.

In retrospect, Kohli's decision when he chose me as his successor was based primarily on his trust and confidence in me and his observations of my ability to build customer relationships. When faced with the choice of joining Tata Burroughs or staying with TCS, I had chosen the latter and by doing so had indicated my belief in the opportunity, my belief in Kohli and my willingness to take a risk. Perhaps this made Kohli feel I could be trusted.

I was running our operations in America and Dr Jain was running the business in Europe when Kohli stepped down as Chief Executive, and I think most people inside TCS expected one of us to take over. We both had different qualities and Kohli was concerned that the succession process should be as fair and transparent as possible, so before he made his decision he drew up a scoresheet listing our strengths and weaknesses. Before he told me that he wanted me to take over as Chief Executive he called us both into his office separately and went through the scoresheet with each of us.

Overall, I think Dr Jain and I had different strengths, but certainly I tended to be more people- and client-oriented. Ultimately I think Kohli recognized that the qualities he saw in me, especially my emphasis on customers, were perhaps best suited to the challenges TCS would face in its next growth phase.

So in September 1996 I was faced with one of the biggest moments in my life. Having started as a trainee in 1972, twenty-four years later I found myself at the helm of the company. Suddenly from working for someone, I was now the boss.

Nobody is ever ready for the top job, despite what they may say. As long as there is at least one management layer above you, you are shielded. The management takes the final decisions and carries the ultimate responsibility for those decisions. Once you are at the top, reality hits and you feel the umbilical cord being cut. Now the buck stops with you. I felt that I had not been exposed to the business to the extent that I would have liked. I knew the US and UK markets which were responsible for 75 per cent of our revenues, but I had not been very involved in continental Europe, Singapore, Japan or Australia which were TCS's other main markets. When I looked at the task ahead, my job as CEO seemed to take on enormous proportions; it looked to me like ten jobs all rolled into one.

While I think Kohli and I shared a common vision for TCS, our management styles were very different, and this was immediately apparent to TCS employees. Kohli had a direct management style and exercised very tight control. He was intellectual, authoritative and aloof—some even described him as an autocrat. Most young recruits were quite afraid of him, in awe of his wisdom and wary of his sharp tongue. As Jayant says, 'You did not ever want to deliver bad news to him because you always felt it could be a career-limiting move.' When it came to taking decisions, Kohli tended to keep a distance from the TCS staff. He would take in all the inputs from colleagues and then, almost out of a black box, reach a decision.

In contrast, I consciously tried to be very participative and actively sought to foster debate and discussion, and to ensure that everyone with a valid view had the opportunity to contribute to a debate and express themselves. If there was a problem I tried to apply strong analytics to it in order to understand what had happened, why it happened and what could be done to try and prevent it from happening again.

I made a point of trying to understand what the individual talents and capabilities of people were, and then encouraged them to analyse problems and consider the pros and cons of specific actions before reaching a decision. I also used to take copious notes at meetings and provided feedback to all concerned, a habit that has remained with me till this day.

Wherever possible, I tried to meet and listen to lots of people and then condense what they had to say into very crisp clear statements: 'This is what I heard, and this is what it means to TCS.' And I tried to avoid simply stating a principle, for example, 'We must be more transparent with clients.' Instead, I would often try and turn the principle into a story. 'I met so-and-so and this is what he said and this is what happened and these are the types of things that happened. And by the way all of this means that we must be more transparent . . .'

I think this anecdotal approach is a good way of fostering strong management skills and getting management to buy into a process. In meetings, what is important is to get people to express their opinions and to get others to either agree or provide alternative points of view, and then to try and come up with a consensus. If that was not possible I would of course bring the discussions to a close and reach a decision myself. But even when I was giving an order I always tried to give it as a suggestion, for example, 'You might want to try this . . .'

I think one result of this policy of active inclusion was that TCS employees tended to stay with the company much longer than their counterparts at other firms. I also tried to ensure that after joining TCS, people changed their roles every two or three years in order to broaden their experience and ensure that they had new opportunities and challenges.

This wide exposure to different people and a variety of situations also meant that TCS employees quickly absorbed the culture of the company, for example, the importance of integrity and putting the customer first, no matter what the cost. Today, TCS is becoming more rigorous about explicit internal messaging. Even so you still learn a lot from the work environment around you; it is very much like informal schooling.

After five years it is usually pretty difficult to tell the difference between someone who has been trained inside TCS as a new recruit, and an old-timer. If they are sitting around a table together they are almost interchangeable. They subscribe to the same value systems and share the same leadership DNA.

As a manager, I think it is very important not only to *listen* to what people are telling you but also to *understand* what they are saying and *how* they are saying it. Of course it is important to select the right people for a job, but it is also important to hold them totally accountable and to be upfront and direct with people if they make mistakes.

I remember on one occasion I was meeting with a relatively junior employee and was asking him a series of questions that appeared to get him flustered. His manager was there and was trying to help him out by giving him the answers. I told the manager afterwards, 'If you go on answering my questions, how will he learn accountability, he will keep shifting the work up to you and never learn.'

I could be direct with managers when called for, pointing out their weaknesses and the issues they needed to address. But I think if you asked them what my main weakness was they would say that sometimes I overdid the participative style and allowed people to talk too much before reaching a decision.

Nevertheless, on the whole I think the participative model worked. For example, we came up with the 'Top 10 by 2010' target through a participatory dialogue. In contrast, under Kohli you would submit suggestions, hear nothing for some time—and then out would pop the right answer.

I created a think tank and brought in Pankaj Ghemawat, a respected professor from Harvard Business School (now with IESE Business School, Barcelona) to lead the think tank strategy sessions. These meetings helped push the TCS structure towards a much more participative style with open discussions—it was a total departure in style from the past and something that we desperately needed to do at the time. We had some outstanding people amongst us and I felt that not leveraging their ideas would be a gross failure on my part.

I also encouraged the creation of transparent internal policies that everyone understood and to which there would be no exceptions. I felt it was better that there should be zero exceptions and that everything should be decided by the policy. If you didn't like it, you could go back to the person who created the policy, hold them accountable for setting it and argue the case. This transformed the culture at the workplace because it meant that it was pointless to ask for exceptions. It was all about coming up with a good policy— one policy for everyone.

Today, succession planning has become a core aspect of good corporate governance, unlike at the time of my taking over as CEO. It is a matter discussed in the boardroom and taken up by the nomination committee in great detail. The process involves looking at potential candidates who will build organization strength, fulfil its strategic intent and be a role model for organizational values. The potential candidate need not necessarily be someone from within the organization. In spite of this there are still plenty of instances where things have not gone to plan. CEOs have been involved in financial fraud; they may have bypassed risks and even been creative with figures. It is ironic that even with governance guidelines in place, implementation of these can still go wrong.

Succession planning when I stepped into Kohli's shoes was an unheard-of concept. Learning on the job and working your way through was the only strategy. So when I took over there were several changes at TCS, some of which can be attributed to my different work style and some which I initiated. In terms of the business itself, we could already hear the rumbles of the Year 2000 (Y2K) problem that would soon become a game-changing opportunity for us.

## THE Y2K PHENOMENON

AS THE TWENTIETH century came to a close, the Year 2000 (Y2K) problem which afflicted almost all computer code developed for mainframe computers since the 1960s, threatened to cause chaos in leading economies and bring key defence, health and transport systems to a grinding halt.

At its core, the problem had arisen because, in an effort to save valuable memory space, many early software programs used two digits rather than four to designate the year in a date field. That meant at midnight on 31 December 1999, the date would become '1/1/00' and any calculations based on the date would fail.

Understandably there was considerable fear and apprehension among both private sector companies and governments alike regarding the possible failure of their systems. By now computers had become mainstream and an intricate part of businesses everywhere, and there were literally thousands of computers around the world running code that needed to be adjusted before the turn of the century. Even the date field, if the year was two digits, would have to be increased from a yy/mm/dd to a yyyy/mm/dd format. This meant that wherever there was a date field in a file its size would increase by two digits or characters, and this was not as simple as it might sound at first. Corporate IT departments and IT consultancies in countries like the US lacked the manpower to deal with a problem of this scale so they inevitably turned to India which had a huge and largely untapped pool of low-cost labour.

For the Indian IT industry as a whole, the Y2K problem created an enormous opportunity to expand its client base. For existing Indian IT companies, it presented an opportunity to raise their profiles, while for others it was a reason to get into the software business.

Of course TCS had the 'early bird' advantage, so Y2K provided a big opportunity for us to scale up our operations. In fact Y2K was important for TCS because it played to our strengths in two ways.

First, TCS had built its original business around migration— from one system to another or from one language to another—and we had designed software tools to automate this process. All our migration business was based on tools that we had built internally. Of course everybody at TCS used to build their own software tools and that was a challenge because sometimes we had ten tools for the same thing—but it was a good problem to have. We realized early on that Y2K was also a migration issue that involved importing a huge number of programs and lines of code into TCS systems, identifying where the date references were, correcting the date, testing it, then shipping the corrected code back to the customer. It could therefore be addressed using the migration tools we had developed years ago.

Second, addressing the Y2K problem did not call for pure programming talent. We were able to adopt a factory assembly line approach towards correcting the legacy Y2K code. We established the first software factory in Chennai because Y2K was largely a mainframe-oriented problem and Chennai was where we had most of our mainframe capabilities. We also partnered with a number of smaller companies and were able to borrow their programmers. We trained them on the application suite, on our process discipline and our tool sets. These tool sets essentially helped identify the elements in a computer program that would be affected with logical errors when the clock rolled over from dd/mm/99 to dd/mm/oo.

A particular tool set designed for programs written in the COBOL mainframe computer language could, for instance, quickly identify the fields that needed to be converted, a process that would have taken the naked eye much longer. We developed a seventeen-step assembly line process in Chennai and innovated with ideas from the Production Quality Compiler Compiler (PQCC) research project at Carnegie Mellon University to build our tools. Thus we were able to read through millions of lines of code with Y2K problems and apply remedies in a semi-automated manner. As a result we were able to sign huge new contracts with large multinationals to migrate and upgrade their legacy software.

Our ability to use our own migration tools and the establishment of the software factory in Chennai distinguished our approach to the Y2K problem from that of our competitors and enabled us to deliver a much more efficient, reliable and faster service to our customers.

This approach enabled us to handle between 600 million and 700 million lines of code—far more than anyone else. While other Indian firms also rushed to get a piece of the Y2K work, TCS managed to get the bulk of the business due to our technical prowess in automation tools, technologies and processes. From 1995, the year before Kohli stepped down, to 1999, our revenues ballooned from $125 million to $419 million, and we still managed to maintain 32 per cent operating margins.

The factory approach towards the Y2K problem, coupled with the processes we developed working for IBM Labs and General Electric (GE), also resulted in significant internal changes within TCS. First, we were hiring a lot of people, but not all of them needed to be engineers; so we developed the concept of a business associate. Second, because of the numbers, we had to strengthen many of our processes including hiring, training placement and delivery processes to make them highly scalable.

As a result we ended up with thousands of new programmers who were trained on FORTRAN, PLI and COBOL applications and on migration programs for IBM, ICL, Tandem and other hardware companies. Once the Y2K problem had been successfully addressed, many of our clients wanted the programmers to continue maintaining their applications.

We were able to expand into new segments especially in the financial sector which was more compliance focused. But the Y2K problem had affected multiple industry sectors and we were in a position to proactively leverage what we learned in one sector to help companies in other sectors—and our customers quickly realized this.

The diversity of clients allowed us to cross-pollinate—understand the best practices in a particular sector and find uses for it in another. Clients therefore began to ask us to tell them what they could do better. Our continued engagement with these customers went well beyond Y2K. We were challenged to help our clients build their own intellectual assets and differentiators. As we became more engaged with these sectors, we realized that to constantly enhance our value-add, we needed to acquire domain expertise.

TCS's domain expertise was built by focusing initially on those sectors that absorbed technology fastest. The financial services sector had the largest rates of absorption of IT globally, and was also one of the first in India to adopt information technology.

Several foreign banks and securities firms had an early presence in India which enabled us to recruit high quality financial service expertise domestically early in our history. Similarly, we developed an expertise in insurance because many of the migration projects we had undertaken were for foreign insurance companies.

Our telecommunications domain expertise grew out of our work as a subcontractor to IBM on contracts with Canada's Nortel Networks and with British Telecom (BT). Nortel began to look seriously at India because the telecommunications sector was opening up and as part of the liberalization of the 1990s, a new Indian telecommunications policy was drafted.

The new policy allowed overseas companies to make direct investments in the Indian telecommunications market for the first time and encouraged foreign institutional investors to invest in the sector. The changes resulted in a number of private domestic and foreign telecommunications companies making an entry into the Indian market.

At the same time, Videsh Sanchar Nigam Ltd. (VSNL) and Mahanagar Telephone Nigam Ltd. (MTNL), the two government-owned organizations in charge of international and domestic telecom services respectively, were beginning to modernize their networks and were looking to procure new equipment. Until then telecom links within India and those between India and the rest of the world were obsolete, unreliable, slow and expensive.

TCS spotted the opportunity and although distance and the lack of international bandwidth was a problem making collaboration difficult, we began scouting for telecom business in Canada and the US. Much of the time potential customers cited poor bandwidth as the reason for not doing business with us. But with the new Indian telecom regime in place, Diju Raha, who oversaw Nortel's expansion in India at the time, recognized the potential of India to supply the back-end services that would fuel the tech boom of the 1990s.

Diju betted on India at a time when few western technology companies looked towards the country. He was convinced that partnering with a local Indian software company would create a beachhead for Nortel and demonstrate the Canadian company's commitment to India. He felt that if Nortel proved its willingness to invest in India, it would be better positioned to win the orders from Indian telecom companies when they came.

The relationship between Nortel and TCS which began then was unique in many ways and demonstrates the vision of many of those involved. In the 1990s Nortel was a leading supplier of telecommunications equipment and an R&D powerhouse having acquired Bell-Northern Research (BNR), a joint venture between Bell Canada and Northern Telecom.

BNR's researchers pioneered the view that a telephone switch (PBX or central office) was best regarded as a special form of real-time computer. Traditionally a switch had been viewed as a relatively dumb piece of hardware that could only handle basic telephone calls. But features such as conference calls, call forwarding and voice mail required much more flexibility leading to the development of the modern computer-controlled digital switch.

Diju recognized that Nortel could tap India's emerging expertise in software development and engineering to keep its new digital switches ahead of the competition and position the Canadian company for growth in India at the same time. He brought a Nortel delegation to India to see what was happening on the ground and when they returned to Canada the president of BNR told him, 'So long as you tackle the infrastructure, things can move forward.'

That endorsement made Diju's job easier, but he still had to overcome the key infrastructure problem—the lack of high speed communications links between Canada and India. He decided the only option was to pay VNSL upfront to install a dedicated high-speed data link that would link Mumbai to Ottawa, and from there to BNR's development labs. The data link (64 KBps), which also supported videoconferencing, was maintained and supported by BNR at the Canadian end and VSNL at the India end.

The next challenge was to persuade a sceptical BNR development team that project work should be transferred to India. Diju devised an incentive scheme under which he promised that for every $1 of project work moved to India, the R&D team in Canada would receive $1 in funding. Since costs in India were about one-third of those in Canada, he knew that even with the incentives, the investment still made sense.

As part of the project TCS and BNR set up a joint research lab in the Borivali export zone in the Mumbai suburbs and installed a selection of switches sent by Nortel from Canada. This was the first time TCS had set up a captive office in a secure bonded area, a move that gave Nortel the confidence that its intellectual property was safe.

With the infrastructure in place, the next step was the transfer of knowledge to TCS. Nortel selected a team of people whose job was to coach the Indian team for the new project, help with the transition and then with testing and maintenance.

Instead of sending software code stored on tapes back and forth between Canada and India, the dedicated high-speed data link meant that Nortel developers in Ottawa could remotely access the new software running on the switches in the TCS–BNR Borivali lab and test new features before releasing the updated code to customers in the European and North American markets.

At the peak about a hundred TCSers were working on the project which was unique at the time because it demanded both hardware and software integration, and a tremendous coordination effort between geographically dispersed teams. It was a bold move for Nortel to bet on India in the 1990s but it was also an important milestone for TCS because we demonstrated that with the right infrastructure and bandwidth in place, we could deliver on time and within budget.

The Nortel project helped TCS build its telecom domain expertise, gave us the confidence to set up other dedicated customer development centres and proved the viability of the offshore software development model. Following the success of the Nortel–TCS partnership, Ericsson, AT&T and later BT all established development centres in India. The Nortel experience also paved the way for TCS to win the contract to provide IT services for Tata Teleservices which was established in 1997 as a joint venture between Tata and Bell Canada.

Not only did this enable us to deepen our domain capability expertise in telecom, TCS was also able to use the systems and solutions we built for Tata Teleservices to win other customers in the telecom industry. As a result telecom became one of our largest areas of domain expertise and accounts for about 15 per cent of TCS revenues today.

The growing importance of domain expertise led to a significant reorganization within TCS. Before 2000, our domain-driven business was still relatively small and mainly focused on financial services and telecom, but after the turn of the century, I reorganized the company around industry practices, service practices and sales on a geographic basis. The industry practices were charged with building the domain capability and the service practices were responsible for ensuring we had the necessary technical capabilities for application building and for developing or buying the software tools we needed.

The reorganization fuelled another growth spurt for TCS because of the opportunity to cross-sell and upsell to customers. Each region was dealing with multiple industry practices and multiple service practices so they would try and find out what more TCS could do for a particular customer.

For example, if the customer was a multinational in the US, we would ask, what more can we do for you in Europe, or can we do something for you in Asia? Similarly, if the customer was a utility company, we would ask if we could provide engineering services for them, could we contribute to the design of a hydraulic distribution system for them or could we perhaps design for them an asset management system.

As a result new service practices like engineering services emerged. Similarly business process outsourcing (BPO) emerged as a speciality because the sales people were tasked with finding out from customers the areas of their business where TCS could value-add. This in turn led to further geographic expansion because if you are doing a lot of things for a customer, it may make sense to locate yourself close to the customer, whether they are in the US, Uruguay or China.

Fortunately in the years following Y2K, a rapid improvement in global and Indian telecommunications capabilities expanded the range of software development services that we could offer. In particular, databases located in developed countries could now be accessed remotely to offer new services such as real-time database management, quality assurance and web services.

The reform of the Indian telecommunications system eventually led to the introduction of Internet Protocol (IP) telephony and ended the state monopoly on international calling facilities. This in turn was the catalyst for the growth of IT-enabled services (ITes), the BPO industry and inbound call centres. Telemarketing services and data processing centres mushroomed in India. The reforms also opened the provision of telecommunications to the private sector and were critical to the growth of IT services, particularly the offshoring of business processes to India.

Our earlier successes in providing software services to overseas customers gave them a sense of comfort when they considered moving business activities to India. Because of our past engagements, their concerns about security and continuity were eased.

Since 2001 TCS had been operating a small call centre operation as a joint venture with another Indian company and in early 2003 acquired a small provider of BPO services to the airline industry. These were both moderately successful businesses.

In the wake of the Y2K furore, companies turned their attention and resources to the Internet revolution and our customers turned to us to Internet-enable their business applications. Then in 2001 when the Internet bubble burst companies began to cut costs dramatically and looked once again to offshore or outsource non-strategic, IT-enabled, back-office operations, and the BPO market began to take off.

The turn of the century also saw a lot of change within TCS itself. Taken together, Y2K, the growing importance of domain-led services and the formation of industry and service practices fuelled the need to recruit ever larger numbers of talented professionals.

Between 1997 and 2002, the number of TCS professionals more than doubled to over 20,000—and we realized that our future growth would depend not just on recruiting the right employees with the right qualifications, but also on recruiting sufficient numbers.

# 4

# TRANSFORMING FOR
# THE FUTURE

## NURTURING TALENT

THE TCS IPO in 2004 was oversubscribed several times over, but what were investors really buying into? Certainly not our campuses, our software or our mainframes. They were 'buying' our collective knowledge, skills, ideas and talent.

All of this value resides in our employees, so when someone leaves the organization, out goes that knowledge. People are, without question, TCS's greatest asset. That meant that as the Indian IT industry matured and competition increased, selecting the right people and holding on to them became the single most critical task for the TCS management.

The TCS business model, since its inception, was based on the premise that India was not short of talent, and that if harnessed and steered in the right direction, this talent could be leveraged effectively. People like Kohli consciously invested time and money to build a people-centric ecosystem by forging relationships with academia—especially the IITs and the country's premier engineering colleges—which provided most of the early recruits.

I extended this ecosystem by creating an academic interface programme that brought together the heads of premier educational institutions to deliberate on industry trends, curriculum adaptations and collaboration opportunities on an annual basis. The programme now encompasses 535 Indian and 116 global academic institutions.

By the mid-1990s, the number one career choice for most Indian engineers was the IT software and services industry. The exciting nature of the work, the opportunities to travel and work overseas, and relatively good salaries all worked to its advantage.

Today approximately 1 million students show up for the IIT-JEE examinations each year; of these 50 per cent or so will eventually join the IT industry where companies like TCS will make a further investment in their training to make them ready for jobs. Since 1968 when TCS was formed, roughly half a million people have benefited from TCS's training and experience. So in addition to generating billions of dollars in export revenues, talent building has been the Indian IT software and services industry's biggest contribution to the Indian economy.

From the beginning, the industry has attracted the very best. An elite group from the IITs or from US universities such as MIT, UCLA and Harvard who had returned to India made up the initial TCS team. All of them heard about TCS through word of mouth and joined because of the entrepreneurial spirit and vision they found in TCS and the opportunities it offered them.

Over time growth necessitated a somewhat more structured organization with a recruitment process based on an aptitude test and the ability of a candidate to demonstrate analytical and logical thinking capabilities.

When I joined TCS almost everyone was pretty much the same age, between twenty-six and thirty-five, with the exception of Kohli and Yash Sahni, who were somewhat older. We were, however, a very close-knit group and we pretty much knew everybody else in the organization. This created a close 'family' kind of office atmosphere.

Camaraderie notwithstanding, each of us had to be accountable for our time in office. Offshore work involves charging customers according to people time, so timesheets played an important role in TCS in the early years. Even those of us who were in mid-level supervisory positions had to fill in a timesheet every day detailing how many hours we worked and how we used our time.

These timesheets would record, for example, how much time we spent in the library studying, how much was spent working on a project, what sort of project it was and whether it was billable or not. The timesheets were collected by Kohli's secretary and at the end of the week he would look through them to see how people had spent their time. If someone had not been that productive, he would call them to a one-on-one meeting to discuss the issue or ask the project manager why a team member was not being used to their full potential.

People were always encouraged to use the library and every TCS facility had a well-stocked library given the fact that TCS was operating in a knowledge intensive business. Employees who thought they could exaggerate the hours they spent in the library, or go there to rest, were mistaken. If you put down on the timesheet that you had spent five or ten hours in the library, Kohli would call you in and want to know what books you had read. Sometimes he would even look at the books that were issued to you by the library staff so that he knew which books people were reading.

Luckily for me, I loved reading just as much as he did and would happily share my thoughts on what I had read. My reading habit was to serve me well in later years when Kohli and I travelled together, because it always gave us something to talk about.

To systemize things, every project or assignment undertaken had a record number. The appropriate project record number had to be entered on timesheets and was used to capture all the data related to a specific project, like the number of people allocated to it, and to assess billable hours. I am pretty sure we were the first consultancy in India to have this system.

From the beginning there was also a big emphasis on performance management. We had a comprehensive self-appraisal system. Once a year employees were asked to assess themselves based on a series of quantitative and qualitative criteria. Answers were recorded in a thick booklet and were subsequently discussed with supervisors. If there was disagreement an employee could take the matter to the next level.

Project leaders and supervisors were encouraged to mentor and coach people and would typically go through the self-assessment form and suggest opportunities for improvement. The role of HR was simply to administer these forms.

In addition, when a project was completed everyone was expected to fill out a project report that included a complete history of the project that could then be shared with colleagues. That was one of the ways in which we captured institutional knowledge; it also provided another chance for an individual to discuss their own performance with the project leader.

It may seem quite unusual by today's standards, but Kohli believed that there should be a clear separation between financial rewards and performance assessments. Your ability to do a particular job, or undertake a particular role or function, should be entirely distinct from what you got as a salary. In fact supervisors played no role in setting salaries or deciding on pay increases. That was done by a few top people. The advantage of this system was that while you might disagree with your supervisor about their assessment of how well you had performed on a project and whether you had been a good team player or successfully written a code without bugs, there could never be a dispute between you and your supervisor about pay.

While most people think that if they score high on their appraisal, they should automatically receive more pay, the prevalent view in TCS was that the potential of people should be considered. Some people are very steady workers, while others are very good at taking on additional responsibilities or rising to the challenge of leadership. Kohli argued that an individual's performance should be judged by the degree to which they fulfil their potential, while financial rewards should be based on the company's performance.

Of course we always felt deep down that we were paid less than we should have been, but we never bothered to dispute the issue because the difference was not worth arguing about.

Today, every TCS professional has a biannual performance appraisal and receives feedback highlighting areas for improvement. We operate a variable pay scheme linked to the company, unit and individual performance. We reward and recognize exceptional performance through differentiated compensation which helps us retain and motivate the best talent.

The paper-based system of people management worked well while TCS was a small company operating out of just a few buildings. But by the time I took over in 1996, we had grown considerably bigger, and we needed a new and more systematic approach to issues such as recruitment, training, manpower allocation and the HR function.

When we were recruiting say a hundred people a year we were able to cherry-pick the best graduates from the IITs and IIMs, and most training was informal and 'on the job'. But after 2003, the markets began to look up and I foresaw the potential for tremendous growth.

Scaling up in the IT software and services business has always been about adding people. At the time we were hiring in batches of 500 to 1,000 people but in the future we would need to recruit by the tens of thousands. I realized that in order to do this we would have to hire people with many different skill levels. In addition, although the company had a systemized process for entry-level hiring, we did not have much experience in hiring the more senior people we needed from sectors outside IT that would bring in domain and consulting skills, and add diversity to our employee base.

We clearly needed to adopt a different approach towards both recruitment and training if we were to maintain the quality that TCS had come to be known for. In fact one of my top priorities at the time was to establish a human resource management system that would serve the TCS of the future.

When I thought more deeply about the situation I realized that although an HR function existed at TCS, it operated primarily as a back-office administrative system. Its main roles in the early days had been to manage self-appraisal forms and to ensure compliance with regulations. It played little or no role in scouting for new talent which was primarily done by project managers.

HR and operations were also quite distinct, and most HR managers had little or no operational experience. This was not entirely satisfactory from a business perspective because one of the key functions in an IT business is allocating people to projects. The challenge is to match the person with the right skills to a project at the right time while minimizing the 'bench time' that someone spends between projects.

This is a critical task and the efficiency with which it gets done directly impacts the bottom line. I felt that having someone with operations experience would be an advantage here. There was another consideration: we were expanding our global reach at a fast pace, with plans to set up centres in continental Europe, China and Latin America, and that meant we would be recruiting and transferring people imminently. I was also considering growth through acquisitions.

I knew we needed an institutionalized process and we could not manage all this growth with the ten-odd people in our HR department that had served a 5,000-strong organization. All these changes required a major restructuring.

After much thinking I picked S. Padmanabhan (better known as Paddy) for the job of overhauling HR. He was a mild, soft-spoken person who had worked for TCS for twenty years and had experience in building an operation from scratch. I called him and his wife over for breakfast at home when I planned to make him the offer.

I chose home because it was a more informal and personal environment and I anticipated that Paddy would be surprised by my offer. I was right—he was taken completely by surprise and told me I had chosen the wrong guy! He said he needed time to think, but his hesitation clearly meant that he was not exactly jumping at the offer.

He called me again when he got home to ask me why I had chosen him. I told him that I had consulted with many people and they had all said that he was the best person for the job. But I could understand his hesitation. TCS did not have the best image from the HR perspective. We were perceived as body shoppers, a cost-arbitraging company with ordinary HR skills and competencies. We also had a fairly high attrition rate. People would join TCS, learn new skills and then leave. Paddy thought this move would effectively sideline him, but I wanted him to take up the challenge and change things. I truly felt he was the right person for the job.

At the same time I brought Mahalingam (Maha) in to head the finance function—a post that had fallen vacant after the previous

CFO left the organization. It was a turning point for TCS because for the first time these two critical functions—HR and finance—were integrated into the operations of the company and run by people with real operations experience.

Under Paddy we restructured the HR function and moved to a geographic structure with HR experts from India's best institutes staffing the new positions. New IT systems for the HR organization were built, roles were defined and processes that built efficiencies, allowed scaling up and were just and fair to employees were put into place.

A lot was happening at the same time and HR was under pressure. Just as we were expanding organically and adding new capabilities internally, TCS acquired CMC in 2002 and Tata Infotech soon after, so integration became a top priority. I am sure Paddy spent many sleepless nights, but eventually the HR engine was cranked up and morale slowly but surely began to rise.

On one occasion Paddy decided to meet a US client to try and find out why TCS had lost a particular project. The client told him that their employees had felt threatened by our proposal team—it was an 'all-male Indian team' while their workforce was all American and of equal gender. It was a lesson in the value of diversity and that is when we started hiring local sales people and stepped up the hiring of women in all geographies.

The biggest success of this transformational exercise was to win over line managers and persuade them that HR managers were on their side and essential to their growth. To me, that was the litmus test of complete HR integration with the business. Since then, the whole of the HR function has been further modernized to focus on five key areas: productivity improvement, talent retention, talent acquisition, succession planning and leadership development—and finally scaling for future growth.

## Recruitment

In recent years, excluding the 2008–10 downturn, TCS has been recruiting about 30,000 people each year. I am often asked how the induction and training of such a large number of new recruits happens. This is a skill that TCS has mastered, developing a very well-oiled system that transforms young adults into confident and competent professionals ready for a global career.

The growth of the IT industry in the early '70s and '80s created a sudden and huge demand for software engineering skills. True to its pioneering spirit, TCS developed its own dedicated training programme to ensure it had access to the skills needed to take advantage of the new opportunities.

Different TCS branches were responsible for ensuring they had access to people with the skills they required. But to ensure standardization and integration, TCS also established a centralized programme. In 1993 we decided to establish a corporate training facility in the lush green and peaceful environment of the Technopark in Thiruvananthapuram.

The first batch of the Induction Training Programme recruits started in Technopark in 1997 and the following year TCS commissioned its own Corporate Learning Centre (known today as Bodhi Park) with a capacity of 700. What evolved from these initiatives was a formalized and integrated training programme. Over time, in addition to software development, we added soft skills like foreign language courses and cultural integration workshops to the course curriculum. In 2003, because of increasing recruitment numbers and diversity in learning styles, the focus shifted from training to learning and the Induction Training Programme was re-christened the Initial Learning Programme. The curriculum was once again augmented and dovetailed with business needs, incorporating ideas from industry leaders and subject matter from academic experts.

During this phase we added tailormade modules to the programme designed to suit professionals like MBAs and chartered accountants. We also established new training centres at Thiruvananthapuram (Peepul Park, 2007), Ahmedabad, Guwahati (2008) and Chennai (2010) to help manage the increasing volume of new recruits.

Today, new recruits are initiated into the TCS way and the Tata culture in a two-and-a-half-month-long day programme with a curriculum and methodology that is continuously adapting to the changing business requirements.

I strongly believe that in this business, learning must be a way of life at all stages of one's career. That is why TCS has a

Continuous Learning Programme for its experienced professionals. This spans issues like business strategies, project needs, technology and business directions. Aside from meeting individual aspirations, it also addresses the long-term, short-term and medium-term needs of the organization.

As individuals progress professionally, our Leadership Development Programme is designed to turn them into future leaders for the company by carefully assessing leadership potential and then putting the leaders through rigorous training which may include attending a premier business school programme. I am particularly proud of TCS's achievement as being one of the real pioneers in training. We have even heard informally about a general belief in the market that people trained at TCS do not need an interview or test and are considered good enough to be recruited.

Personally, I value people who have a quest for knowledge. For me, talking to a film critic on a flight is as engaging as discussing a new technology with a business colleague. Convergence is bringing different disciplines closer, even humanities and science. You never know where a good idea will come from. I have always encouraged TCSers to use facilities such as libraries, to nurture hobbies and to take part in outdoor activities, because I believe they must grow beyond technology expertise. In my talks to young students I always emphasize this need for multidisciplinary skills.

## Maitree

My strong belief that TCSers should have a well-rounded educational background and opportunities for professional growth resonated with an idea suggested by my wife Mala which appealed instantly to me.

Mala had watched TCS grow and was a bit concerned that the young people we were employing did nothing but work, while their wives fended for themselves with no outlets for using their time productively. Mala suggested that we should find a way to engage our rapidly growing workforce—we had 17,000 associates at that time—and their families in activities that would bring them closer together. That was how the concept of Maitree—which means friendship—was born in 2002.

The idea was to bring people together through interest groups, cultural festivals and sports. At the same time, Mala thought Maitree could function as a support group that a young wife (like she had been) could lean on when she found herself setting up home in a foreign country, with a husband who was too busy to be of help. I thought it was a great idea and gave it my full support.

We thought a knowledge management company like TCS should be able to use its expertise to aggregate and make available to these newly-placed couples all the 'knowledge' about strange cities, the schooling system, the places where one could find Indian spices etc. A website for this purpose was started. This has slowly become a lively and colourful repository of vital information and a vehicle for informal exchanges between the associates.

The members of our young workforce were mostly far away from their families and without friends in new cities, so Mala felt that there was an urgent need for a psychological counselling service as well. The surprise was when no one availed of the service initially! The stigma attached to seeking help for psychological wants had to be overcome. The idea that we could easily make the service available online was shot down by the Maitree team—every computer had a unique number and could be identified! Of course within a few years there were counsellors in all the locations, and their calendars were quite full.

Although today Maitree is a part of the HR initiative and is serviced by a corporate team in Mumbai with coordinators in every region, it is actually managed by the TCS associates themselves. Over 40,000 associates are engaged in Maitree activities ranging from a toastmaster's club to salsa dancing classes and hiking; the activities are partly self-funded. Dancing and theatre workshops are not only fun but they also boost self-confidence and improve body language, which is otherwise so difficult to teach.

The toastmaster's club operates globally, so if you are posted to the US or Japan you can continue the activity there; this provides an important sense of continuity. For TCSers who needed to enhance their communication skills Mala thought that the many qualified spouses could be engaged. This would be a win–win situation for the corporate and the spouse. But apart from the astounding success of one wife who was fully engaged in Bangalore, there were, disappointingly, not many takers. The idea of setting up a crèche met with the same fate. The idea was floated that TCS would provide the space and any wife willing to put up a crèche could do so, reserving 75 per cent of the seats for children of TCSers. There were surprisingly no takers! Many other ideas were explored to set up a crèche especially as the number of women employees at TCS was growing at a rapid rate. Unfortunately nothing bore significant fruit. This led to my often-quoted belief 'thou shall never give up'—and the passion must continue.

Maitree has played a critical and supportive role in engaging with employees on issues such as global warming. Talks at every TCS location in India were conducted by partnering with an international organization. A Green audit was initiated with all the administration representatives sensitizing them towards waste management and reducing water and power consumption. The collaboration with *Sanctuary Asia*, India's premier wildlife and ecology magazine, provided employees the opportunity to visit wildlife parks and be inspired to join the campaign to save the environment. The partnership also led to the release of a coffee table book titled *India Naturally*. Similarly, when the Right to Information Act was promulgated in India Maitree facilitated talks across TCS locations by experts. All of these were attempts in awareness building and sensitization of individuals to their own and the organization's larger role in society.

Maitree volunteers have engaged in a wide range of community projects such as providing employment opportunities for the differently abled and HIV/AIDS education programmes which have now been accepted as best practices by TCS. Spurred on by Maitree volunteers, TCS has pioneered an Advanced Computer Training Centre (the first of its kind in India) for the visually impaired, and has subsequently employed more than thirty visually impaired people in the company; many more have found jobs in other companies and banks.

As Mala had predicted, we also found that there were a large number of TCS associates who wanted to undertake community work, so we started work in rural areas in India working with children who needed better care and teaching. The community project started in the suburbs of Mumbai five years ago and initially involved teaching conversational English to the children of a primary school in Wazapur village, Panvel. Spurred on by the deeper involvement of TCS volunteers, it grew to embrace broader aspects of education, improving the local water supply, combating illiteracy and empowering village women.

The Maitree team set up a school computer and science lab using solar power while the empowerment programme focused on training women in activities that would generate income. To improve the water supply and provide clean drinking water to the villagers, the team checked dams, deepened wells and instituted a rainwater harvesting project. Today this holistic programme is impacting the lives of 600 children and 2,000 adults. TCSers have truly made a difference to these lives. This model has been adopted at many other TCS locations and TCSers have truly made a difference to many lives.

The Maitree model has attracted a lot of interest in part because of its uniqueness: I don't think there is another volunteer-based employee engagement programme elsewhere in the world. Maitree has won awards and appreciation not just in India but overseas as well where community initiatives by an Indian company attract even more attention.

While not all Maitree initiatives have been a success, the Maitree culture has become deeply embedded in TCS and Maitree members are extremely enthusiastic about the organization and the friendships they have formed. In fact we have so many Maitree-ites who have married within the group that someone suggested we should set up a matchmaking service!

The formation of Maitree and its full integration into HR was not without pain; like any new idea, there was resistance. But the Maitree experience strengthened my belief that sometimes in a large organization, you need to nurture an idea like a start-up and take it under your wing until it reaches a level of maturity that enables it to stand on its own two feet. Indeed some new ideas need to be nurtured outside the system for them to stabilize.

For this strategy to succeed, support from the top management as well as mentoring is essential, and, as I have discovered, it is always important for an initiative to be led by people who are passionate about the project. I also believe it is important to take risks. For example, in TCS we have never waited for a position to open up before recruiting someone special. If I came across a good person, even if he or she was not relevant to TCS at that time, we still brought them into TCS and then tried to create a function or activity around them. If we at TCS can do something that enhances their individual capability and engages or challenges them, it may connect with the mainstream activity at some stage.

You can think of it as a form of research or innovation, and I believe this type of experimentation is very, very necessary in an organization that seeks innovation. Over time I have often used this strategy, especially in a training initiative that I thought held great potential.

## Ignite

In 2005 a few of us in TCS got together to discuss the future of talent management in the Indian IT software and services industry. What was different about this meeting was that it began with the premise that we may be missing out on some of the best potential software professionals because traditionally an engineering degree was a prerequisite to joining the IT industry.

But looking at the global landscape, we could see that information technology was not the sole preserve of engineers. There were science, social science and even arts graduates who were helping shape the future of technology services on different continents, bringing their own special talents to this melting pot. So we asked: 'Should qualification be the sole criteria, should being part of India's educational elite of engineers be the only route into an industry growing at 40 per cent annually? Why not broaden the criteria to those possessing the basic skills of logic, cognition and reason coupled with high interest levels and a propensity to learn?'

From these questions, the idea of bringing the IT growth story to a new audience of science and math graduates was born. We decided to go ahead and experiment. Thus not only was a new national career option born, but it allowed the IT industry to go national—to even more towns and cities, to the farthest corners of the country.

It was also clear to me that the IT industry's demand for engineers would continue to increase. There was already growing concern outside the IT industry in India that the IT sector was siphoning off all the best engineering graduates. I also felt that while the remarkable growth of the Indian IT software and services industry had created jobs and considerable wealth for engineering graduates, a whole section of the population with non-engineering degrees was being completely left out—especially women and those from small rural communities.

To 'net in' a larger pool of bright minds, in 2006, a year after the idea was generated, I launched a new initiative within TCS called Ignite. A six-person team led by Dr Raman Srinivasan was put together to develop the Ignite training programme—which they did in just nine months, that too on a shoestring budget.

They used a high-tech, high-touch approach, which was reflected in a specially designed facility in Chennai that offered flexibility for individual and group activity, face-to-face and distance learning. One of the first challenges was to develop new and cost-effective ways of talent sourcing. A new digitized selection process was designed to test for communication abilities and team skills in addition to more common questions related to aptitude, logic and reasoning, and analytical capabilities.

Then the team travelled to more than 234 colleges in twenty-five cities across nine states including some like Kerala, Assam and West Bengal that had not traditionally produced many IT professionals. Between 3 and 13 per cent of the candidates interviewed were offered jobs with TCS and placed on the inaugural Ignite course which launched with 500 trainees in the purpose-designed facility in Chennai in December 2006.

The first batch of trainees came from diverse socio-economic, cultural and educational backgrounds and a wide range of disciplines including mathematics, statistics, physics, chemistry, computer science and IT. Over 60 per cent of them were first-generation graduates, 65 per cent were women, and over 60 per cent came from 'Tier 3' towns, rural areas and villages. The Ignite team was as passionate about the opportunity to transform the students' lives as the students were themselves about the doors that would be opened to them.

In keeping with the vision of the programme, Ignite training focuses on active participation and collaborative learning rather that the more traditional teacher-centric approaches. Ignite also makes use of the latest learning technologies like real-time classroom response systems, personal growth monitors, intelligent software tutors, gaming technologies and creative communication workshops.

Aside from learning programming, trainees are actively encouraged to take an interest in the arts—and a selection of world-class Indian musicians have performed at the Ignite facility. The teaching methodologies and training approaches used in Ignite are so unique that we have applied for patents to cover them.

The early results from Ignite have been very encouraging. The first batch completed their training in December 2007 and since then another 2,500 trainees have graduated from the scheme and have been successfully integrated into projects. Not only has the feedback from their projects been exemplary, but a majority of them have also enrolled for a higher degree (MCA) as a part of a tie-up with Sastra University.

More generally, Ignite has demonstrated that operational excellence and innovation go together. Ignite has established global benchmarks in cost leadership in the corporate training space. It has also shown that with the right learning methodologies, science graduates can be empowered with knowledge and skills relevant to this sector, thereby developing new sources of talent to sustain the growth of the Indian IT industry.

The success of the Ignite experiment also highlights other larger possibilities which to my mind are even more exciting. The technology-based approach and learning platform of Ignite could lend itself to training in other areas as well. Virtually any sector that is training-intensive, even teaching a vocation, becomes possible with a low-cost, technology-driven, scalable model.

Skill development is perhaps India's greatest need today and this model squarely addresses the challenges of scale and reach. Once India's villages are connected with broadband links, the trainer, the content and the trainee can all be connected no matter how remote the village is or which part of India it is in.

## Mentoring, career development and leadership

Both the Maitree and Ignite experiments have been successful and are now integrated into the larger TCS system, but in the initial years I needed to mentor both projects personally—something I learned earlier from mentoring people.

From the beginning, it was ingrained in all of us at TCS that part of a project leader's job was to spot and promote high potential employees. As we grew in numbers, I began to be concerned about whether our formal processes would limit our ability to spot talent and mentor individual people.

We actually tried to formalize mentoring and tried a number of simple things like asking the top 100 managers to become mentors, but we quickly discovered that this did not work. Not everyone can be a mentor, and that was proven beyond doubt. We also tried allocating five or ten people to someone who wanted to be a mentor, but again that had very limited success because it was a regimented process. If a system like that is to work, you need to see your mentee on a given day for a given amount of time, and that was just too difficult to arrange. So I discovered that formal processes are not appropriate for everything.

I think mentoring is simply an inborn passion and not something you can learn in a classroom. It can only be mastered by observation and practice. I also realized that most mentees select you, and not the other way round. The mentor's role is to create a sense of comfort so that people can approach you and hierarchy has no role to play in that situation.

The mentee has to believe that when they share anything, they are sharing as an equal and that their professional well-being is protected, that they won't be ridiculed or their confidentiality breached. As a mentor you have to create that comfort zone. It is somewhat like being a doctor or a psychiatrist, but mentoring does not necessarily have to take place only in the office.

For example, if I was travelling I would often take along a junior colleague to meet a client. I made sure they had a chance to speak and then afterwards I would give them feedback and say, 'You could have done this or that'. Similarly, if I observed somebody when they were giving a pitch or a talk, I would meet them afterwards or send them an e-mail to say 'well done' or coach them about how they could have done better.

This trait of consciously looking for the bright spark amongst the crowd has paid me rich dividends. I spotted N. Chandrasekaran (Chandra), TCS's current Chief Executive, when he was working on a project in Washington, DC in the early 1990s; the client said good things about him so I asked him to come and meet me. We took it from there.

Similarly urging Maha and Paddy to move out of their comfort zones and take up challenging corporate roles was a successful move. From a leadership perspective I believe it is important to have experienced a wide range of functions within an organization.

If a person hasn't done a stint in HR, finance or operations, or in a particular geography or more than one vertical, they stand limited in your learning. A general manager needs to know about all functions. You don't have to do a deep dive—a few months exploring a function is enough so long as you have an aptitude to learn and the ability to probe. This experience is very necessary today even from a governance perspective.

I also believe firmly that once you place your trust in a person, you must delegate and empower them. If you hold onto everything and do not share, it never works. We have seen too many examples of projects failing because a manager held all the cards too close to his chest. A lot of people are frightened to delegate because they fear they will lose control, but unless you do it, you will have only control and nothing else. At the end of the day you are going to be measured not just by what you did, but by what you left behind.

That means if you do not build a set of people around you with a varied set of capabilities, you will not have created an institution that has the inherent strength to run without you, and in a manner that is better than what you left behind. That fundamental belief is what drove me to get the best group of people around me, to challenge them to the full extent of their capabilities and to help them to grow into the positions.

The result was that the closing of a chapter on 6 October 2009 when I stepped down as Chief Executive and handed over to Chandra was as easy as anything. I never felt, 'Oh my God, I kept so many things to myself, my successor is going to wonder what is going on, or curse me for not sharing completely.'

I think this sensitization was driven by my own experiences. I was put in that position myself in 1996 when I took over from Kohli. I had quite a few deficiencies: I had no exposure to Europe or Japan or South-East Asia which were like black boxes to me. Similarly some parts of the Indian organization were relative unknowns too.

Even though I used to keep my ears open, I felt I lacked key information and understanding about some of our operations—and that made me determined that I would never put those who follow me in the same position. As a result I deliberately accelerated the sharing significantly—I virtually became a human real-time information highway. My team got used to getting a barrage of calls from me at any given time. It could be a real-time client update of a meeting concluded a few seconds ago, or an e-mail at 3 a.m. Sharing, and sharing with speed, became an obsession with me.

Being a gadget freak, I rely heavily on digital communications during my extensive travels and I am sure my office and my colleagues always feel that we are connected because I am always just a phone call or e-mail away.

I remember a comment made by a Tata Group colleague. He had just concluded a meeting with me and taken a flight soon after. On the flight he met someone from my leadership team, so he mentioned our discussions to him. To his surprise this person was completely updated already, thanks to a call I had made to him. Of course I had no idea that they were both on the same flight. I had called merely out of habit.

This has worked well for me in my relationships with colleagues. I like to answer every mail I get within twenty-four hours, even if it means getting up at 4 a.m. to check my mailbox. I truly believe that if someone has taken the trouble to write to you, they deserve to know that you have read what they had to say, and responded to. It does not matter if that someone is a young TCSer who wishes to share a thought with the CEO, or a Harvard professor; they both deserve a timely response.

My experience has taught me that the secret to managing people at work is to understand that they are human beings first and professionals second. With 160,000 employees to manage it is a fine balancing act for any organization to make its systems and processes as human as possible. It is, however, an ideal worth aspiring to.

## THE INNOVATION JOURNEY

THE PENETRATING VISION of Jamsetji Tata, together with his act of philanthropy, created the Indian Institute of Science in 1909. Seven decades later, a similar vision and the same commitment towards the pursuit of knowledge led his successor J.R.D. Tata to set up India's first software research centre, the Tata Research Development and Design Centre (TRDDC) in Pune.

The idea of an IT research centre in India was first mooted by Kohli who believed there was a need for a facility that would foster technology research. He believed that if anyone could do it, the Tatas could. He felt that all the technology knowledge India had at that time was in semiconductors which was really the domain of physics, not computer science. He was of the view that India didn't have the knowledge base required for us to do advanced research in India, but he felt confident of the support of some of the best North American universities.

A small team from the University of Waterloo in Canada and MIT, together with a couple of Indian researchers, were commissioned to study the issue and prepare a report on the need for such an institution. Their recommendation was strongly in favour of the Tatas establishing a technology research institute.

Although J.R.D. Tata was not a technologist, he was very well informed about technology and foresaw the benefits of setting up such a facility. The Tatas had already set up three great institutions: the Indian Institute of Science in Bangalore, the Tata Institute of Social Sciences (TISS) in Mumbai and the Tata Institute of Fundamental Research (TIFR), which undertakes research in mathematics and physics, also in Mumbai. JRD believed people were the most important raw material in India. He said there was one more thing he wanted to do for his country—to create an institution that would apply science and technology for the benefit of the Indian industry and the Indian people. It was with this aim that the TRDDC was established in 1981.

The university town of Pune was chosen as the location for TRDDC because it was close enough to the TCS headquarters in Bombay, and yet separate from it. The scope of research was set intentionally wide because Kohli was convinced that computers would become a tool for all sectors of industry. He rightly felt that design played a big part in the R&D process, after research but before development. Hence the emphasis at TRDDC was not on 'R&D' but on 'R, D & D'—research, design and development.

E.C. Subbarao, a renowned materials scientist and a distinguished academic from IIT Kanpur, was appointed as the first director of TRDDC and came to Pune where he set up residence in a bungalow at the corner of the Tata Management Centre. After he moved out the bungalow continued to be used as part of TRDDC.

Although TRDDC was part of TCS, its mandate was to work with other Tata and non-Tata companies, including the public sector. From the outset one thing was clear: the focus was to be on applied research that would have a direct impact on industry. This required working closely with industry. Equally importantly, TRDDC provided a base for Indian scientists working abroad to come back and set up in India. This was something that the government had also tried to do in the 1970s by setting up the Council of Scientific and Industrial Research (CSIR) but had had met with limited success.

Naturally, because Dr Subbarao was a material scientist, the first research group set up at TRDDC in 1981–82 was focused on material science. The Tata name drew talent to TRDDC and its reputation spread mostly by word of mouth.

It was a true research atmosphere. As Dr Subbarao remembers, 'The team sat in close physical proximity to—literally rubbing shoulders with—each other. That's when intellectual exchange takes place naturally, and ideas from one discipline rub off on another.' TRDDC quickly became home for a wide range of academic disciplines and a melting pot of ideas from non-software fields like process engineering, metallurgy and engineering services with software engineering.

Much of the early research work found its way into industry outside TCS's ambit. For example, TRDDC worked on projects for Tata Steel, Tata Chemicals, Hindustan Zinc and Hindustan Copper and did some important work with Associated Cement Companies (ACC) in which the Tata Group had a big stake but later as a part of rationalization sold its stake. TRDDC researchers worked closely with ACC to develop online process controls and to improve performance. By 1999 the project had matured into a product that was adopted not just by ACC, but by other cement companies as well. Ultimately this was the foundation for what became known as the manufacturing systems group in TRDDC. Subsequently the same team studied the automotive industry and industrial processes to see how they could improve them. Today that group is very large and forms a very important part of the engineering services unit within TCS.

At the same time the TRDDC software group was working on process improvement but often found it difficult to persuade business groups within TCS to adopt their solutions.

When I took over I felt it was important that the output of TRDDC research be used. So I decided to put them in touch with the sections of TCS which I felt would benefit from their research.

I began with the TCS unit in Delhi working on banking systems and I told those who baulked at the idea of using the TRDDC technology, 'If you do not want to use it, tell me why.' That was of course a very difficult question to answer. Ultimately our cross-banking product branded as MasterCraft emerged from this collaboration and was sold to clients from 2000 onwards.

Joseph Mathai, a professor of computer science at the University of Warwick who had earlier worked at TIFR for seventeen years, joined TRDDC as Deputy Director in 1997 and became Director eighteen months later in 1999 when Dr Subbarao retired. When he took over, his initial focus was to see if TRDDC could be self-sufficient, in other words, whether or not it was able to support itself. But when he looked at the figures, it was obvious that

TRDDC was covering just a small fraction of its total costs. The main problem was that while the researchers were bright, productive people, they were not necessarily good at marketing and they spent far too much time chasing small external projects that brought in revenue, rather than undertaking valuable research. As a result the basis upon which researchers were evaluated was changed, so that the revenue they generated from external companies was no longer an important factor in their appraisals.

We also established a balanced scorecard to show what it was that TRDDC was putting into TCS through project engagements. We did not attempt to estimate the particular value addition that the TRDDC contribution made, because that is very hard to do. Instead we tracked the total number of project engagements that TRDDC had with TCS and estimated what the value of those projects was. That was one measure of success. We also measured the number of times TCS support units resolved a problem or issue using something developed by TRDDC.

Further, instead of working on immediate problems we refocused the research on longer-term projects recognizing that we needed to take some risks and would probably make some mistakes, for that is what research is about. So in software, we set up tool foundries that could deliver tools for people's customized requirements and turn them around in about a month's time. Many tools came out of that process and mainly went into use in TCS. Once we had developed a tool—for example a Java code checker—and persuaded project teams to take it on board, it just became standard practice to use it.

In order to find out what the TCS business units needed, I encouraged Prof. Mathai to visit different sites. Sometimes I would suggest to him that he take a look at a particular project that had run into problems, and see whether something TRDDC had been working on might help. On other occasions, if I knew a project team was having problems, I would suggest that they talk to TRDDC.

Initially project managers would want TRDDC to send people to join the project but we had to explain that was not how it worked. Instead TRDDC would send a few people to assess the problem and then deliver a software solution or tool to do the job.

Of course most project managers were working under enormous pressure. They had deadlines and they had things to deliver to clients. If the project faltered, in the back of their minds there was often a belief that they could 'hack it somehow', and that if they could just get through the project acceptance stage, they could fix it later.

This was a mentality TRDDC needed to overcome. It was a long struggle and involved a lot of time meeting project managers and others, but now I think it is fairly well established that if a project runs into a problem it can be escalated to TRDDC to find a solution. Like many other things, it takes nudges and encouragement, but at the end of the day, you can often achieve a lot through personal interactions.

Gradually the perception people had of TRDDC changed. The project managers began looking ahead and recognizing that they needed to work with TRDDC and other research organizations. That was a big change that I think came about because the business became much more stable and balanced.

Conversely, we also needed to be careful that TRDDC did not become too embedded in day-to-day processes, because R&D needs time. You cannot drive R&D much faster than it is going to go. There will be mistakes and you have to tolerate a certain number of them, but that in turn takes the pressure off the scientists.

I also felt that it was important to establish partnerships with top universities on long-term research that would not only benefit TRDDC's work, but would facilitate the funding of long-term research which was becoming an issue for us. We could fund research projects that had a horizon of three to five years but not beyond, since business was too volatile for longer-term projections. So I encouraged Prof. Mathai to develop relationships with universities and establish research partnerships in areas of mutual interest. As a result, TCS established research partnerships with Stanford, Georgia Tech and several UK universities including University of York and King's College, London. Typically, there would be exchange visits and then a TRDDC member would be assigned to the project at the university for its duration. We also made it attractive for the people who went overseas to take higher degrees which I think worked very positively for them.

Today other Indian and global companies have set up research centres in India, validating a model that we pioneered; back in the 1980s, TCS was unique in having set up a research centre like TRDDC.

## Strategy and innovation

One obvious difference that was felt at TCS when I took over the helm was the change in leadership style. I was keen to introduce a 'collegiate team' atmosphere in TCS and I wanted to mould a core group of people into a leadership team, a team that I could trust and whose opinions I would value.

First I brought Chandra in as my executive assistant in 1996, and I made a fundamental change by bringing TCS veterans, with IT expertise, into key corporate roles such as finance and HR—Maha with his accounting background took over finance while Paddy took over HR. I also wanted to create the role of a Chief Technology Officer and after some transitory moves, I appointed Ananth Krishnan in that role. Later I also created the functions of the Chief Information Officer and Vice President–Transformation.

My core leadership team comprised Maha, Chandra, Paddy, Ananth and Ravi Viswanathan, head of TCS operations in Chennai. Often we just gathered together informally on a Saturday or a Sunday morning at my home in Worli, or at the TCS guest apartment in the same building. We would discuss whatever was of consequence at that point in time. I recall long discussions on the digitization of TCS and exchanges on our quality initiatives and the application for the Tata Business Excellence Model.

Soon I asked Chandra to move into the same building to make access easier. We often discussed issues during a morning stroll, held a quick meeting or compiled a quick list of actions after returning from a lengthy business trip. I found being together in Mumbai certainly drove greater management efficiency and except for Ananth and Ravi, all of the team eventually moved to Mumbai.

I was also on the lookout for a coach of sorts on strategy planning and I already had Harvard Business School professor Pankaj Ghemawat in mind. I had first heard of Pankaj from Kohli, who knew him. When my son, Tarun, joined Harvard and I went there on a visit, I met Pankaj and asked if he would be willing to work for us. After we had worked out the finer details of the engagement, he agreed to join us and quickly became part of the strategy 'huddle group'.

I wanted Pankaj to join us because I felt a completely outside view on strategy would be of great use. I was also concerned that most of the members of the core leadership team were too grounded in operations—something that can be limiting when thinking about the big picture. I thought someone like Pankaj would balance that out.

I had also been introduced to the case study approach at MIT. I had found it of immense value and I knew that Pankaj could introduce this analytical tool into our way of doing things at TCS. Finally, I thought that it would be easier to win acceptance for a change in strategy, should that be required, if it was backed by the views of a Harvard consultant.

After Pankaj became part of the core group, the nomenclature of the meetings changed and we began to call the core group the 'Think Tank'. Funnily enough our meetings with Pankaj then came to be known as the Pankaj Ghemawat sessions—and later the PG sessions. Sometimes we would meet him as a group, sometimes it would be me alone. Often Chandra would follow up with him.

On one occasion we decided to meet in Boston, away from our respective work environments. The Charles River session, as it came to be known, was a milestone. We got to know each other really well and developed a sense of comfort with each other. I believe the sense of 'one team' was formed at that meeting.

I am sure it helped some of the younger team members like Chandra, Ananth and Ravi to overcome their initial uneasiness. Over time we developed a heightened sense of communication; we knew exactly what each of us was thinking just from body language or the tone of voice. This was extremely useful especially in meetings with clients.

Each of the PG meetings threw up a whole list of further actions, but I began to get frustrated because people would often wait till the next PG session before acting. So I asked Ananth to start taking minutes at the meetings and to list the actions we agreed upon. At the next meeting everyone had to report the progress they had made. It became a cyclical process—learning led to action and deployment. Learn–act–deploy, learn–act–deploy—that became our mantra.

But we also had to learn to prioritize our efforts because there were too many things happening at the same time. I realized that there was no way we could do it all, so we decided to take up only the top items on the list of actions for each year.

One of the first things we needed to focus on was the need for information: billing, time sheets, delivery metrics and so forth. We knew enough about global best practices through projects with clients like GE. So we borrowed best practices like Six Sigma and the quality management system (QMS) and adapted them to our needs.

## From research development and design to innovation

TCS's research efforts were concentrated in Pune but I was convinced that this model was a very limiting one. I wanted to adopt a distributed research model and to spread our R&D efforts around geographically. I believed that we had to go where the researchers were, rather than asking everyone to come to Pune.

I knew that innovation and R&D in TCS would play a key role in our future strategy and would help keep us differentiated from our competitors. We needed a more systematic approach towards R&D, and we needed to broaden and widen the foundation on which we built our new services and products. I chose Ananth Krishnan for this role; Ananth was young, hungry to learn and had a great appetite for technology and its application.

We expanded our research facilities in Hyderabad, Chennai, Mumbai and Delhi and in the UK and the US. Today TCS has nineteen innovation labs across these three countries. Meanwhile, we created a Corporate Technology Board in 2006 to formalize the governance of innovation in the company. The Board provides these research centres with a forum for strategic and agenda-setting discussions, a consolidated face to the external world and mechanisms for aligning the innovation strategy with the needs of the TCS businesses.

To build the TCS of the future we knew that we needed to widen our participation within active innovation networks and to seek out new capabilities and new platforms for markets and technologies. Our labs have collaborated over the years with many external entities including academia, industry thought leaders, other research labs, various start-ups and venture funds.

These relationships served as a template for a more collaborative and open model of co-innovating. TCS formally launched the Co-Innovation Network (COIN) in January 2007. COIN is a rich and diverse network of academia, venture capitalists, start-ups etc. that together drive innovation in an environment of open communities. The Corporate Technology Board, led by the Chief Technology Officer, decides and reviews the 'Innovation Investment Portfolio' and monitors the governance of the lab and COIN processes.

TCS, together with the Co-Innovation Network partners, invest in radically new technologies that could lead to breakthroughs for the future. When COIN was launched, a respected IT industry analyst said, 'The TCS Co-Innovation Network has set the bar high for global IT providers.'

At TCS, we see innovation serving our business in two ways. First, it creates a funnel of options for future growth while ensuring that we are delivering continuous improvements and differentiators in our current business. Second, it helps combine creative thinking with sophisticated R&D to deliver solutions for our customers that help them stay ahead in their lines of business.

We also discovered that as this was happening, the organization itself became more sensitized to the need for a 'culture of innovation'. We encouraged this through initiatives such as the launching of the TCS Innovation Awards, a separate career track for innovators, practices such as academic sabbaticals and greater efforts in promoting collaboration amongst people and projects.

In the span of just a few years we had launched several major initiatives and implemented them, had scaled up recruitment numbers and simultaneously scaled up our training capabilities too. We had also established a distributed delivery model, as well as distributed R&D. Strategy was finally leading to deployment and it was reflected in our first billion-dollar revenue year in 2003.

When we achieved annual revenues of $1 billion we crossed a psychological barrier. Traditionally TCS had shied away from publicity, but when we passed the $1 billion mark we behaved in a most uncharacteristic manner. We wanted to celebrate the occasion; we invited the media to the Taj Mahal Hotel in Mumbai and, decked out in specially designed T-shirts and caps, the TCS leadership team strode in one by one to the theme from *Chariots of Fire*, throwing our caps in the air as we walked on stage.

We made the big announcement—we were the first Indian IT company to achieve this milestone and we cut a celebratory cake. Each of us felt a mixture of emotions; we were proud of our teams, and proud of every TCSer—for they were the real heroes. We felt we had climbed a mountain. But in our hearts we also sensed that there were going to be many more summits in the future. The excitement had just begun.

## The Tata Business Excellence Model

The period 2000–04 was a period of tremendous change and one of the most productive and dynamic periods in TCS's history. TCS was buzzing with new ideas and new processes driven by the strategy emerging from the PG sessions. Initiatives such as Ultimatix, the TCS digital intranet, and Knowmax, a convergence of knowledge management processes that connected the organization with its customers, suppliers and partners, came into being one after the other.

Other initiatives that we implemented during this period included iQMS, a sophisticated project management system; a delivery dashboard with twenty-five parameters that could be tracked; and an intensive sales training programme based on Revenue Storm methodology. Revenue Storm was a sales consulting firm that had programmes by which sales teams were trained to create rather than capture demand. This meant that they had to study trends, analyse implications, look at possibilities, and then come up with solutions which would help the client. It also involved refining the 'sales engine', using market research for lead generation, making the sales funnel more productive by the process of classifying accounts, mining and qualifying accounts. This programme took several years to implement and we used an external agency (Revenue Storm) to help roll it out on a global basis.

All this change excited the TCS troops immensely; the whole organization was in a dynamic mode, learning new skill sets and then applying them. This was one of our most accelerated, productive, integrated and collaborative periods. We were all quite pleased with the positive impact of these initiatives, and decided to apply for the Tata Business Excellence Award, otherwise known as JRD QV, in 2004.

The Tata Business Excellence Model (TBEM) was based on the Malcolm Baldridge framework and was designed to enhance operational quality and performance standards. By signing the Tata Brand Equity and Business Promotion agreement in 1998–99, TCS had earned the privilege of being labelled a Tata enterprise and being able to use the Tata logo; it had also committed to abiding by the Tata code of conduct. Most importantly it had also begun its journey in business excellence the Tata way.

The TBEM measures seven aspects of a business: leadership; strategic planning; customer and market focus; measurement, analysis and knowledge management; human resource focus; process management; and business results. One of the changes I initiated after becoming CEO was to put in place a cross-functional team reporting directly to me that would work towards improving processes within the company and specifically on all seven areas of the TBEM. To reinforce this, communication to employees went into overdrive to sensitize people to what the organization was moving towards.

Quality and the drive for the TBEM had to become a part of our everyday lives, part of the DNA of the organization. Our human resources capabilities had already come a long way. We had integrated formal competency management systems into the learning management systems which were aligned with the TCS performance management system. Our digital information management framework, Ultimatix, provided the ideal platform to introduce a variety of HR initiatives including an employee satisfaction survey called PULSE and a performance management and personal development programme called SPEED. Slowly but surely we were able to put in place a complex and comprehensive system of processes that built on our strengths and enabled us to target the excellence we sought.

If the TBEM score of a Tata company exceeds 600, the company wins the JRD QV award, a coveted quality award amongst Tata companies named after J.R.D. Tata. Like the TBEM, the JRD QV award is modelled on the Malcolm Baldridge National Quality Award, but integrates beneficial attributes from other quality awards as well. The annual award recognizes a Tata group company that has achieved the highest levels of quality, and is presented at a glittering award ceremony held on 29 July, the birth anniversary of J.R.D. Tata.

Fortunately my confidence in the TCS team was not misplaced. In 2004 TCS won the JRD QV award, becoming only the second company—after Tata Steel—to do so. For all of us at TCS it was the recognition we needed and deserved. But for the first time in Tata history, when the award ceremony took place on 29 July 2004, neither Ratan Tata, the Tata Group Chairman, nor the Chief Executive of the winning company—myself—was present.

There was a simple and exciting explanation for this break with history. The TCS IPO was under way. But more about that in a later chapter.

## THE GLOBALIZATION OF TCS

WHILE MOST COMPANIES begin by serving their local or national markets and then expand their operations overseas, TCS did just the opposite. It took on a challenge that very few corporates in very few countries have taken on: to look outside the home base and establish a presence in a foreign market—in this case the US, a market that was and continues to be the most advanced in terms of both the production and the consumption of technology.

We had no choice but to be a 'global' company from the start. We would have liked to build our business in India, but there was no real domestic market at that time—so we went overseas. We went westwards to the US, built 'knowledge pipelines' back to the East and sent people back and forth. Very few companies have attempted such a model.

Underscoring our push into overseas markets was the belief by the founders of TCS that technology is like a raw material used to create a new kind of service that would help us do things better and ultimately improve society. Just as water is used to generate hydroelectric power and iron ore is the raw material for steel production, they believed that technology—imported from the West—would drive change in India.

It was this kind of thinking that attracted some of the early recruits to TCS. Without this lofty objective there was no reason for Indian computer scientists like me who had done our Master's in the US to come back to India. We came back because we wanted to make a difference. We wanted to be identified with an organization that had the potential and the vision to build for the future, even though at the time there was no model to follow. We had to start from scratch.

## Evolution of the business model

For the first twenty years TCS had to sell not just its service offerings, but had to market India as well. Potential customers did not believe an Indian company could provide IT consulting services to a US company. Even in the early 1990s, many people still had their doubts and asked, 'What do these guys know?' Before we could win a new customer we had to educate them about the skills that were available in India and the ability of TCS to leverage these skills and deliver value-adding services.

When we first contacted a potential client, their perceptions were against us. Two or three meetings, or two or three months later, their opinions would generally have changed dramatically. The most important ingredient in our sales strategy was the high calibre of the computer professionals we were able to recruit in India. Even though they may initially have done rather basic-level work, these people were not software code writers, but highly educated and skilled computer science or engineering graduates.

This was in stark contrast to programmers and system analysts in the West who often had little job experience and just a high school education. Our customers in the West quickly realized that we had capabilities far beyond the work we were doing for them, so they slowly began giving us more complex work requiring greater skill, but also paying considerably more. The kind of work we did evolved from migration to maintenance to optimizing systems and eventually to developing the system itself. We wanted these challenges and were ready to take the risks; we demonstrated competency. And there was also the associated reward of going overseas.

The opportunity to work on the latest hardware enabled us to continue to attract the best computer science graduates from the Indian IITs, despite the fact that the majority left the country for further studies. The IITs in turn attracted the best brains in the country and were formed with global collaboration. For example, IIT Kanpur was set up with American knowhow, IIT Bombay with Russian collaboration, IIT Madras with German collaboration, and IIT Delhi with British assistance.

Having created the offshore model, TCS began looking for ways to win projects that did not need people to sit at client locations. The focus at this stage of our development was predominantly on migration, conversion and re-engineering. Migration was about sophisticated tools running on one software platform being made available with the same functionality on another software platform, conversion required some redevelopment while re-engineering required total redevelopment.

So, for example, if a customer told TCS that they wanted to move from their current computing environment to a different one, we had the tools to automatically go through their current system, understand the functionality and the logic, and to generate the code needed for the new system. This was what TCS specialized in.

The idea was to create an offshore-centric model with just a few people onsite with the customer. There was no Internet, no networks and no mobile phones in those days. We had to send the software code back and forth on tapes—one small change meant a week's delay. As a result we could only do project-based work. Since we had no real-time system access, we could not do support or maintenance work. If something failed at the customer's premises we could not fix it from India.

The work we chose to do initially was not domain intensive because that would have required us to put a lot of people onsite, which would have driven up our costs and potentially caused visa problems. But in the 1990s things began to change. In particular, the development of the X25 data communications protocol enabled PC-to-PC links so we could exchange data with clients in real time. We no longer needed to fly tapes back and forth between continents.

In 1991, we won our first large-scale support contract with Nortel Networks, the Canadian telecommunications equipment group. The contract involved the real-time maintenance of Nortel switch software using direct data links from India to Nortel's facilities in Montreal, Ottawa and Toronto. In turn it led to pilot projects with GE and eventually to a large GE support contract.

In 1995–96 a large procurement team with representations from several GE companies arrived in India to evaluate Indian service providers including Tier 2 companies. In a very transparent and involved process, they examined all companies on quality benchmarks, ability to scale, adherence to process rigour etc. I was personally involved in these negotiations with GE and we eventually won and established a partnership. I was told later that a personal comfort with TCS, our display of commitment and presentation of our capabilities won their favour.

TCS's partnership with GE in the 1990s was a major learning experience in our globalization journey. We ended up setting up a dedicated Offshore Development Centre (ODC) for GE at SEEPZ in Mumbai. Although we had imbibed quality benchmarks from an earlier Motorola experience, the GE relationship gave us the confidence to build scale with the right process rigour in a very short time. The ODC catering to multiple GE units enabled us to get domain capabilities across several areas.

GE believed strongly in the India model and was aggressive on wanting a value proposition. TCS in turn looked at the engagement strategically and in totality; we evaluated what we stood to gain beyond mere revenue terms but in terms of learning quality processes and performance benchmarks. In achieving that we were highly successful, as the TCS team got a firm grounding on delivery excellence, managing relationships at different levels and an unwavering customer focus.

Our work with GE moved up the value chain from conversion projects to migration work to small developmental and maintenance projects. We offered to do production support and Internet-enabled work and would proactively offer new services. Their openness and our willingness created for a dynamic and fruitful business relationship. For instance, GE had embraced Six Sigma—a quality benchmark that helps improve the quality of process outputs by identifying and removing the causes of defects and minimizing variability in business processes—in a big way, so TCS offered to build capabilities in Six Sigma, and we mandated within TCS that every project manager in TCS must be a Six Sigma black belt. This helped TCS build a culture of 'quality certification'; we ensured that every project had at least one quality champion, and encouraged people to take the very tough Certificate of Quality (CQA) examination. GE looked at Internet deployment in three ways—for sourcing, selling and operations. This kind of thinking helped formulate our own strategy when we built our digitization platform Ultimatix.

Another expertise we acquired as a result of the GE partnership was in managing accounts. Before this we had no real experience in managing multiple accounts; we would complete one project and move on to the next. But there were over forty companies within the GE umbrella, and in dealing with them we learnt the art of relationship building and subsequently appointed account managers to look after our principal accounts. Today of course account management is a well-entrenched process at TCS. Incidentally, GE also became a big reference customer for TCS. When we bid for similar types of work to what we did for them, they were quite willing to give us a reference.

In a reverse process, TCS too helped drive innovation in GE. 'Support Central', a next-generation collaboration and business productivity platform which TCS helped build, was one of the biggest innovations for GE and became one of its most popular productivity tools.

GE has always been very price-sensitive and this pushed us towards superior level execution which TCS takes pride in even today. After the IPO we surprised investors and competitors who now had a visibility on our margins which proved a lot of sceptics wrong.

In 1993 India adopted a new telecommunications policy and as new data links became available we stepped up our bids for support work and for domain-related projects that involved both support and maintenance work. So in the space of just a few years we went from offshoring migration projects to offshoring for production support and maintenance. At the same time the BPO market was beginning to take off and lots of new companies had joined the arena.

Around 2001, we noticed that all our customers in Europe, the US and the UK had started to look at the emerging markets for growth. We realized that when they set up in emerging markets, they would need support. We talked to over a hundred of our top customers, sixty of whom were either present in China or were planning to go there. By 2002, we were ready to make a foray into emerging markets ourselves. We decided to focus on three locations—China, Eastern Europe and Latin America—and we identified the customers we would go with. We did a location comparison and presented it to GE and made a case for Hangzhou in China and for Hungary.

In Latin America we realized that a different pattern was emerging. The homegrown companies in these emerging markets had global multinational aspirations, so we decided that when TCS entered these markets we would not only do offshoring for our global customers, but also create relationships with the local companies as they expanded overseas.

We decided not to create franchises, but to go in with our own people. We declined local partnerships and chose instead to create our own employee base and replicate the very model we had established in India. We also decided to use the same training and quality systems that we did in India. We thought about translation issues in different languages but eventually decided to retain English as the medium of communication across the company for all processes.

iQMS was our main quality and process system. We wanted the use of it to be institutionalized across TCS, so we decided not to create multiple instances. We had learned that providing copies to different locations meant that local changes would be inevitable, and ultimately every system would be different. Instead, we decided that everybody had to log on to the core system. Some minor changes were built to accommodate customization such as weekly payroll for some countries but beyond that, the primary system was common across all locations. This strategy has worked very well in ensuring a single standard being adhered to across the organization.

Our value proposition for our global customers was *one* global service standard, whether we served them from China, India or Latin America, and we branded it as the Global Network Delivery Model (GNDM) in 2002. The difference between GNDM and other models was the one global service standard it enabled—it also enabled the resulting globalization of the workforce. It was as if everyone was working in the same building.

We also integrated employees at a customer level. This meant that from day one, a person in Mexico or China working on the General Electric account reported to the overall GE head sitting in New York and not to the country head. This further tightened the 'one global service standard' we were creating. I believe this was a key differentiator for TCS. Other companies operated through country practices such as a Latin America practice or a Europe practice, and that model came with certain drawbacks.

While the evolution of our business model drove much of the globalization of TCS, we also expanded our geographic presence in order to access and support our expanding customer base, and to be close to the companies on the leading edge of technology development.

## Global footprint

While I was in New York setting up our US operations, Silicon Valley in California was where technology was being created, and I knew that we had to be there physically to participate in the developments. The first offices we opened in the US outside New York were in Boston—where there was a technology cluster around Route 128—and in Silicon Valley. Our presence enabled us to absorb new technologies and gave us an opportunity to work with technology companies like HP, Tandem and IBM.

We imported their machines to India and learned to work with the technology—so Chennai became an IBM hub, Kolkata a Digital Equipment Corporation (DEC) hub, Mumbai a Burroughs centre, and so on. We also persuaded these companies to give us project and development work and we leveraged this knowledge to help customers who were migrating from say Burroughs to IBM or to HP, where we could use the tools that we had created.

This took us to other cities in the US and we began setting up offices in places where we had customers. A resident manager from India would begin scouting for work where we had a customer and begin generating some money that we could use to fund further growth. As part of this expansion, we set up offices in New Jersey, Chicago, Minneapolis, San Diego, Buffalo, New York and in Arizona.

We also sought out places where the Tata Group already had a presence. For example, in the UK the presence of Tata Limited in Grosvenor Road in London enabled some early projects in 1974. Like the US, the UK was also a technology source because ICL was headquartered there and Burroughs had UK operations as well. Maha was sent to the UK in 1977 to take care of this part of the business, so our UK foray was quite early in the TCS journey.

Europe was also a potential market since Burroughs's European operations had to be serviced. There were some small migration projects in Yugoslavia, Russia and the Netherlands which we serviced out of the UK. For Switzerland we took a slightly different route. We knew the Burroughs people there were willing to look at new opportunities and to work for TCS. We eventually set up a joint venture company called Teknosoft (TKS) with Pierre Page, an ex-Burroughs person, and Jacob Schmidt, also from Burroughs. TCS held a majority stake in the company. Page had Burroughs experience and the necessary local contacts and knowledge which enabled us to sell our services and bootstrap our way into the market. Our direct business model in Switzerland gave us a key strategic opportunity and enabled us to undertake projects with the Swiss National Bank and later with SEGA.

The Swiss company eventually expanded its coverage into Austria and France. Tata also had some presence in continental Europe and while it did not really help us win new business, it was useful to have access to someone with knowledge of the laws of the land and a physical place to sit. In that sense the connection with the Tata Group was useful for us.

From 1982 onwards, we were exploring Australia, New Zealand and Japan but the expansion was minimal, very fragmented and project specific. Similarly, I had visited Singapore along with Kohli to see whether we could leverage any of the Tata Group's contacts there and we subsequently started a one-man office there. Later we also established a one-man office in Japan, but here, like in most of the operations in the Asia Pacific, business grew quite slowly. Our presence was not as strategic as we would have liked it to be; it had been more opportunistic—unlike our presence in the US, the UK and Switzerland.

Much of the specific regional geographic expansion took place after 2000. Until 1996 I had been primarily involved in our North American operations. Europe and South-East Asia were looked after by Nirmal Jain. So these regions were new for me. When I took over as CEO I scouted around for someone who had local knowledge, and I brought in Girija Pande, a former banker with extensive international experience, to head our Asia Pacific operations. While moving from a specific domain to IT was unusual, I took a chance because I wanted to bring in someone who knew the region and could recruit people locally to build operations and construct a model that would be localized for the region. Pande's brief was to consolidate the Asia Pacific operations and look for expansion of a TCS version 2.0 in the region.

Around the same time, we also began to look strategically at Latin America and I began to look for someone to head it. I first met Gabriel Rozman in Mumbai in 1996 during an Ernst & Young consulting committee meeting and then again several years later in 2001, after he had retired from Ernst & Young. He made a presentation to Chandra and others in London about some plans he had to set up an IT services firm in Latin America and was looking for some venture capital. After the presentation Chandra told him, 'We have some good news, and some bad. The good news is we liked your presentation. The bad news is that we are going to do it ourselves, so you better join us.'

That's how Gabriel came to head TCS Latin America. I think joining TCS was a bit of a shock for him because he had been used to Ernst & Young salaries and perks, which included limousines and first class air travel. He went to our offices in SEEPZ in Mumbai and said he thought the roof was going to fall on him. But he also said the TCS culture was refreshingly entrepreneurial; I think that excited him. Gabriel and I have become close friends since then. To some extent we saw Latin America as a testing ground for our strategy in the emerging markets and under Gabriel's leadership we opened offices in the region and grew from zero to 5,000 employees in five years.

Today TCS Latin America has over 7,000 people on the ground, of which 90 per cent are locals. Similarly in China, we have a Chinese leading our presence of 1,300 people with 95 per cent local Chinese-speaking employees. The head of our marketing in the US is an American and our marketing head for Europe is British.

In countries where English was the dominant language, we could station Indian nationals but we found that when operating in countries where cultural differences were more pronounced, it helped to have local people. The other benefit of having locals was of course the local language capabilities it brought to TCS, so our Chinese employees could help service the Japanese and South-East Asian markets, while the Spanish-speaking Latin American employees could help service European companies' requirements.

Today 6.7 per cent of our 175,000 employees are non-Indian and they come from ninety-nine different nationalities. We have come a long way from the time in 1993–94 when we recruited our first overseas employee, Jim Thomas from IBM, who remained the only non-Indian in the company for several years. As part of our employee development strategy, we now have many non-Indians serving in our India offices so that they can absorb what they learn in India and facilitate a higher level of integration with the company when they return to their home base.

Our biggest challenge now is to continue transforming ourselves from a completely Indian company to a global company without losing the values and principles and passion that have brought us so far, and without compromising on the Tata values and culture. We take this very seriously and our mission incorporates cultural initiatives through employee interactions and presentations. Our Tata legacy has been captured in numerous films which are shown across TCS offices and every major TCS office reception area has LCD screens carrying the same messages through to our visitors. We also have a foreign language initiative that is completely devoted to culture and language orientation.

In 2002 we were only 30,000-strong; since then there has been an exponential growth in our employee numbers and we now add 30,000 to 50,000 people—that is the employee strength of a mid-size company—each year. While it is relatively easy to integrate IT systems and processes, culture and behaviour changes take longer to happen, so integration remains a continuous endeavour at TCS even today.

Today over 90 per cent of our revenues come from outside India, including a growing proportion from emerging nations. We have achieved this by following the simple principle that small victories give you the confidence to do bigger things, and small pieces can eventually be connected together to form a larger whole. Our business today is spread across 145 offices across forty-two countries, which means just as many cultures and just as many legal systems to manage. This is truly reflective of the long distance TCS has traversed in its globalization journey, and I think we have proved beyond doubt that we can adapt our business model to local environments successfully.

## DIGITIZATION AND THE CREATION OF 'ONE TCS'

THE HEAD OF every organization is perhaps paranoid about having a good grip on the numbers and data that help run the business. For a complex and dynamic industry like IT services, accuracy and real-time information are the keys to our operational efficiency.

In 1996 when I took over as CEO, I found it somewhat overwhelming. The view from the top suddenly seemed very expansive and the sheer scale of TCS and its reach across the globe struck me forcefully as if for the first time. Most of all, I felt I needed to have basic information about the business in hand in order to be able to manage effectively.

For example, I needed to know total employee numbers, numbers by location, by technology skills, hiring projections, the number of projects being worked upon and their status. The need for this data was made even more acute at the time because we were growing so rapidly in the run-up to Y2K, and adding more than 10,000 employees a year. Pankaj Ghemawat put it very well when he said, 'If you are riding a rocket which is intrinsically risky, some sort of guidance system is useful.'

But when I asked for these numbers, I often got a vague estimate or I would be told that they would come back later with an answer. On some occasions, I got no answer at all. When I did get an answer, it was often too late and when I cross-checked the figures, invariably I would end up with conflicting numbers. I realized that a lot of the time, the people I asked were 'going down the totem pole' for information, and at each level people were making adjustments or offering guesstimates rather than providing accurate and authenticated numbers. It became obvious our information management systems were inadequate.

We had created a number of systems that were functional in nature, a separate system for manpower allocation, one for quality management, yet another for keeping track of people and one for customers. These had been developed in the pre-Internet era. I discovered that there were actually about 1,200 applications running inside TCS. They were fragmented because they had been developed at different times by individual departments and business units using disparate technologies. Moving data between them often involved a loss of accuracy, integrity and timeliness. From an accuracy, time and cost point of view this was just not acceptable.

The irony was that while we were building extremely sophisticated integrated systems for our clients including stock exchanges and banks, our own internal systems were both archaic and non-integrated. We needed to create a single unified system—the digital backbone for 'One TCS'.

So I asked Chandra, who at the time was heading our GE business, to put together a team to investigate possible solutions to these issues. What emerged from these discussions was a blueprint for the transformation of TCS using a unified information system we called e-TCS, which would include an executive dashboard and would support the organization's exponential growth.

The Y2K problem and the beginning of the new century was a signal of major changes for TCS. I felt the growth we were already experiencing was bound to bring about changes organization-wide, some which we could anticipate and others that we had no clue about. Around this time I decided to appoint a Chief Transformation Officer (CTO), something that I don't think any other Indian software company had done previously and which was sufficiently unusual that it generated a flurry of newspaper stories. I selected Paighal S. Viswanathan who had worked for HCL and earlier for Johnson & Johnson and hence had a background both in technology as well as sales and marketing. I realized for the job at hand we would need someone to 'sell' new ideas internally and help influence behaviour. The first thing on his plate was the new internal information system we were planning.

Viswanathan's early contribution to the digitization project was to rebrand the e-TCS package that Chandra's team was working on as 'Ultimatix'—which really stood for 'the ultimate system'. He also suggested that rather than roll the new system out in phases, we needed to adopt a 'big bang' approach and switch everyone in India over to it at the same time. The view was that if Ultimatix was rolled out alongside the existing applications, no one would switch over. So it was agreed that we would launch the Ultimatix system in India on 1 April 2002. This called for an investment in technology to the tune of $40 million.

It was a significant commitment for a company whose annual revenues at that time were about $700 million. In fact the investment was big enough to warrant a presentation to the Tata Group Business Review Council (there was no Board as we were not public) for ratification of the investment. We put together a presentation that was made at the Taj Hotel's ballroom in Mumbai using, for the first time, the concept of reverse video. Images from prototypes of the system were beamed on the screens specially put up for the Council members.

The aim of Ultimatix was to digitize all processes, create a system that was slick, real-time and scalable, that would enhance efficiency multifold and enable the company to move forward to the next level of growth.

We put together a team of about 140 people that began work on the project in 2001. From the planning stage to project launch took three months, even though the concept itself had been under consideration for a long time. From the outset, it was clear in our minds that we wanted a system base that was architected for the future, not something repurposed from the past.

We used an enterprise resource planning (ERP) package as the core of the system together with other best-of-breed software packages and built an integrated system that also enabled us to showcase our middleware technologies. The team began work in July 2001 and the whole project was completed in nine months. Ultimatix was launched in India on 1 April 2002, the date we had targeted.

Six months before the rollout, Viswanathan launched a consumer product-style teaser campaign aimed at generating a buzz around the launch with the tagline, 'Your world is going to change'. Over the next six months we trickled out more information about Ultimatix and then on 1 April 2002 people arrived in their offices to find balloons everywhere—and the new system live.

Viswanathan jokes that he and his team had to wear protective clothing over the next few months because some of the reactions to Ultimatix were extreme. I think he got yelled at a lot. Nevertheless, people gradually got used to the new system which was used for everything from filling in timesheets and expenses to completing the semi-annual self-appraisal forms.

Over time Ultimatix became enormously successful and made the idea of 'one TCS' possible. Management could view dashboards and we started to get real-time data which enabled us to become operationally efficient. For example, we were able to significantly improve the utilization of consultants by reducing the mean time from bench to project allocation, adding $75 million to the bottom line.

Ultimatix was a state-of-the-art system at that time and enabled us to bring together, on one platform, data about projects, clients, employees and prospects, capturing relationships between them. The impact was very visible at Bombay House, the Tata Group headquarters, and Ishaat Hussain, Group Finance Director, used to say that the way the numbers came together was 'like magic'.

After we deployed Ultimatix in our India operations, the next challenge was to deploy it in our overseas operations, particularly those in the US, and in our subsidiaries. Within a few years the same people who had objected so strongly to its introduction were saying, 'How did we ever live without it?'

We also learned some lessons in the process. For example, while Chandra's team was drawing up the specifications for Ultimatix, I also asked another team led by Ravi Gopinath, who was Vice President–Engineering and Industrial Services, to map every single business process in TCS with a view to finding ways in which they might be streamlined.

Unfortunately, however, there was a bit of a disconnect between the IT systems teams and the business teams who did not understand process mapping. So, instead of improving processes and then digitizing them, we decided to digitize the existing processes rather than try to change them, which would have delayed the rollout and might not have been successful. As it turned out, Ultimatix itself began to change the processes because it integrated the IT and the business processes iteratively—and that ended up being a far more effective way of doing things than having a separate team trying to work on the business processes themselves.

Certainly from a management perspective, Ultimatix made a huge difference and we have continued to improve it, adding in new functionalities and applications over time. Recently we have introduced a number of Web 2.0 and enterprise networking applications like question-and-answer forums, an idea generation platform and blogs designed to help the associates share knowledge and ideas and collaborate with their peers. Originally Ultimatix was introduced to address the digitization requirements of a fast-growing business, but it has gone far beyond that. Today the Ultimatix system is the backbone of TCS's Global Network Delivery Model, a collaborative, best-in-class framework of people, processes and infrastructure that makes it possible to provide one level of service globally.

As we progressed on the digitization front with Ultimatix we were also simultaneously progressing on the quality journey. Our obsession with quality benchmarks led to a period around the year

2000 when a lot of different quality models were being adopted by us. Amongst these were the Capability Mature Model (CMM) and the People Capability Mature Model (PCMM)—the Software Engineering Institute's (SEI) model of software engineering that specifies five levels of maturity of the processes of a software organization; then there was the Customer Operations Performance Centre (COPC) certification for BPOs, and finally ISO 20000, the first international standard for an IT service management system from the International Organization for Standardization. Since our operations were widespread and every centre had to be certified separately, we seemed to be going in for certification every day in one location or the other. It was like giving an exam every day. We thought there had to be a better way of doing this.

So TCS decided to examine all the quality processes being used at that time and create a model of our own that would be a superset of all the existing models. There were some processes such as 'customer handling' that was not present in any other model but could go into our superset. With this idea we approached SEI, the keeper of all these models. We added twenty new process areas to the forty-five that were already present in CMM and PCMM. It was decided to take the uniqueness of our model and write a quality management system that would detail all these areas and take into account the processes of all other models; this would be called the Integrated Quality Management System (iQMS).

SEI was approached and we requested them to audit our model as a sufficient benchmark for us to get all certifications at one go. Nobody had ever approached them with a request like this; while they thought it was a great proposal, they came back to say that they did not have an assessment method for what we were asking. Ron Raddice, an independent assessor who had great credibility, then got some people to write the assessment method for this integrated model, for which TCS even got royalty. Ron helped us convince ISO, and assessors were then trained on the new method; finally we made iQMS available throughout TCS to every employee through Ultimatix. We had to train nearly 80,000 people. This mammoth task was achieved through a variety of ways including face-to-face training, Internet-based training and self-learning modules. For ease of use we created a 'wiki' on iQMS whereby any employee on the project could look up any process without interrupting their work at all. It was of course an instant hit.

iQMS was a path-breaking achievement—it created IPR for us and established TCS as a thought leader. From doing thirty different assessments we had gone to only one, yet another aspect of 'One TCS'. We had a big celebration at the Taj Mahal Hotel in Mumbai where Ratan Tata was also present. It was a big moment not just for TCS but for the entire Tata Group.

It's been almost ten years since Ultimatix was introduced, and from a scaling point of view, it can probably serve us for the next five years as well. However, when we devised Ultimatix we did not envisage the extent to which we would became a global business, with employees representing ninety-nine nationalities. Today we have in mind a system for the future which would incorporate next generation technologies and would accommodate processes for a global workforce, rather than one that is designed for an Indian workforce and adapted for global use.

Ultimatix has become the backbone of TCS's business processes, connecting us with all stakeholders in the value chain from suppliers and academia to employees and our customers. We are particularly proud of the transparency with which customers can track through a dashboard the progress on their projects. Ultimatix gave us the confidence to position ourselves strongly by promising the customer an experience of certainty.

## INORGANIC GROWTH THROUGH ACQUISITIONS

FOR THE FIRST thirty years of its existence, TCS had grown exclusively through organic means. We felt no need to grow in any other manner. We were too young a company, in learning mode ourselves and not too well known globally. Although we had projects across the world, our presence was mainly in the US, the UK and in Switzerland, so our global footprint was limited.

By the turn of the century IT services were growing at a frenetic pace. It was boom time. After I took over as CEO, I realized that in order to pursue a differentiated growth strategy we would also need to look at acquisitions, particularly niche acquisitions that made a difference to TCS either by adding intellectual property content, or by expanding our servicing capability in a certain region or area.

There was no mergers and acquisitions (M&A) 'master plan' as such, but our first real opportunity to put our acquisition skills to the test came in 2001 when the Indian government put CMC up for sale as part of its first privatization programme.

We had actually identified CMC as a potential takeover target several years ago because it was a prime contractor to the Indian government and its agencies. In CMC I saw a strong R&D culture and a good solutions business—and very strong hardware–software integration capabilities which had been demonstrated in national projects. CMC had also established a strong position in India's domestic transportation and energy markets which I felt had very good growth potential.

I thought the combination of TCS's and CMC's capabilities would create an unstoppable force in the IT and IT services industry.

The origins of the Computer Maintenance Corporation are interesting. CMC was started in 1975 as a private limited company by the Indian government which held a 100 per cent stake until it was converted into a public limited company in 1977. When IBM wound up its Indian operations in 1978, there were several IBM machines being used across the country, including a few used by the Indian government. CMC took over the maintenance of these IBM machines and others that the government bought subsequently.

For the Indian government, therefore, CMC became a mission critical company because it supported a lot of its computer systems and IT projects. In fact, by the end of the millennium the Indian government accounted for 34 per cent of the total domestic IT market and CMC had grown into a sizeable company in its own right with 3,000 employees and annual revenues of almost $120 million.

In 1996, the government appointed a Disinvestment Commission with a mandate to evaluate all public sector companies and make recommendations for the divestment of non-strategic non-core companies. Despite its importance, the Commission decided that

CMC was a non- strategic and non-core business that the government could divest and transfer to the private sector, and made a recommendation to this effect in 1999. Meanwhile the Indian IT industry had grown substantially, and its success had encouraged many new entrants and increased competition for established companies like TCS. This provided the government with the confidence that selling CMC would not create a dominant, monopolistic player and that market forces could be allowed to take over.

Incidentally, a similar move to privatize VSNL, the government-owned telecommunications group, took place in 2002 after the Indian telecom market had become a competitive market with several players involved.

In 2001 the government sent a dossier on CMC out to investment banks—including DSP Merrill Lynch who were advising us—and invited sealed bids. I discussed the possibility of tabling a bid for CMC with my colleagues who agreed that a TCS bid made sense. Ultimately we made four presentations to the CMC board.

I was convinced that CMC would be a good acquisition for us because it had successfully executed some of the largest and most complicated domestic turnkey projects including the Indian Railways reservation system IMPRESS (Integrated Multi-train Passenger Reservation System). IMPRESS went on to become a huge success and was eventually deployed all over India, facilitating over half a million transactions every single day and cutting wait times for passengers dramatically. The Indian Railways system which runs 6,000 passenger trains carrying over 10 million passengers a day is not only one of the largest employers anywhere in the world, in India it is the one system that touches the lives of almost every citizen. The automation of the system therefore was a major milestone. Before IMPRESS became operational, Indians needed to make rail travel bookings months in advance and booking processes were, at best, opaque.

CMC had also developed a real-time cargo handling system that integrated all the complex and varied activities that take place in container terminals—a system that was implemented in several Indian and international ports. It had also built an online transaction processing system for the Bombay Stock Exchange that today handles 5 million transactions every day.

I knew therefore that CMC would not only increase our footprint in the domestic market, but it would position us advantageously when we bid for big government and public sector contracts.

Since it was TCS's very first acquisition, we were not well versed in processes like conducting due diligence on a company; so we relied heavily on the DSP Merrill Lynch team to handle those aspects of the bid. When the sealed envelopes containing the bids were finally opened there were fourteen bidders, five international and nine Indian. Ultimately, however, only two—CDC (which was basically an association of CMC employees) and Tata Sons on behalf of TCS—remained in the fray. CDC could not come up with a bank guarantee for the funding so we won the auction.

In October 2001, at a ceremony in New Delhi, Ratan Tata, Chairman of Tata Sons, handed over a cheque for $33.8 million to the late Pramod Mahajan, the Union minister for information technology, in payment for a 51 per cent stake in CMC.

Interestingly, many of the larger IT companies in India were not really that interested in bidding for CMC because, with 83 per cent of its revenues derived from India, they viewed CMC as a domestic asset. At that time, most Indian IT companies were focused on the fast-expanding offshore IT services market. We looked ahead and I knew that as the Indian economy grew, the domestic market would present big opportunities for IT software and services.

At the time the acquisition of CMC was not generally viewed as being very logical or as a popular move. Even internally there were a lot of doubts on whether it made sense. Some people worried that it would not be an easy asset to manage. They were concerned that the government's way of functioning and running a company was vastly different from the way TCS was run, and that changing the culture would take enormous time and effort. Nevertheless we stuck to our conviction and staked our reputation on the transaction. It was tough to integrate CMC into the TCS fold and make it work the way it does, but I think we were able to overcome the internal and external scepticism and answer our critics.

In the meantime, we had also begun to think about targeting Latin America for geographic expansion and we drew up a strategic road map for the region that included both organic and inorganic initiatives. We initially looked at potential acquisition targets in both Brazil and Mexico but did not proceed with either because of valuation and other issues. Instead, in 2003 we formed a JV in Brazil with Grupo TBA, an Internet service provider and IT services company, which enabled us to become familiar with the local market. We then bought out our joint venture partnership three years later.

In Chile we acquired a local company called Comicrom in 2005. This was an important strategic initiative because it enabled TCS to expand into other Spanish-speaking markets. It also bolstered our position in the back-office BPO market. Comicrom already handled between 80 and 90 per cent of the banking transactions in Chile and its acquisition gave us the scale to grow the entire banking back-office function in that country.

The same year we also acquired Financial Network Services (FNS), an Australian company with a retail banking software package called Bancs24. We needed them because some of our competitors had begun to target that market segment with their own IP. Bancs24 was a very comprehensive package and we were able to successfully win the systems integration contract for the State Bank of India (SBI) Group for implementation of core banking. Since we had invested considerable effort in customizing and strengthening it we felt acquiring FNS would be strategic for our products business. During our initial dealings with FNS and its feisty owner Tony Ward we learned to our surprise that when the product was being developed in the early 1980s TCS had deputed its programmers to Sydney to work with Tony and his team to help develop the product. Since the acquisition we have been able to deploy the FNS software package, rechristened 'Bancs', extensively with a number of domestic clients. Today close to 50 per cent of the banking transactions in India are processed by Bancs, thereby justifying the acquisition we made.

While we had begun to make carefully selected acquisitions, we also identified some non-strategic assets for disposal. In particular we decided we did not want to be in the call centre business so we decided to sell our 50 per cent stake in a company called Intelenet to Housing Development Finance Corporation (HDFC) for $37 million. Conversely, we acquired the outstanding stakes we did not already own in joint ventures with Swissair and Singapore Airlines.

In 2005 we undertook a major project in the UK when we entered into a deal with Pearl Assurance to process all their closed life insurance policies. At that time the deal was worth almost £500 million and was the largest insurance project for TCS. As part of the deal we had to absorb over 1,000 employees of Pearl; to do this we created a special purpose vehicle called Diligenta located in Peterborough, UK. With this we acquired a large British workforce which had to be integrated with our culture. In addition we learned the business processes in pensions administration and annuities. We also won favour with local politicians as no jobs were lost locally, and instead the workers' skills were upgraded.

Two other important consolidation deals happened in 2006. First we wrapped up the purchase of TKS-Teknosoft in Switzerland which consolidated our business in the continental European markets, and then completed the acquisition of Tata Infotech from Tata Sons. The Tata Infotech purchase was particularly pleasing for me personally because it effectively closed a circle. Tata Infotech was the rump of the Tata Burroughs–Tata Sons joint venture which had been formed in 1978. At that time, if some in Tata Sons had had their way, Tata Infotech would have absorbed TCS and brought about a premature end to the TCS story. In an irony of sorts the exact opposite was now about to happen. In the wake of this deal we sold off Citel, a call centre business that Tata Infotech had run.

Our acquisitions have always been driven by strategic long-term goals. In 2008, just when the global downturn was beginning to be felt, we made our most recent and costly acquisition, that of Citicorp Global Services (CGS). That deal was primarily driven by a desire to extend our abilities to provide end-to-end BPO services for the financial services industry. CGS, which has more than 12,000 employees, was already one of the largest providers of BPO services within the banking and financial services sector, and the $505 million purchase catapulted TCS into pole position in the sector.

It was a landmark acquisition for TCS, helping us not only acquire new capabilities in the banking domain, but also underscoring the importance of our long-term, sustainable relationships with our large customers, including Citicorp itself.

Looking back, we have spent close to $1.2 billion on acquisitions over the last ten years. We have also formed joint ventures in China and other countries to enhance our business in these regions. Meanwhile we have sold off a handful of businesses in areas like call centres and a small engineering design joint venture with GE called Engineering Analysis Centre of Excellence (EACOC). GE and TCS had entered into this JV in 1999 to provide engineering analysis, design and software development services to GE aircraft engineers and GE power systems.

I am proud that none of our acquisitions have fallen apart. Some have done very well, others not so well, but none have blown up in our faces. It is difficult to be precise about the numbers, but we reckon that about 15 per cent of TCS revenues can be attributed to the acquisitions we have made and the return on our investment has been considerable. We have proved that we are ready to experiment with M&A and to supplement organic growth with acquisitions where they make sense, but we are not very aggressive so we do not look to strike too many deals.

I think that TCS's acquisitions have encouraged us to look outwards and have broadened the mindset of TCS employees. I believe acquisitions do have a role to play in our strategy. But this is a people business and we are mindful that integrating acquisitions in this type of business is very difficult and that many large deals in this sector have failed. Overall, I do not expect the Indian IT industry to become very aggressive in terms of acquisitions because the reality today is that most companies can grow organically much faster and achieve better returns by reinvesting in organic growth than in acquisitions.

## BRANDING

AFTER BEING IN existence for about thirty-five years, TCS had built a formidable presence for itself as India's premier IT software and services firm. We had done this in the typical Tata way— quietly. We did not consciously market ourselves and we believed that our work would speak for itself.

As a result, the TCS brand meant different things to different people. In the minds of IT buyers in the US and Europe, there was a general lack of awareness and little differentiation between Tata and TCS. They often used the names interchangeably.

We, as engineers, had done little to change these perceptions. While we were intensely focused on exploiting our technical prowess and on delivering value to our customers, we had paid little regard to marketing and the need to build a brand that could compete on an equal footing in the global IT services markets with the likes of IBM, Accenture and HP.

TCS was also a wholly owned division of a privately held limited company whose owners—a charitable trust—did not want to be in the public glare. The Tatas themselves were by nature shy people who shunned publicity. So for the first thirty years or so TCS did not have a formal marketing or sales organization. That does not mean that we did not sell or market our services. Obviously we did some of these things, but it was not the main focus.

At that stage we did not even have a legal department or a professional HR department. For quite a few years, our PR department consisted of one retired public relations manager—and he was not really a public relations expert, but a former journalist. This did not really matter in the early days. We felt that because we were a Tata company we did not give adequate attention to public relations because we believed—perhaps mistakenly—that our work would speak for itself.

But it soon became apparent that we could not be complacent about our positioning and about the need to establish and reinforce our brand. By the mid-1990s, we began to see some of our more publicity-savvy competitors' names in the news more often than TCS, even though we had essentially built the Indian IT industry from scratch and pioneered the techniques and business models that had made it a success. It was becoming apparent that, outside the network of our own customers, TCS was less known than some of our competitors—even though they were relative newcomers to the industry.

We also realized that if we did not speak about ourselves, no one else would, certainly not our competition. In the absence of our voice in the media, the industry and the press portrayed Infosys as a pioneer of the offshore outsourcing concept, which was actually not true.

Within TCS our employees began to feel that they were working for a company that was not that well known and it began to affect our ability to recruit the brightest and the best graduates. For example, if somebody was joining TCS, their parents might say, 'Why are you joining them, why don't you join Infosys or Wipro, they are better known.'

The other factor that spurred us on was that we knew we would eventually go public. We realized that we would constantly be in the public spotlight, that our financials and operations would be scrutinized every quarter by share markets—and that we would then be on a level playing field with the top global IT services companies.

It was clear to me as I looked past our IPO that the IT services business was going to be dominated by a handful of global giants. We did not want to be known as just one of the Indian players, an also-ran in a global marketplace. In fact we believed that the IT software and services industry would become centred on three top companies. I was determined that TCS should be amongst them.

Initially some of the senior TCS managers needed convincing that TCS would benefit from a marketing arm because as engineers, we believed we could do everything ourselves. But I became convinced that we needed a very strong marketing department and a well-established separate sales force, so I appointed Jayant Pendharkar as head of our global marketing. We also took some other initiatives to regroup and retrain our sales force to use the collateral created by the marketing department as a calling card when we met potential customers, and we revisited the question of advertising.

During Kohli's time at the helm, the only advertisements we ran were the recruitment ads and advertisements for the products that we were selling. Later on we ran one brand-building campaign around a series of advertisements that featured chess players, and then before we went public we ran the TCS global campaign in the domestic financial papers.

It was not really until after the turn of the millennium that we began to think about the TCS brand and to recognize that the public perception of a brand can be as important and valuable as the company's technical abilities and other assets.

One of the first issues we had to face when we decided to get serious about the TCS brand was that TCS already had a tagline: 'Beyond the Obvious'. But as Jayant noted, 'It became obvious that it was beyond anybody's comprehension what it stood for—because it could stand for anything.'

In fact 'Beyond the Obvious' had become our tagline almost by accident. Someone in our Bangalore office had liked the phrase and put it up on his wall. Then one time when Jack Welch, the GE Chief Executive, was walking through the facility he had commented that he liked the sign, and from then on it became our official tagline.

The problem was that whenever prospects or customers asked us, 'What does the tagline mean?' we had no clear answer; more often than not it was left to individual interpretation. I decided that we needed to undertake a more formal exercise and define what TCS really stood for, so I asked those most directly involved in marketing TCS in India, the US and the UK to get together and come up with some recommendations.

The group held a two-day meeting and came up with some ideas, but we quickly realized that we actually needed the involvement of an external source, because a brand is what the outside world sees you to be and not what *you* think you are. So we began looking for a firm of strategic brand consultants to help with the task. It took some time because we had to define and articulate exactly what we wanted from this agency.

In the end we shortlisted six companies, but finally chose the New York-based firm of Siegel and Gale because they had already done a fair amount of work in the IT services business. We had already undertaken some research of our own on the IT market, so we didn't feel that it was necessary to undertake an extensive external market study. Rather, we decided to ask Siegel and Gale to focus on two key questions: First, what is it that makes TCS special? Second, what is it that our clients really value and desire?

We wanted to find a way to articulate the answers to these key questions in an interesting and compelling way that differentiated us from our competitors. The Siegel and Gale project team began by reviewing our existing research and marketing collateral. They conducted numerous interviews with TCSers spread across the world, sometimes meeting them face to face and at other times speaking on the phone, even at odd times of the day and night because of the time difference between India and the US.

It was an interesting process because for the first time TCSers were having to think about what TCS was really about. When I was interviewed, I had to restrain myself from talking too much—after all I had spent over thirty years in the company. After some deep thought, I tried to articulate as succinctly as possible what I thought was the essence of the company.

But we also felt it was important for the Siegel and Gale team to get an external perception of TCS, so we invited them to attend our US customer summit and to meet and speak to our clients. What the team discovered after talking to both internal and external audiences was that there was an overlap between the in-house and customers' views of TCS that represented our real personality.

Dennis Riney, who led the enagagement from Siegel and Gale, described the project as being 'about revealing the soul of TCS from the inside and trying to find a compelling way to explain that to customers'. It was, he said, more 'inside out' than 'outside in'.

'That's a perfectly valid way to create a brand position in our view in B2B (business-to-business) markets, less so in consumer markets,' he said. 'I think generally in consumer markets you need that customer insight, but in B2B markets where there are a limited number of competitors, it is different.'

Siegel and Gale told us: 'Look, you can aspire to be anything you want, but can you support that? Is it believable? If you say I am a true business adviser, will people believe you? If they do not believe you, it will not stick with them and the advertising money you spend will just be wasted.'

They told us that our customers saw us more from an operational perspective—for example, that we did work on time, we had good people, we knew the technology—rather than from an aspirational perspective. For this reason they argued that we needed to adopt a two-step approach. First,we should establish a brand position and tagline that could be defended and that would help us differentiate ourselves and pull us away from our competitors, then go to the next step—our aspirational goal.

One option that we considered was to highlight the innovation at the core of the TCS service offering, but IBM was running its 'innovation' campaign at that time and Siegel and Gale was not sure that the message was the right one, particularly with the economy in a down cycle when innovation might not be as highly valued as during an upswing.

But what did come through very, very clearly in all the discussions that the branding team conducted was a notion of 'certainty'. When TCS undertook a project for a client we looked them in the eye, told them what needed to be done and how long it would take, and then, come hell or high water, we delivered—even if that meant adding more people to the team and on the rare occasion even losing money on a project at the cost of delivery priorities. This came from a strong feeling that once we made a commitment to a client, it had to be met.

It was something that the Siegel and Gale team heard time and again during their interviews, and so the first idea that the team presented to us was that TCS stood for 'The Science of Certainty'. The tagline was meant to convey the notion that TCS had cornered the market on the science of how you make IT systems work 100 per cent of the time, how you make them reliable.

At TCS we liked this concept, but we felt that we wanted the brand to be more closely identified with delivering business solutions, so we sent the Siegel and Gale team back to think about the word 'certainty' a bit more. They then came up with several alternatives and the one that eventually emerged as the strongest was more of a declarative statement: 'Experience Certainty'.

While the words could be interpreted in several different ways, Siegel and Gale argued that the intention behind them was to issue a call to action or a bit of a dare along the lines of: 'If you're looking for an IT provider, come to us and you'll experience certainty. You know you won't experience that elsewhere.'

We did some testing around the phrase 'Experience Certainty' and it seemed to resonate both inside TCS and with clients. The 'Experience Certainty' tagline conveyed the message that TCS provided IT services, business solutions and outsourcing with a level of 'certainty' that no others could match.

Since then the evidence has shown that our clients value the assurance of getting their unique requirements met on time, within budget and with high quality. It means they can be more responsive to the business, be more efficient and shift investment to strategic initiatives rather than tactical functions. Experiencing certainty comes from achieving real business results and allowing clients to transform their operations—not just maintaining them.

The other problem that we needed to solve—and we actually spent more time on this—had to do with the three little lines that we put next to the TCS initials on our communications: IT Services, Business Solutions and Outsourcing.

Initially we thought about highlighting six or seven competencies, but Siegel and Gale persuaded us that no one would remember that many. Instead they suggested that we should take a lesson from Accenture which for many years has had the three words, 'Consulting, Technology, and Outsourcing', to describe themselves. Instead of trying to encompass everything we did, they thought we should focus on the three broad areas that we were really good at.

After a lot of spirited back-and-forth discussions, we came up with IT Services which described a whole range of things that we did, Business Solutions which was meant to capture the emerging software platforms that we had, not just in financial services but in engineering as well, and Outsourcing which encompassed BPO as well as other forms of outsourcing.

We also spent some time considering whether the company should be called Tata Consultancy Services, TCS or something else. As you can imagine, in an organization packed with smart people, everyone had a view. So we had long debates on this topic. But the final consideration was that TCS was still majority owned by the Tata Group and it was felt that dropping the Tata name was not an option.

Some people were in favour of changing the company's name to the initials 'TCS' which they felt put the company on the same footing as our competitors like IBM, HP, EDS and CSC, and was both simple and effective on marketing materials. The initials TCS were probably already known by the top 10,000 IT managers in the world, so the real task was to reach out to the million or more business decision-makers who might come across the name in their boardrooms. For them, and most other business people, you still had to explain what TCS was, and what the initials stood for.

As opponents of a name change pointed out, why would we want to drop a reference to India's most important and celebrated industrial group? On the other hand, the Tata Group already had a number of two-name companies. Tata Iron and Steel Company had become Tata Steel and Tata Engineering Locomotive Works had become Tata Motors. Other two-name Tata companies included Tata Chemicals, Tata Finance and Tata Capital.

The Tata Group would have liked us to call ourselves Tata Systems or Tata Consulting, which we seriously considered. But in the US, 'consulting' meant sending experts, and we did a lot more than that. We also considered Tata Services, but that could refer to cleaning services or catering services and the like, so we dropped the idea.

Either way, it seemed we would lose out if we dropped one or the other of the two descriptors in Tata Consultancy Services. If we called ourselves Tata Consultancy, we thought there might be a perception that we were not involved in providing services, and we risked losing some of the 70–80 per cent of our revenues derived from services; and if we dropped consultancy, we would be dropping the aspirational part of the name because we wanted to be seen as a consultancy. Ultimately we decided that maybe J.R.D. Tata and Nani Palkhivala were right when they came up with the name Tata Consultancy Services, and that the name conveyed the right messages to our partners and customers.

But we did decide on a naming convention for our products that was actually contrary to a Siegel and Gale recommendation. They wanted us to preface our products with the whole name 'Tata Consultancy Services', but we decided that the products from TCS should be prefixed simply with TCS; so, for example, we had TCS Financial Services, TCS Banking Solutions, TCS Healthcare Solutions and so on. We also refer to TCS R&D and TCS Research, so in a sort of quiet way we were creating a brand TCS without having to go to Bombay House (the Tata Group headquarters) for the Tatas' approval.

We also needed help developing our own brand architecture that, while it followed the guidelines of the Tata Group, would also express our individuality and stake our claim to be a unique company in our own right. We wanted a distinctive visual brand architecture that reflected the attributes of our business: the ones and zeroes of binary code and the concepts of repeatability and consistency.

To meet these requirements Siegel and Gale developed what we now call the 'Tata weave' which we managed to get approved by the Tata Group and which now appears on our stationery, business cards, brochures and other TCS documentation. (Before the branding exercise we had some twenty different templates for our PowerPoint presentations!)

After the Siegel and Gale and TCS teams came up with the Tata weave I invited them to my apartment to prepare for a meeting with Ratan Tata, Chairman of TCS, in Mumbai. We had to think how best to present the new branding including the weave pattern. Ratan Tata is an architect by training so I guessed that anything visual that was well done would appeal to him. I guessed right because he saw the logic of what we had done. As luck would have it, we also discovered that Alan Siegel, founder of Siegel and Gale, was Ratan Tata's contemporary from Cornell, so there was a connection. To our surprise, Ratan Tata asked Dennis whether he thought we were not going far enough. He wanted to know if our proposals were dynamic and exciting enough, compared to Microsoft's, for example.

The next step was to spread the new branding message and the 'Experience Certainty' tagline throughout TCS, and to ensure that everyone not only used it but bought into the thinking behind it. The agency had warned us that this would be the most difficult task.

So we prepared a 'Certainty kit' and over a period of a year the marketing team went to every major branch in the US, UK, Latin America and the Middle East. To make it popular, we also developed an audio-visual with a jingle; in many TCS offices if you ring us up you will still hear the 'Certainty' jingle.

Family send-off at the airport on the way to UCLA, 1969

Bachelor digs in Los Angeles, 1969

His first car—a Beetle, 1970

On a visit to Yosemite National Park as a student, 1970

The wedding ceremony, 1972

A few relaxing moments with Mala at home

In Queens, New York with Mala and Tarun, 1980

Tarun's thread ceremony, 1987

## TATA CONSULTANCY SERVICES

ADM/SRD                                   February 23, 1972.

Mr. S. Ramadorai,
Bombay.

Dear Sir,

Further to your letter dated the 2nd December 1971,
addressed to Tata Incorporated, New York, this is to advise
you that we are pleased to offer you employment as Asstt.
Systems Programmer & Analyst in our organization, on a consolidated salary of Rs.1,000/- per month during the first year.
You will also be entitled to house rent subsidy as per the
Company Rules.

2.      You will be on probation for a period of twelve months,
on satisfactory completion of which you may be considered for
confirmation in a suitable grade.

3.      Your appointment will be subject to your being found
medically fit by our Chief Medical Officer at the commencement
of and during the course of your appointment with the Company.

4.      Your appointment is subject to the following terms
and conditions:

   (a)   The Company reserves the right to alter or
         modify its working hours or to increase them
         so as to require you to work upto 48 hours
         in any week or 9 hours on any day.

   (b)   The public holidays observed by the Company
         are subject to adjustment or reduction from
         time to time.

   (c)   The facilities, amenities and leave granted
         to employees in excess of statutory require-
         ments do not form part of the conditions of
         the service, and are subject to revision at
         the discretion of the Management.

   (d)   You will be governed by the Service Rules of
         the Company and you will be entitled to
         Provident Fund (on confirmation), leave and
         other benefits in accordance with such Rules.

.. 2

CONSULTANCY SERVICES

: 2 :

   (e)   The Company reserves the right to utilise or
         transfer your services to any of the Company's
         divisions, offices, work sites, or affiliated
         company on the same terms and conditions in any
         part of India.

   (f)   Your services may be terminated at any time by
         giving you one calendar month's notice or by
         payment of one month's salary in lieu of notice.

   (g)   In view of the fact that the Company will be
         incurring considerable expenditure in training
         you, you will be required to execute an agree-
         ment to serve the Company for a minimum period
         of 3 years from the date of joining duty,
         failing which you will have to pay an amount
         of Rs.5,000/- (Rupees five thousand only) to
         the Company as compensation.

5.      Please return the duplicate copy of this letter duly
signed as a token of your acceptance of the above appointment
on the terms and conditions mentioned above.

                          Yours faithfully,
                     TATA CONSULTANCY SERVICES


                          (F. C. Kohli.)
                          General Manager.

TCS's appointment letter signed by F.C. Kohli, 1972

The early TCS team, 1973 (Ramadorai is standing second from right)

The Burroughs B6700, 1976

With his mentor F.C. Kohli, 1990

At the TCS leadership team retreat, 1998

The senior executive development programme at MIT's Sloan School of Management, 1993 (Ramadorai is third from left in the third row)

Handing over the cheque for the acquisition of CMC to Pramod Mahajan, 2001

Launch of the TCS IPO at NSE, 2004

August 4, 2004

Dear Ram,

Having spent the past 10 days with you on the Road Show, I just wanted to let you know how proud I was of the way you handled the meetings. You have built TCS into a great enterprise, and of course it will need to be further nurtured as we go forward as a public company.

I value your colleagueship and look forward to working with you to make things happen.

With warm personal regards,

Yours sincerely
Ratan

Ratan Tata's letter after the TCS road show, 2004

Dear Ram,

My heartiest congratulations on your selection as the Businessman of The Year 2004. This is indeed a well-deserved recognition of your achievements at TCS over the years. It is good to know that a person who goes about quietly building a great company without loudly proclaiming his achievements, is finally recognised and rewarded for his efforts — a rare occurrence in today's environment. The lead story on you in Business India is also very well presented.

You have a hard task ahead of you to keep TCS in its leading position but I have no doubt that you will succeed. However, in this process, please do take care of yourself.

With warm regards — and all good wishes to you and Mrs. Ramadorai for the New Year,

Yours sincerely,
Noshir Soonawala

Warm wishes from Noshir Soonawala, former Vice Chairman, Tata Sons, 2004

Receiving the *Business India* Businessman of the Year Award, 2004

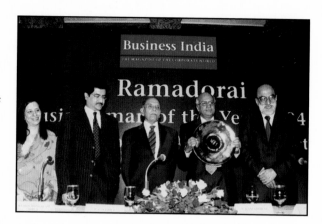

Receiving the *Economic Times* Company of the Year Award from Prime Minister Manmohan Singh, 2006

Receiving the UK Trade and Investment Special Recognition Award for TCS's exemplary contribution to Indo–UK economic ties from Tony Blair, 2005

Receiving the Padma
Bhushan from President
A.P.J. Abdul Kalam, 2006

With Ratan Tata at the
inauguration of TCS
House, 2007

TCS House

At the twenty-fifth anniversary of TRDDC with Dr A.P.J. Abdul Kalam, 2007

Receiving the CBE from Vicki Treadell, former British Deputy High Commissioner, 2009

In his office in the Air-India building

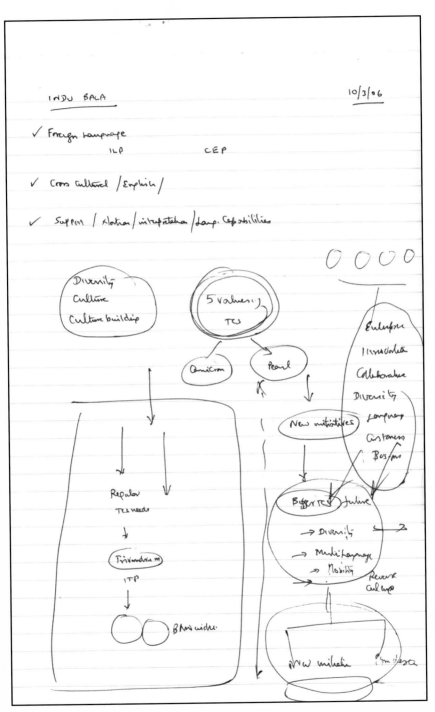

The scribble from which the Ignite idea germinated

With David Cameron, 2006

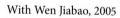
With Wen Jiabao, 2005

With Colin Powell, 2007

With Martina
Navratilova, 2007

With Antonio Calabrese of
Ferrari, 2007

With Gabriel del Torchio
of Ducati, 2009

With Larry Summers, 2008

With Swiss architect Mario
Botta in Lugano, 2011

Launch of the TCS JV in Beijing, 2007

Distribution of school bags to children—a Maitree initiative

With N. Murali, President, The Music Academy and renowned clarinet artiste A.K.C. Natarajan in Chennai, 2009

The TCS Board of Directors, 2009

Jogging at Worli sea
face to keep himself fit

Mala Ramadorai

Tarun and Purnima at their
wedding ceremony, 2007

Overall, we approached the task with almost missionary zeal to ensure that everyone from the company drivers to the top executives understood what the brand stood for and what it meant for them. We urged everybody to think about how best they could perform their roles with our brand in mind.

What I like about the tagline 'Experience Certainty' was that it was something to live up to at any time and all the time. If a customer or a prospect came to India for the first time, I would like the TCS chauffeur to feel inspired to be there on time to receive him, wearing a starched white uniform and driving a nice clean car. We wanted to ensure that 'Experience Certainty' started from the smallest detail and extended all the way up to the top. But we also had to explain to our staff that 'certainty' was not a legal guarantee and could not be put in a contract. It was meant to be an expression of intent and confidence.

Since the new branding was adopted in 2005–06, supported by a media advertising campaign which ran until the recession intervened, we have tracked its impact and we believe it has been a success. Indeed, TCS-commissioned brand surveys have shown improved awareness and increases of more than 20 per cent in positive brand perception across many TCS attributes.

In fact I would say it became a strategic initiative for us, not just some marketing gimmick. A lot of measurements were done internally and they showed that we do indeed deliver a certain experience and that we consistently outperform the industry average and our nearest competitors.

The branding exercise itself won the Gold Award for Marketing Excellence in the category of Sharpening Brand and Competitive Differentiation by the IT Services Marketing Association (ITSMA). The 'Certainty' campaign was recognized for differentiating TCS's positioning and offerings in the areas of innovation, execution and business results. It also awakened a sense of pride amongst TCSers.

However, we always saw 'Experience Certainty' as a transitional message and we have now begun a second exercise with Siegel and Gale to assess where we are today, and whether we are ready to adopt more aspirational messaging.

# 5

# GOING PUBLIC: THE TCS IPO

IT IS NOT often that you see the 'propah' business suit-clad bankers conduct themselves like backslapping boys in the dressing room. But that was exactly the mood on 25 August 2004 at the Taj Mahal Hotel, Mumbai.

They had good reason to celebrate—the TCS initial public offering (IPO), one of India's largest, most complex exercises, was hugely successful. Five years of preparatory work including two years of frenzied activity had enabled the carving out of India's largest IT services company from its parent holding company, the Tata Group. This was no mean feat—and had no precedence at all.

The IPO work had brought together a group of people working towards a common vision. The time spent together, whether during the hectic road shows or when managing the enormous back-end work, created personal bonds and friendships. The Crystal Room at the Taj that evening reflected that bonhomie. The bankers, not known for humour, outdid themselves, playing the generous hosts at a party for the Tata–TCS IPO team. The menu had some delectable fare that evening, but also on offer was some light-hearted fun. The bankers put up a show: a parody of the Tata Group and its key players which in a good-natured way poked gentle fun at the TCS team—how they had started diffidently but quickly learned the ropes and come out with flying colours. Since it was also the birthday of one of the team members a big cake was rolled out with great fanfare. Ratan Tata—at his best—even wondered if Hemendra Kothari, in true Wall Street banking tradition, would get a striptease artiste to leap out of the cake!

In the hall were teams from DSP Merrill Lynch, Morgan Stanley and JP Morgan, TCS and Tata, along with Tata directors and Chairman Ratan Tata. The mood was festive and charged, the excitement visible on every face present in the room. I felt overwhelmed by the moment and the impending changes that were round the corner. The TCS IPO party was the culmination of an effort that had begun over five years ago but it was also the beginning of a new phase in TCS's journey.

## Leading up to the TCS IPO

Ever since TCS had been set up it had been run as an independent division of Tata Sons with its own CEO. Effectively it was run as a company within a company with its own Chairman and an executive team, which I had led as Chief Executive since 1996.

TCS had proven to be extremely successful as a Tata Sons division, but inside TCS we believed that in order to take the business to the next level in the global marketplace, we would eventually need to be an independent public company.

The issue of restructuring came to the fore in the late 1990s, because it was a necessary precursor to floating TCS on the stock exchange. As Ishaat Hussain who took over as Tata Sons' Chief Financial Officer in 2000 recalls, 'There had been a long-standing view held by certain people inside TCS and some even on the Tata Sons board who felt that it would be a good idea to corporatize TCS and to make it public.'

At TCS we were always very keen that we should emerge as an independent entity for our own business reasons, but for Tata Sons this was obviously a very sensitive topic and a complex issue because it required a massive restructuring exercise. As it happened the restructuring took nearly five years. Finally the Tatas pressed the button to go ahead with the TCS IPO. May 2004 was the target date and there was a huge sense of relief and excitement.

## Why go public?

The momentum to restructure Tata Sons and float TCS on the stock exchange picked up in the wake of the bursting of the dot com bubble and the subsequent market adjustment. To some extent, it was driven by the fact that two of our competitors, Wipro and Infosys, were both listed companies. Inside TCS and within Tata Sons, the listed status of Infosys and Wipro was viewed as having given them a huge amount of brand value and an advantage in the marketplace, particularly in the US where Infosys was also listed. In addition, these quoted companies were able to offer stock options which we could not do.

India's leading investment bankers were eager to facilitate a TCS IPO and pursued Tata Sons relentlessly on this issue. It was such a large project, described by one investment banker involved at the time as 'a one-in-a-hundred year event', that it attracted the attention of all the investment banking firms in India at the time. Indeed there were few bankers in the country who did not make presentations to Tata Sons during this period. Noshir Soonawala and Ishaat Hussain, both Tata Sons directors, fielded most of the bankers' unsolicited thoughts on restructuring the business. Most of the time the bankers were told that while the issue remained on the table, the Tata Sons board was not ready to act.

Tata Sons realized that by floating TCS it could get a pot of money upfront but that it would lose the cash flow. As Ishaat says, 'On balance it was felt that it was not in the interest of the shareholders at that point in time to go ahead. As far as the brand issue was concerned I do not think there was consensus that it was really such an important competitive disadvantage.'

So in early 2000 when investment bankers and others approached Ishaat Hussain and warned him that he was missing out on an opportunity he would take a piece of paper and ask, 'Listen, how am I missing out?' Then he would calculate the share price based on the price-to-earnings (PE) ratio and point out that because TCS was growing so fast, Tata Sons would lose out if they sold off a stake in TCS too early.

'I remember having this argument very often with all those who continued to push for an IPO,' says Ishaat. 'But I think by about

2002 TCS had developed sufficient scale and size that the amount of cash that Tata Sons would realize through an IPO and the amount of cash flow that would be forgone were falling somewhat into balance.'

Indeed, in 2002, TCS broke another record by becoming India's first billion-dollar software company. Its revenues for the fiscal ended 31 March 2003 reached $1.04 billion, up from $908 million a year earlier.

There were many who believed that the TCS IPO should have happened sooner. Dr R.H. Patil (then Chairman of the NSE) was one of them. He recalled a conversation with me before the TCS IPO, where he conveyed his view that there was considerable merit in taking TCS public. In his words, 'A back-of-the-envelope exercise based on the then prevailing PE ratios, especially for the best IT companies, showed an enterprise value in excess of Rs 100,000 crore for TCS. So, even a small dilution of ownership could unlock tremendous value for the Tata Group's ambitious plans.'

Fortunately for the investment bankers, there were so many changes happening in the IT industry at the time that every few months there was a reason for them to revisit the subject and go back to the Tata Sons management with some new angle. By about 2002 an 'in-principle' decision had been taken that Tata Sons would go ahead with a TCS IPO.

## Tata Sons' considerations

It was a very difficult decision for Tata Sons for several reasons. As a division of Tata Sons, TCS had functioned as the cash generation engine for the group at a time when—in the wake of economic liberalization—there was a tremendous need for capital. TCS effectively anchored the aspirations of the Group in non-IT businesses as was evident with the entry of the group in the telecommunications and retail space. TCS's cash flows were used from day one, but by the mid-1990s, the cash had become material because TCS had its first big growth spurt through the Y2K boom. We evolved a practice of retaining half of the profits generated within TCS, with the balance being used by Tata Sons. As a result, Tata Sons had access in a very strategically efficient and tax-efficient way to a significant part of the cash flows of TCS which were steadily increasing. TCS's cash requirements for acquiring computer systems and buying office space were met through the funds retained for TCS. However, the business of TCS itself never required any significant investment. In the early years of software exports the government had allowed all of the software export revenue to be set against the overall tax liability of the exporting company. This was a huge benefit to Tata Sons as they were able to use the TCS software export revenues to reduce the tax exposure on the dividend income.

The TCS model produced incredibly high returns on capital employed and only a small part of it really needed to go back to fuel growth. Growth basically meant sending more people overseas to client locations in those days. They did not even need to sit in our offices; often they sat in the client's offices. The component of the work done in India at TCS's offices at that stage was low—that transition really started after 2000–01.

As a result, Tata Sons had the ability to leverage its balance sheet against those cash flows and pursue Ratan Tata's agenda of enhancing ownership in group companies and funding their requirements aggressively through preferential issues.

For that reason alone, the decision to turn TCS into a subsidiary and then conduct the IPO required a lot of thought because the moment it became an independent company, Tata Sons could only rely on the dividends received by it. There were also issues relating to structural efficiencies. The whole process of carving out a division and creating a separate legal entity is challenging in any country, and certainly in India, because until then there had been no instance of anyone having gone through such a large-scale exercise. People had tried it before, but the implications from a tax perspective were never on the same scale, so we had to be very, very careful about how the new entity was created.

Unlike any other IPO, this was hugely complex, as Amit Chandra (at that time with DSP Merrill Lynch and now with Bain Capital) remembers: 'There were internal and external stakeholders, it was important to consider what was right for the Tatas, for TCS, for independent shareholders and for the regulatory framework. And indeed we were walking a thin line; there was a deep commitment within the Tata Group to be fair to all stakeholders and satisfying everybody is always a difficult task.' Amit who had by then handled several similar transactions remembers the TCS IPO being one of the most complex and challenging.

As expected, the process of extracting TCS from Tata Sons was not just extremely complex but time consuming as well. To do this a team of about twenty to twenty-five people was assembled, in addition to the accountants and lawyers who were brought in to work out the most efficient way to pursue the transaction. For example, the way the tax code was worded at the time, if Tata Sons had simply corporatized and floated TCS it would have faced a huge tax bill, since at the time the IPO was being considered the tax authorities did not allow a carry forward of tax benefits in the event of restructuring. Fortunately a subsequent amendment to the tax act has remedied this.

The tax rules had never really envisaged a situation where a holding company would corporatize an entity and then sell it immediately. So we had to wait quite some time for a suitable tax code amendment to be passed. At the time of corporatization of an existing division, the usual practice is to have an inactive corporate entity acquire the division; the new entity can then be renamed. The Tata Group had a few such companies and we chose one which was not completely owned by Tata Sons. This company was Orchid Prints which was owned 90 per cent by Tata Sons and 10 per cent by the shareholders of Tata Sons. The majority shareholding in Tata Sons is held by charitable trusts and in the 10 per cent outside shareholding, a substantial part was held by the charitable trusts as well. The IPO of TCS was for the purpose of diluting the stake of the promoter group to 85 per cent. When the IPO took place, we had a combination of secondary sale—that is, sale by the existing shareholders of the new entity—and primary issue, that is, sale of new shares. In the secondary sale, the charitable trusts also took part and they raised significant sums of money which were then used for charitable purposes. This act was very revealing of the Tata way and of the Tata philosophy of giving wealth back to the people.

The whole process took about two years; sometimes I am sure even Ratan Tata thought it was all taking too long, but there were a lot of hurdles to overcome. Crucially, Ratan Tata said he did not want to let go of TCS until he felt he was getting the value he deserved for it.

To satisfy this condition, the project team came up with an ingenious court-approved scheme that included a 'condition precedent' which ensured that the extraction of TCS from Tata Sons only became effective after TCS was floated. In other words it was only when the underwriting agreement was signed and after Tata Sons had got the price that they wanted that TCS would become a new and separate entity.

It was a unique court scheme that had never happened before or has happened since. It took a long time to develop and prepare the proforma accounts for the red herring prospectus that TCS submitted to the regulatory authorities at the start of June 2004. This was finally approved by SEBI on 16 July 2004.

Even though TCS had no plans to list outside India, the investors would include funds from the US and other overseas jurisdictions and the prospectus was designed to be SEC (United States Securities and Exchange Commission) compliant and the accounts were prepared in accordance with the US GAAP (Generally Accepted Accounting Principles) rules.

The prospectus had been eagerly awaited by the investment community because for the first time it stripped away much of the mystery surrounding TCS and Tata Sons. At the most basic level, everyone could see who the Tata shareholders were and what size their shareholding was.

Morgan Stanley, DSP Merrill Lynch and JP Morgan India were appointed lead managers for the issue which was priced at between Rs 775 and Rs 900 per share and comprised just under 55.5 million shares, ensuring that it would be the biggest IPO in Indian market history.

May 2004, the targeted month for the IPO, was round the corner and there was frenzied activity contributing to the build-up. At such times you never seem completely ready. To complicate matters general elections in India took place at the same time, the ruling coalition lost, a new government came to power, and the stock market took a dive. Going ahead with the IPO in such an environment was not advisable. After many consultations with the bankers and within the Tata Group we decided to postpone the IPO to August 2004, the last possible date recommended by the investment bankers for that year. If we missed this deadline we would have had to push it to February 2005. The team was in peak form and felt ready for the plunge but the stress was enormous because the process involved moving targets and we had to remain in a continuous state of preparedness.

The macroeconomic scenario in the country was seeing a fair bit of action. The government disinvestment process in public sector companies had begun a few years ago, with the offer for the sale of the government's residual stake in companies such as the Indian Petrochemicals Corporation Ltd. (IPCL), the Indo-Burma Petroleum Company (IBP) and CMC. In 2004, IPOs from the Dredging Corporation of India and GAIL India, in which the government offloaded 20 per cent and 10 per cent stakes respectively, took place. The last among the lot was the issue from the Oil and Natural Gas Corporation (ONGC), garnering Rs 11,000 crore. The enormous public interest generated by these offerings breathed life into the dormant primary market. Several interesting offerings from Patni Computers, NDTV, TV Today and ICICI Bank sailed through collecting Rs 5,000 crore. The enthusiasm of investors opened the doors for large private sector IPOs such as biotech major Biocon, controlled by Kiran Mazumdar-Shaw.

Following this dream run, the primary market again went into hibernation. After the successful completion of the IPO of NDTV in April 2004, barring the IPO from Vishal Exports Overseas in early May 2004 at Rs 45 per share which mobilized Rs 27 crore, not a single issue hit the market in May and June 2004.

The grim scenario was reversed when TCS, India's largest IT services company in terms of sales, went public in July 2004. The issue was oversubscribed 7.7 times. On listing, the stock opened at Rs 1198.97, commanding a 41 per cent premium on the issue price. The TCS issue proved to be a trigger for the primary market that had gone quiet after the Lok Sabha elections in April-May 2004.

## The TCS road show

The environment at the time of the IPO is important to be considered. At that time TCS was still an unsung story. No one ever denied the fact that TCS had created the industry—that was something that people always gave TCS credit for. But since it was a division of Tata Sons, outsiders always had a very limited visibility of TCS. Only those inside really knew that this was the jewel in the Tata Sons' crown.

There was a very visible perception amongst the investment community, for instance, that Infosys was the company of the future and that TCS was living in the past. As Amit Chandra says, 'The impression that TCS carried in the minds of people was one of the elephant and not one of a tiger.' The media would portray and report the same.

I think when the investment bankers saw the numbers and put them into context it was very evident to them that TCS was at the cutting edge of the industry and that our leadership position was well deserved. Anyhow, we faced the challenge of how to overcome these external perceptions, how to tell the TCS story and how to create an organizational structure that was outward- rather than inward-facing.

I realized we were starting on the back foot, but that only made me more determined to fight on. I had great confidence in our capabilities and pride in what we had achieved till then. We had experienced the birth of the industry and nurtured it through, and we had a depth of understanding that was unparalleled—this was and still remains our strength. I hoped my confidence permeated to others in the team and I believe it did, for everybody rose to the challenge. We would give Infosys a run for their money. Eventually we did: although TCS shares originally traded at a discount to Infosys, it now trades at a premium, demonstrating that belief. Time told its own story.

However, at that time, we were faced with the task of revealing the real TCS to the world, and as part of the book-building process, two teams were assembled for a global road show. One was headed by Ratan Tata and included myself and Paddy; the other was headed by Ishaat with Maha and Chandra. Both started off at the same time. Ratan Tata led the road show flagged off in Singapore and Ishaat led the road show started in Europe.

Ratan Tata was already well known in the investment community, but it was a new and interesting experience for me. Inevitably perhaps, on the road show we were always being compared and evaluated against Infosys and a lot of complimentary things were said about Infosys. Although we were competitors, to hear good things said in international forums about an Indian company made us very happy. When Ratan Tata returned from the road show he wrote a letter to Infosys's management saying, 'I must tell you that I felt so proud that here is an Indian company which is considered a benchmark in governance and transparency.'

There was one aspect to the IPO which we made a point of underscoring during the road show. We told the investment community upfront that we would look at a dividend payout of between 30 and 50 per cent. We also pointed to the record of the Tata Group which has always looked after its minority shareholders. In reality, however, we have never got to a dividend payout ratio of 50 per cent—the maximum has been 30 to 33 per cent.

The two road shows moved from one city to another, making presentations to various investor communities. The schedule was very hectic. What it did for all of us, though, was to bring us closer, developing bonds that last to this day. Exhausted by the day's proceedings, I and the others would crash early, with no late night dinners at all. Besides, I needed my 6 a.m. walk to keep me recharged for the day ahead. I missed home food as I always do when I have long overseas trips, though every hotel I stayed in went out of its way to serve me its version of 'curd rice'. If nothing else I certainly can take credit for globalizing the very modest Indian dish of curd rice.

The road show was hard work. Never before had I canvassed for TCS as I did during the road show. Each day I would contemplate a new strategy, a new angle of TCS to portray to investors. How could I convey the depth of TCS's capabilities in mere words? How could I make them believe in us, trust us and share our confidence? As the CEO of TCS, I sometimes felt that the investors were doing a due diligence on me. The last time I was under the scanner in this manner was way back when my mother-in-law did a due diligence on me before she allowed me to meet Mala! I had passed with flying colours then and I hoped this time would be no different.

This was the largest IPO in Indian history and it happened at a time before the foreign institutional investor (FII) boom in India. Deals on this scale were not common, so we had to educate the investors to get them interested, we had to market ourselves and communicate our value proposition. Money was hard to come by in those days. Once a few large orders came in, it pulled the rest of the market along—but it was a struggle.

The enthusiasm for the issue, particularly among retail investors, was gratifying. At the end of the book-building process the cut-off price for the IPO was set at Rs 850 per share. 'Our intention is to have TCS continue to please investors. The pricing has been fixed at a level that would provide an attractive upside to investors as a token of our gratitude to their overwhelming response to the issue,' said Ratan Tata at the time.

At the issue price of Rs 850, the offering, including a 'green shoe' option, totalled over Rs 5400 crore ($1.2 billion). The retail portion of the IPO was subscribed three times, and the non-institutional portion—for high net worth individuals and corporates—was subscribed twenty-two times.

The strong retail interest was a fitting tribute to J.R.D. Tata, who was at the helm of the Tata Group for four decades and who would have been 100 years old in 2004. His successor, Ratan Tata, would have liked to have allocated all the shares to retail investors. He told us, 'You know it should be given to the people, they have backed us.' But SEBI rules dictated that 60 per cent had to be allocated to institutional investors, leaving 15 per cent for non-institutional bidders and the remaining 25 per cent for retail investors, so that was the way it was.

The road show and the IPO work had me working closely with Soonawala and Ishaat to build the perception of TCS and we took on the financial community head on. I am proud to say that we were able to convince the sceptics that not only were we the pioneers of Indian IT but that we would always aspire to lead and fiercely protect our leadership position. I am happy that this confidence was infectious and Chandra, Maha and Paddy also got into the act and played their part. Ultimately both teams were well received by the investment community. 'It was as though a beautiful girl had unveiled herself,' says Ishaat.

Ratan Tata and Hemendra Kothari, head of DSP Merrill Lynch, who were notoriously bad sleepers on long-haul flights, finally slept peacefully after we successfully won over the analysts. According to Kothari the TCS IPO motivated the market to move up. It proved that there were Indian 'blue chip' companies, and this acceptance would encourage others to enter the market.

## Matters of principle

We wanted to set aside some shares for our employees and, in line with SEBI guidelines, these were to be allocated to people in active service in TCS. These were the employees who had made TCS what it was. The yardstick used for the allocation of shares was a combination of experience and performance. We set aside up to 5.5 million shares for purchase by TCS employees. These shares were granted to the employees under a formula that I worked out with Ratan Tata personally. The list included everyone who had completed a certain number of years at TCS, and TCS employees, including support staff, benefited from the substantial increase in market value of these shares post the IPO.

It was a modest plan by some standards and it did not end up creating a huge amount of wealth for individuals, but it was carefully thought out and was an elegant solution that reflected the ethos of the Tata Group. TCS plays a dual role. As an employer, it is part of the IT industry and therefore to some extent its employment practices need to be like those of other IT companies, but it is also the flagship company of the Tata Group and needs to actively promote the best practices of the Tata Group. In true Tata spirit the focus was not on individual wealth creation but rather on doing the right thing, and I think in retrospect we struck a fair balance between making sure that the concept of employee ownership was introduced via the IPO but it was not done in an ostentatious manner. We set out to conduct an IPO that could serve as a model for others. It was done in a very refined atmosphere and in a manner that was fair to all stakeholders, as against individual gain to a few.

Some years later Ratan Tata was in a meeting with an ambassador who asked him, 'Mr Tata, do you not think that you would have been much better off taking TCS public in 1999 or 2000 when valuation multiples were much higher? You would have created an incredibly valuable entity and would have got so much more cash than you did later.'

Ratan Tata replied, 'But who do you think would have been the loser?' His point was that the dot com boom valuations were clearly unsustainable and if TCS had been floated at its peak the subsequent collapse in the share price would have created only ill will.

As it was, the TCS IPO was widely considered to be an enormous success—a success that benefited all participants and helped consolidate the Tata Group's reputation for fairness while paving the way for the next phase in TCS's growth.

## The big day

I remember the day of the IPO clearly. There was much excitement in TCS offices across all locations. The area around Dalal Street, the hub of stock trading activity in Mumbai, was abuzz. My office staff actually picked up a camera and drove around capturing the scenes outside brokering houses, where people were queuing up for forms. For the first time I watched live the power of what had been built over the years by many of us and those before me. I realized that we had begun a new phase, opened our doors to let the world in. It was an exhilarating moment.

On 25 August 2004, we were ready to list the IPO on both the stock exchanges: the National Stock Exchange and the Bombay Stock Exchange. Of course there was lots of friendly betting on what premium over the issue price TCS would trade at soon. The plan was that Ratan Tata, whom Chandra and I would accompany, would click the mouse to flag off TCS on NSE, while Noshir Soonawala, Ishaat, Maha and Paddy would strike the gong in the BSE's Rotunda Hall—just the way they do on Wall Street.

At 9 a.m. on that momentous day, thirty-six years after its inception, the click of a mouse put Tata Consultancy Services on trading screens and turned the Tatas into one of the most highly valued private groups. With the TCS IPO, the Tata Group became one of the largest wealth creators among private sector companies in India. Eventually the IPO helped the Tata Group enormously in further enhancing the brand. It also created the right currency for the other group companies to further their own mission to become more global.

Incidentally, both the NSE and the BSE, who superbly handled the IPO, had IT infrastructure supported by TCS. It was a strangely satisfying feeling to be 'clients' for our own software.

With all this churning I knew my life as CEO was changed forever. While the IPO was the end of a long-awaited journey, it was also the beginning of a new, more challenging one. I felt that from now on we were under the microscope: we had just stepped up on a treadmill and pushed the start button—there was no getting off now.

# 6

# THE TATA LEGACY

UNDER THE TATA logo at the top of the Tata home page are three words: 'Leadership with Trust'. Many companies have equally inspirational taglines. But Tata is no ordinary business enterprise. It is a confederation of over ninety companies across eighty nations, operating in almost every sector of the economy, that each promise to abide by a set of core values and ethical principles.

The five core Tata values underpinning the way TCS, and every other member of the Tata Group, does business are:

**Integrity:** We must conduct our business fairly, with honesty and transparency. Everything we do must stand the test of public scrutiny.

**Understanding:** We must be caring, show respect, compassion and humanity for our colleagues and customers around the world, and always work for the benefit of the communities we serve.

**Excellence:** We must constantly strive to achieve the highest possible standards in our day-to-day work and in the quality of the goods and services we provide.

**Unity:** We must work cohesively with our colleagues across the Group and with our customers and partners around the world, building strong relationships based on tolerance, understanding and mutual cooperation.

**Responsibility:** We must continue to be responsible and sensitive to the countries, communities and environments in which we work, always ensuring that what comes from the people goes back to the people many times over.

I do not know of any other company that ploughs back two-thirds of its income into community projects. Indeed Tata Sons' holdings in highly profitable companies like TCS, Tata Steel and Tata Chemicals and the income therefrom is returned to the community through various activities of the Tata trusts. Sometimes the community and the company are hard to tell apart—a good example is what Tata Steel has achieved in Jamshedpur or Tatanagar in India's heartland. Studies of the Tata brand by numerous agencies have demonstrated beyond doubt that the name Tata evokes a feeling of trust in the average Indian.

My own joining the Tatas in the 1970s was also an act of trust. My family was one that believed in simple living and high thinking. As a child I observed my parents and teachers day in and day out, and the right and honest way of doing things was inculcated in me, which was why the Tata Group with its principle of doing 'business with ethics' held such appeal to me as a young man. Our values matched.

I firmly believe that within organizations, the way you conduct yourself and lead really matters. In a company, if employees see their managers doing the right thing all the time, it gets reinforced daily and becomes institutionalized. Individuals start understanding what is expected of them and what their responsibilities are. As a senior executive, not only are you responsible for your own actions, but you must always be aware that your actions will be observed and others will follow you. That is how we have integrated the Tata ethics into our operations, all the way down to the project level.

There have been instances when people have said, 'We can get this project for you.' At TCS we have politely refused such offers, and have shied away from projects that were not transparent enough. Without casting aspersions, we simply decided not to bid for the project.

When it came to legitimate contracts, some competitors would find a reason to complain every time they lost a project. In contrast, at TCS we try to analyse internally what we did wrong. Sometimes when we lose the project we ask the customer why they think we lost. Instead of assigning blame we ask ourselves: 'What could we have done better—not cheaper?'

I remember an instance when a group company—Tata Steel—gave a contract to IBM, Ratan Tata offered to intervene on our behalf, but we said 'no'. Later Tata Steel came to us of their own accord. We never demanded the contract; we earned it in the right way and the honest way. This is how a value system is practised. We believed that the others had won the contract on merit and so should we.

In my experience, companies can learn a lot from both winning and losing bids. For example, we waited for eight years before we got our first break with the American Insurance Group (AIG). We never gave up, and ultimately our determination and passion did pay off.

Why do customers like to do business with us? It is certainly not just about dollars and cents. I believe it is because we try to ensure that it is a pleasure to deal with us. We ask all our customers, 'Are you happy with our work?' It is important for us to be just as open about our customers sharing problems and issues with us as well. That is part of the value system built into our DNA, and what I believe distinguishes TCS from other companies. Ultimately the message is simple: Be true to yourself, and question yourself before blaming others. Living these values is the only way to pass them down to the younger employees. As TCS expands, keeping things the 'Tata way' will be every CEO's biggest challenge.

The 'Tata way' is actually what binds everybody together at TCS. What this means is that wherever you are, you must serve the community within which you exist, and be true to the Tata brand and its values. Each Tata company has its own set of philanthropic programmes and projects; TCS for instance promotes IT-based solutions to address community-related programmes. The computer-aided adult literacy programme or IT training for the blind, both developed by TCS, are examples. Also, every company has its own touch points with the community through its own products. The Nano car, the Swach water filter that was started by TCS and further developed by Tata Chemicals, Ginger Hotels, TCS Microfinance and our digital inclusion programmes are examples of this in action.

Every Tata employee who joins the organization pledges to abide by these values and is given a copy of the Tata code of conduct, a Tata bible of sorts. The Tata code of conduct provides an ethical road map for every employee including the CEO/Managing Director, full-time directors and independent directors. The code of conduct has twenty-five clauses which cover all areas of company operations including accounting, insider trading, business gifting, equal opportunity employment, prevention of harassment, conflict of interests, protecting company assets and adherence to local regulations in every country of operation.

Our reputation of trust has been earned through several decades of consistent conduct, and we strive very hard to live up to this legacy. As a Tata group company, integrity is a core value that underpins all our business activities at TCS. To maintain integrity, we conduct all our business activities honestly, fairly and with a high degree of transparency, so that we can always pass the test of public scrutiny.

By tradition, Tata companies have developed pro-employee management practices and are known to look after their employees. Tata pioneered many industrial practices that have now become standard, like the eight-hour working day, free medical aid, annual leave with pay, and workers' provident fund schemes.

TCS is in tune with the Tata tradition of doing the right and correct thing for the professional well-being of employees. Being in the knowledge business TCS assigns a premium on learning and provides several opportunities for every employee to expand their knowledge; in fact ten to fifteen days of mandated learning are assigned for every employee each year. I have always promoted the idea of TCS as a 'learning organization'—one that respects and empowers its people to learn and grow.

Integrity is central to our functioning not just because of the Tata way but because of the way our business works. Providing software services involves having access to customers' business models and data. Confidentiality in handling this is a must. Often our employees work at client sites and are therefore deeply embedded into the customer environment. Personal integrity is vital in such circumstances and violations when they occur can threaten business relationships. I remember an incident when an employee at a client site in the US compromised client information; the matter was immediately escalated to their CEO who wrote to me. I flew down to the US to meet with him and assured him that an investigation would be conducted immediately and that this would get my highest attention. We asked the employee to leave, earning back the trust of the customer so much that when the CEO moved to another company he gave us new business.

TCS being a services-oriented organization, we have a limited supply chain and the scale of procurement activities and the level of inventory is quite small when compared to a manufacturing or trading organization. All big procurement decisions which are mostly for computers, software and offices are made centrally by senior executives with adequate levels of oversight and controls, which makes procurement fraud improbable. Further, as we are in a B2B space dealing with multinationals and large organizations, large cash transactions are non-existent. The scope for embezzlement by staff in an IT services company is minimal—notwithstanding the Satyam fraud where the top management was involved.

My long tenure at TCS, of course, has not been without instances of being witness to fraud or harassment and other forms of wrongdoing. While I am quite satisfied that the adherence to the Tata code of conduct by the TCS community of employees, clients and suppliers is very high—in fact one of the highest in the Tata Group—there have been some unfortunate instances of non-compliance. But when it came to taking action against the offenders, we were strict and no exceptions were made, be it a country head, business unit head or a department head who was involved. In fact I feel that stricter standards have to be applied to senior executives as their conduct has a greater influence on colleagues, especially juniors.

We have taken some hard decisions in instances of misconduct, especially when senior persons have been involved. We have zero tolerance for misconduct and have demonstrated this through swift action. On the other hand, we carefully follow due processes to ensure that we are fair and sensitive in the way in which we respond to and address concerns. Background checks at the time of joining the company tend to limit undesirable behaviour by employees, especially presenting false information on past experience. Adequate control measures are in place to detect inflated expense claims or medical claims. Instances of harassment involving insensitive remarks about minorities or with reference to women associates are addressed after due investigation. Remedial measures include sensitization, but in instances where the underlying problematic attitude persists, the errant employee is asked to leave.

Being a multicultural organization has its share of challenges. Sometimes insufficient comprehension of cultural differences can result in misinterpretations of friendly gestures from co-workers in foreign locations. A friendly peck on the cheek in the form of a greeting or being addressed as 'dear' can be seen as an invitation for intimacy. There have been occasions when such overtures were resented and complaints made. Every representation was investigated and action that was fair to both parties was taken. Also, at TCS, cross-cultural orientation is routinely provided to associates travelling overseas.

On the other hand, when we acquire companies we get 'new' employees who have to learn the 'Tata way'. They may not know enough about the Tata legacy, its values, and our expectations from employees. Films and presentations on the founders, the Tata history and and its growth as a Group form part of the orientation process.

Naturally, in order to appreciate the importance of the Tatas' core values, it is necessary to understand the history, structure and purpose of the Tata Group. Every employee in a Tata company needs to be aware that this legacy comes with a responsibility of high moral conduct that must be lived up to by all Tata employees and directors.

The Tata legacy runs back to 1868 when Tata Sons, the company at the heart of the Tata Group that holds stakes ranging from 25 to

100 per cent in Tata group companies—was founded by Jamsetji Nusserwanji Tata, who came from a family of Parsi priests and went on to become India's most important and visionary industrialist.

Jamsetji Tata's early years were inspired by the spirit of nationalism. He was amongst the leading industrialists of the time who believed in India and its future. Jamsetji said that before political independence is achieved there must be industrial independence, and with a single-minded purpose he laid the foundation of a modern industrial India. Through his bold investments he pioneered several industries of national importance—including steel, power and hospitality—and prepared the blueprint for higher education in science and technology which resulted in the founding of the Indian Institute of Science in Bangalore in 1911.

When India's first prime minsiter Jawaharlal Nehru came to Jamshedpur, the home of Tata Steel, he reminded the audience of the courage and vision of Tata's founder and said: 'Jamsetji was one of the architects of modern industrial India ... We have our planning commissions but Jamsetji formed himself into some kind of a planning commission and began his own ... not a five-year plan but a much bigger plan.'

This tradition was passed down to future generations. J.R.D. Tata was the fourth Chairman of Tata Sons with the longest reign (1938–91) and was also the father of the aviation industry in India. During this period there was tremendous expansion at Tata. JRD was part of a core group of industrialists who developed a plan of economic development for India a few years before Independence, in January 1944. This came to be known as the Bombay Plan or the Tata–Birla Plan. It proposed a fifteen-year economic plan with a total investment of Rs 10,000 crore with large investments in power, mining, roads and railways. Almost 50 per cent of the investment was slated for industrial development, 25 per cent for housing and only 10 per cent was planned for agriculture, which was at the time the predominant industry in India.

Nehru's socialist agenda for development brought a great deal of grief to JRD, as he felt the environment was not conducive to growth of business houses like his. Even so, he worked within this restrictive situation, built bridges with the government and contributed towards India's industrial policy.

The pioneering streak woven into the Tata DNA passed on over the years and more recently, companies like TCS and Tata Motors, which made India's first indigenously developed car (Tata Indica) in 1998, have carried on Jamsetji and J.R.D. Tata's pioneering tradition.

From the outset, Tata companies were committed to returning wealth to the society they serve. In 1892 Jamsetji Tata started the J.N. Tata endowment scheme that provides loan scholarships for higher education. By 1924, a third of the Indian Civil Service (ICS) officers in India were Tata scholars. Jamsetji's sons Sir Dorabji Tata and Sir Ratan Tata founded trusts in their own names which today are two of the main trusts of the Tata Group. There is a history amongst the Tatas of donating vast amounts of personal wealth. This combined with money from the trusts which hold two-thirds of the equity of Tata Sons has helped create national institutions for science and technology, medical research, social studies and the performing arts.

The Tata Group is a loose conglomerate of independent Tata companies, each with its own Board of Directors and management style. There is a great deal of flexibility in the running of the company, which is why a company like TCS has bloomed into an agile and aggressive player in the hard-nosed IT sector. It has played by the rules of the IT market which have sometimes been different from markets served by other Tata companies in other sectors.

In 2007 TCS's corporate headquarters moved to a grand old building in Mumbai's Fort area, christened TCS House. One of the first things we did here was to custom-order busts of two of our founding fathers, Jamsetji Tata and J.R.D. Tata. Placed in the foyer, they reside with us as reminders of the rich legacy that has been gifted to each of us and the responsibility that we carry as a result. Walking past them at the start of each new day never fails to inspire me, as it must inspire all those who share the space.

For the Tatas, evoking such feelings is not entirely unusual. Bombay House, the Tata headquarters (also in the Fort area of Mumbai), often has unlikely visitors, like the elderly man I saw struggling up the steps of the eighty-seven-year-old building with no other agenda but to pay his respects to a bust of Jamsetji Tata, a man whose benign presence lives on to this day.

# 7

# TECHNOLOGY AS THE
# ENABLER OF DEVELOPMENT

## TECHNOLOGY AND INNOVATION

TCS DEVELOPED AN innovation mindset not by choice but by necessity. Software needs hardware to run on and our capabilities in software created dependencies on the IBMs and Burroughs of the world. Back then the computing industry was completely dominated by hardware players and everything else was a value-add around it.

Even so, we always aimed to learn as much as we could and be as little dependent on others as we could. When we imported mainframes we made sure our engineers were trained by the original manufacturers; we learnt to install, maintain and support the machines. In the case of Burroughs our support work in the field exposed us to the problems faced by customers. This feedback from the field made us recommend engineering changes, which would lead to improvements in the next version, in both hardware and software, in the form of circuit boards or patches or operating system improvements.

We exhibited a 'can do' attitude very early on. We had to make do with less. Foreign exchange was scarce, import procedures were complex and time-consuming, and import duties punitive. Almost all our equipment had to be imported. Since our business model was based on software solutions and services and India did not produce computers, we were completely dependent on imports. So we had to innovate in order to survive. Computers were treated as a luxury back then and the government was in no mood for any relaxations in imports. We had to make optimum use of the scarce resources at our disposal and had to go to extraordinary lengths to make the computers productive. Today computing time is a commodity that is available on a 'cloud', and programmers are a scarce resource. In the 1970s it was just the reverse—we could sell computer time for Rs 1,000 an hour, while we started programmers at a salary Rs 800 a month. In fact my own starting salary in TCS was a 'princely' Rs 900 a month! We had to exercise every form of ingenuity to maximize use of the computers, rather than maximize programmer productivity. Many innovations were born out of this necessity but they ultimately resulted in the creation of intellectual property which we could later exploit.

We always looked at opportunities to add value to existing software to enhance the customer experience and built useful tools for disk management or for 'sorting' and used them in our projects. For instance in the early 1970s we did a project for composing and printing of the Bombay telephone directory. We developed algorithms to club similar-sounding names such as Parekh, Parikh, Pareekh etc. Our work was done on a magnetic tape interface which was the technology used then by the computing industry. However, the printing press was using an older technology of paper tapes (as used in the teleprinter). So we had to take the formatted directory from Bombay all the way to the Hindustan Teleprinter factory in Bangalore to convert it from magnetic tape to the slower paper tape. Since the data transfer involved a change of formats and media, we had to develop the solution in the assembly-level language of the ICL 1903 computer. But our commitment to customer focus overrode all the trouble that it entailed, and it was worth it in the end.

By working with almost all the major hardware companies, our engineers learnt multiple architectures; this proved to be a major advantage. Our first software export project in 1974 was undertaken on the ICL 1903 in Bombay for Burroughs. This project required the conversion of a large software package from the Burroughs medium systems (B2500) to the newly architected Burroughs small systems (B1700). The solution we developed was on ICL 1903 which is what we had in Bombay. So our engineers had to know the architecture of three different machines. We developed a 'filter' which accepted the source code of machine 'A' (the Burroughs B2500) on machine 'B' (the ICL 1903), and the output was the source code compatible for machine 'C' (the Burroughs B1700). This innovative solution was so successful that Burroughs asked us to develop a filter to do the reverse, that is load ICL source code onto a Burroughs machine and churn out Burroughs code, with the result that Burroughs was able to compete with ICL and win over ICL customers in their home country (the UK).

The maintenance and support work of these early days is what we have to be thankful to developing in us a DNA for ingenuity and frugal engineering. At one time we were supporting around ten installations worth almost $10 million located in Bombay, Delhi, Calcutta, Jamshedpur and Pune. We did not have adequate spares and test equipment. The environment was hostile with plenty of dust and an erratic power supply resulting in tripping circuits. Even the power protection devices themselves kept burning out. We had to actually design and fabricate frequency stabilizers, reliable fail-safe power supplies to keep the computers running on a 24x7 basis. Sometimes we even had to get spare parts fabricated locally, as imports were prohibitively expensive and the process to import very time-consuming.

Our printers were used round the clock since we undertook many print-intensive jobs such as examination results processing and utility bills printing. I remember that some of the characters on the printer slugs used to get worn out more than others, particularly o, 1 and the symbol '-'. To print 'o' we would switch the circuits to use the letter 'O' in place of o which had worn out. We used to get the slugs etched with the new characters as each slug had four characters and only one had to be fixed; by replacing the whole slug we would have wasted the other three good 'characters' on the slug.

The tough environment we worked in conditioned our minds to think in a particular way. We became problem solvers, always looking for better and more cost-effective ways of doing things. Even in terms of people we were highly productive. The TCS team which undertook Burroughs hardware and software support in India consisted of only half a dozen engineers. In the US or Europe there would have been a team at least four times as large for the same work.

As a natural progression of our innovation, in the early 1980s we set up the Tata Research Design and Development Centre in Pune to design and develop productivity tools not just for software but also for materials engineering. We created mathematical models for soft simulation of furnaces and kilns to optimize fuel and raw material requirements. We created a software foundry which designed and developed the jigs and fixtures for software development. Assembly manufacturing techniques were adapted to software manufacturing, which resulted in reusable components being created. Not only did this result in quick prototyping but the resultant code was tested and reliable as it was machine generated.

Some of the earliest software productivity tools we developed by ourselves, based on the experience we had gained in Burroughs machines, were data dictionaries which helped maintain and keep track of all the names used in a program. This was particularly useful when software had to be changed and the impact of the change had to be studied. We named the tool ADDICT (Advanced Data Dictionary). Subsequently it became a strong value proposition when we were working towards a project with Firemans Fund Insurance Company in San Rafael, California, so we developed a data dictionary on an IBM platform and called it CasePac.

We leveraged both these experiences to develop MasterCraft, a high-level language generator which included features such as code generation and a data dictionary. With this business analysts could develop Cobol or C-language source codes by describing business rules in easy-to-learn and intuitive English and supplying them as parameters to MasterCraft. In addition analysts could also decide on the hardware and software environment such as an IBM or HP mainframe. The analysts did not have to be concerned with idiosyncrasies of the hardware and software. This way complex projects were completed in TCS in much less time and with higher reliability.

At TRDDC many conversion migration tools were developed which automated the process of converting not only programs but also data from one computer platform to another. These were the earliest examples of an Indian IT company creating intellectual property. Projects within the healthcare industry encouraged us to build low-cost diagnostic kits for tuberculosis, and the 'silicon locket' to monitor heart parameters that could send alerts to healthcare providers over mobile telephone networks. Researchers from MIT and Carnegie Mellon who had joined TRDDC were early drivers of such initiatives.

In 2000, we had a strategic discussion on how our research agenda must expand beyond the work of TRDDC to a more distributed model that reached out to a wider canvas of people and technologies. Our Hyderabad advance technology centre, our embedded system and chip design work in Bangalore and the radio frequency identification (RFID) work in Kolkata was an outcome of this thinking. Our innovation footprint soon expanded to other locations including overseas destinations.

In TCS we have firmly believed in building deep alliances with academia. Our first alliances with leading technology institutes in India were with the IITs and with IISc. In North America we had alliances with leading schools such as MIT, Stanford, University of California at Irvine, University of California at Los Angeles, University of Washington at Maryland, University of Waterloo in Canada and many more. We had exchange programmes for faculty and joint research programmes between our researchers and the university academics. For example, with University of Maryland and University of Waterloo TCS developed FALCON, one of the earliest versions of the Local Area Network (LAN) which allowed single-user PC users the benefits of multi-user capability and connectivity. In fact this was the only instance of LAN being developed indigenously, and it enabled many Indian corporations to connect PCs over a network.

In the 1990s, when the National Stock Exchange was set up and TCS was appointed as systems integrator, the design called for all

NSE brokers in India to be connected in real time to the NSE computer. But conventional telephone lines did not provide the reach and pan-India connectivity that was needed. We therefore decided to go in for a heterogeneous network of satellite communications and conventional leased phone lines. This had not been attempted for a stock exchange, which has to handle large volumes of data to be processed with a very quick turnaround time, before. When the initial RFP was prepared the architects had envisaged volumes in the region of 10,000 trades a day with a peak of 100,000 trades a day. To meet these volumes we selected the Stratus Central Processing Unit with fault tolerant hardware and limited scalability at the CPU level. The system was so successful that the exchange was doing 100,000 trades a day within eighteen months. Very soon we would run short of processing horsepower. To meet this contingency TCS engineers split market architecture and configured more CPUs to handle larger volumes. Again, this had never been attempted before. Today the NSE handles about 5 million trades a day on the same architecture. Other stock exchanges that handle such volumes have to do so on hardware on a magnitude of scale. This was one of the extraordinary challenges we met—the rest is history.

Looking at new horizons of technological advancement, TCS realized that with one of the largest population of engineers, we must progress to using software techniques for engineering. We set up an Engineering Industrial Services unit with R&D into CAD/CAM applications. Joint facilities were set up with jet engine, passenger jet and automobile manufacturers. One can literally say that TCS was into 'rocket' science!

The growth in the distributed model of research and innovation to over twenty global innovation laboratories made us realize the need for a structured 'distributed' model. In March 2006 we appointed a Chief Technology Officer for the governance of innovation. New developments in technology were happening not just in R&D centres of global companies but in incubation labs and entrepreneurial teams spread across the world. It was time once again to change our innovation model to envelop this enlarged community. TCS's Co-Innovation Network worked through the network of start-ups, R&D, academics and venture capitalists to co-create cutting edge technologies in a short period of time.

TCS's span of vision when it came to innovation extended not just beyond India's shores but deep within India's heartland as well. Bringing affordable technology to the global marketplace and products and services based on these affordable technologies to India was a dual goal we have always had.

In the 1970s India was not ready to embrace technology; today it sees this as the key enabler that will help it ramp up the pace of growth and development. India is now a country on the rise, a country that aspires to achieve global leadership and a significant role in the global arena. A lot of people talk about the China–India race but in my view, it's not about winning a sprint between two countries; rather it's a game of golf, where you compete with yourself. We need to improve our own score by bringing growth-led opportunities equally to all Indians; in doing that, if we emerge as a powerful global force, that's great.

As a country we can truly realize our potential if every Indian has an equal opportunity to succeed. The aspiration of India's vast rural folk is simple—they want jobs, two square meals a day, good health and a life of dignity. We must equalize the undulations between the two Indias, and reach the benefits of development to the remotest corner of the country.

Herein lies the challenge, because the complexity does not get any bigger than this. When you are a country of 1.2 billion people with eighteen national languages, belong to different religions, live across an expansive landscape that ranges from sub-zero temperatures on the ski slopes of Gulmarg to the sunny shores of Kovalam, with a disparate distribution of wealth where tribals in the deep forests continue to live like they have for centuries while the vibrant cosmopolitan population in the cities drive the latest BMW models, what you have is many mini-worlds within each other. Sometimes I wonder what keeps it all together, what is the 'Indianness', the unique common thread that somehow syncs us all. But perhaps that is something that will always remain the great Indian mystery.

No other country in the world faces such complex challenges. We have no examples to learn from, no reference point; as Indians we will have to chart our own developmental path. However, one thing is certain: our demographic dividend is central to our success. The window of opportunity to leverage this is limited—maybe twenty years or so—before the dividend could become a disaster.

Education, healthcare and employment are the foundations of development—and naturally these are the focus areas of every Indian government. However, India does not have the luxury of time to build brick-and-mortar schools, training institutions and hospitals to meet the needs of its large population. We have to find smarter ways out. This is where technology can be a big enabler. A hub-and-spoke model can connect a teacher in a classroom to several classrooms nearby where good teachers are not available. Distance learning and online education are other ways to educate and skill people remotely. Similarly telemedicine, eHealth initiatives and mobile healthcare can be an answer to the lack of access to doctors. We will need to think of out-of-the-box solutions to address issues of scale and reach.

Neither India nor China is following traditional patterns of growth. In some cases they are leapfrogging technologies, as in telecom, where Indians have taken to mobile phones in a big way, almost obliterating the use of landlines. Both countries are better placed to adopt breakthrough innovations because they do not have the baggage of legacy technologies. Their needs are unique and this will drive the move to indigenous local solutions which will keep in mind sensitivities of cost, access, language and relevance.

A *Harvard Business Review* article correctly assesses that India with a far smaller per capita income is happy with 'high-tech solutions that deliver decent performance at a low cost'. Born at the cusp of cutting-edge technologies and the need to keep costs low, Indian markets are triggering the emergence of several innovative products and services. These 'new' innovations, however, do follow some old rules. They need to pass the tests of access, affordability and appropriateness, or else they stand little chance of success. This is driving what some call 'reverse innovation'—where products and services are developed in emerging markets and then taken to global markets where they can create new markets of their own. The simple interface of these products hides behind its immense complexity.

The Tata Nano, mobile phones that sell for around Rs 1,000, and the low-cost Tata Swach water purifier exemplify the unique needs of the Indian market. While these products may seem basic and the user interface simple, they belie the complex technology behind them. The Tata Nano may be a relatively inexpensive car but behind the modest exterior is some very advanced technology, right from the material used for the body to the engine parts. Thirty-seven inventions have been filed for patent protection to cover all the innovations in the car; its Powertrain design alone has thirty-four patents. Similarly the water purifier Tata Swach has necessitated research on very advanced materials. The key component of the Swach is its cartridge, the Swach bulb. This runs on a unique patented TSRF technology (path breaking nanotechnology) that uses rice husk ash, a widely available natural waste, as the base, with nano-silver particles bound onto it. Fourteen patents have been filed around this technology so far.

These products have markets beyond the Indian shores and so, in a reversal of sorts, 'more with less' is becoming India's export signature; we are rewriting the value proposition. In the services sector it is affordable call charges that has driven India's telecom revolution and relatively inexpensive yet good quality medical treatment draws medical tourism to India.

India's domestic market is driving the democratization of technology. The scale and volume of the Indian market is an irresistible enticement to global companies, but to be successful you have to pass the 'desi endurance test'. Indian companies which leverage this kind of understanding of the market for competitive advantage can become serious multinational competitors in the future. Multinationals too are realizing the need to rethink strategy on their homegrown models. GE's portable ECG device for rural India and the portable ultrasound machine developed for rural China are examples of products created for cost-conscious markets, which have potential to do well in the western mobile healthcare and emergency services markets as well.

Coupled with the democratization of technology, there is another phenomenon that has potentially game changing consequences. That is the democratization of information. India has not yet addressed this adequately but has invested in a system that will bring about change in the future. Many believe that corruption and malpractices thrive when there is a premium on information and it is available with only a few. It took us two decades to build a nationwide voice platform with a digital network and wireless access. India is working towards developing public information infrastructure by building six national platforms: broadband for villages, universal identification (UID-AADHAR), geographic information system (GIS), cyber security, application and payment. As these systems are implemented they will have an exponential benefit in all spheres including business as well as the implementation of large-scale government programmes.

A lot of good work is already happening in the areas of digital and financial inclusion and healthcare across the country. Often, however, innovation remains isolated and confined to pockets of excellence. We must find a way to bring these successes out in the open, at a national level and on a national platform. We need an 'India innovation platform' where innovations can be shared across sectors and communities to enhance collaboration. I truly believe we should not waste time reinventing the wheel. Instead we should be focused on scaling up innovations and making a real difference at the ground level. We need to connect the government, businesses, NGOs and citizens in powerful new ways and present them with a basket of solutions that they can choose from. We need to connect the buyers and the sellers and the intermediate support structures such as banks and funding mechanisms.

Such an initiative will require an investment in nurturing a strong ecosystem. Attention to building the ecosystem is not a very well-recognized factor and often a reason for failure. TCS's early investments were in developing the ecosystem for the computing industry (as it was known back then) and we continue to do so. Today we are benefiting in tangible and intangible ways because of a vibrant ecosystem comprising academia, governments, the financial community and the society at large.

A great example of a supportive ecosystem is that of Silicon Valley. If you were a start-up in Silicon Valley during the boom, you were offered the best possible chance of success; the 'plus' factor came from the strengths of the connections within the web of academia, start-ups, venture capitalists and the government. In comparison, in Europe, there is clearly no lack of innovative minds, but there is a commercialization gap in the ecosystem. Many outstanding European software companies are focused on their home market rather than growth on a global scale. This leads to stunted growth and a limiting ecosystem. There is a lesson for India in this.

TCS has continually moved up on the innovation barometer, embracing new technologies to design better solutions for its global customers. In turn these customers have been able to innovate within their own markets and offer new products and services. There is no reason why technology cannot be a key enabler for innovation in areas where we need it most—health, education and sustainability. TCS was able to achieve what it did because we simultaneously passed on our learning to our resource pool—academia and suppliers—so that they could adapt themselves to the needs of the market; in doing this we created the ecosystem we needed.

India has the scientific capabilities and the technological expertise to leverage technology to address its developmental challenges. However, in order to leverage its power to the fullest, the ecosystem has to be enabled as well. Rural broadband connectivity must be supported by mass IT literacy and the democratization of education must be accompanied by access to funds for the rural poor. Bringing in the technology is the easy part; transforming the ecosystem is our challenge.

## TECHNOLOGY AND INDIA

TWO DECADES AGO if you asked the question, 'Where is cutting-edge R&D happening in the world?' India would not have figured in the answer. But times have changed. Indian institutions, particularly the IITs, are at the forefront of research. IIT Kharagpur has an internationally recognized very large scale integration (VLSI) group, IIT Kanpur is leading the way in algorithms and complexity, IIT Delhi in computer vision and graphics and IIT Bombay in open source and affordable computing. Similarly Indian Institute of Information Technology (IIIT) Hyderabad, leads in language technology, while IIT Madras has many incubated companies focused on low-cost wireless technology and on applications for rural India. India's private sector is increasingly investing in research. The Indian IT industry alone has 594 R&D centres across India. The research climate is undergoing a transformation.

Zinnov Management Consulting, a globalization advisory firm, in its white paper titled 'IP Capacity Landscape in India' reveals that the number of patents filed in India has increased at an average of 11 per cent per year for the last three years to reach more than 36,000 patents annually. According to a Duke University survey, Indians account for 13.7 per cent of international patent applications. They are also driving entrepreneurship—a quarter of all technology companies in the US have at least one founder who is a Chinese or an Indian immigrant.

India's position as an emerging global research hub is also reflected in the investments that multinationals have made. For example Microsoft, which started its R&D centre in India five years ago with just twenty people, employs over 1,500 people today. India is SAP's largest R&D centre outside Germany and employs 4,200 people. Google, the Internet search and advertising giant, chose Bangalore as its first R&D centre outside the US, and Cisco, the networking equipment market leader, has filed more than 600 patents from India.

These companies are investing in India because it makes pure economic sense to develop products in an emerging market like India, home to one-sixth of the world's population. From their perspective, hiring local researchers enables them to better tailor products at the right price and value-add to these markets of the future. India's economic and socio-cultural diversity means companies can test their products in one of the toughest environments and then adapt them for local markets.

The government too must use a similar strategy. Towards funding for large national missions such as energy, water, urbanization and education it must incentivize 'frugal' innovation originating in India, and coming from Indian companies as well as MNCs. The focus of government funding must be on the 'cash to ideas' phase of R&D to create new intellectual property, while industrial research should aim to monetize 'ideas to cash'. Clearly success will come from ideas and technologies that have a social, national and global relevance. The IT industry is emerging out of a licensing mode into another, where service is the utility. The service is taking over the product, much like the iPod, which is really a service in the form of a product and business is created from the number of songs users download. Supercomputing lends itself well to this model, as is being leveraged by Tata who have built EKA, one of Asia's fastest supercomputers at 133 teraflops. Addressing the big challenges in nanotechnology, weather prediction, security and microelectronics, it is also of great relevance to drug discovery and clinical trials. The pharmaceuticals industry, wary of the patent regime, is moving towards the 'drugs discovered by an Indian company' model. Cost of R&D in India could be as low as one-fifth the spend of discovering a drug in a developed nation. While there are several high-impact technologies, some like cloud computing, mobile technologies and nanotechnology stand out more than others because of the sheer scale of transformation they make possible.

## Mobile technologies

Currently 41 per cent of the Indian population is unbanked. This lack of access to affordable financial services is a recognized constraint to India's growth impetus. India is looking at a new model where banks can be brought to people's homes. Alternate channels for delivery such as through post office services or home banking through business correspondents who use handheld devices to transact are being experimented with. Technology is adapting to support interoperability between the suppliers, service providers and delivery mechanisms. Mobile phones are yet another channel for the delivery of services. The financial services sector needs integrated technology frameworks that seamlessly tie up e-banking and mobile banking with core banking systems and third-party applications. At the same time advances in biometrics and cryptography are required to support network authentication, and open standards architectures that offer multi-channel, multilingual and multi-connectivity functionalities need to be explored.

There are over 600 million mobile phone users in India—almost half the country's population. With this kind of penetration, phenomenal reach can be achieved by leveraging the mobile phone to connect with the customer. Simple, affordable services on the mobile targeted at rural populations is a huge potential business opportunity because although fiber-optic cables provide backbone broadband connectivity, the 'last mile' physical infrastructure is missing in rural India. The applications could vary from education and entertainment to health and agriculture.

By almost any measure, the growth of the Indian mobile sector is extraordinary and is reflected by the number of mobile service providers operating in India—fourteen at the last count. This growth has been facilitated by the policies of the Telecommunications Regulatory Authority of India (TRAI) which has overseen the creation of a regulatory framework designed to ensure that telecom services are offered to Indian consumers and businesses at affordable prices. The TRAI has actively contributed to the competitive landscape in the mobile market by encouraging the entry of new players and implementing several initiatives to encourage competition, including the introduction of mobile number portability, the national broadband plan and the recently completed auction of 3G licences. These developments are expected to benefit end-users by fuelling competition among operators and putting further downward pressure on tariffs, which are already among the lowest in the world. Fifteen million new mobile subscribers are being added each month—faster than any other market in the world. This growth is expected to continue and the total number of mobile subscribers could exceed 1 billion by 2014.

New business and governance models, unthinkable until recently, have now become possible as a result. As an example TCS has developed mKrishi, an agro-advisory system for farmers. Using mKrishi, the farmer sends a query either by pressing an icon or by responding to a voice or text menu on the mobile handset. The query reaches a central server through a CDMA cellphone network. Experts access this information on their computer and reply with their advice in the native language using Roman script. mKrishi's features include weather forecasts—a seven-day forecast of precipitation, cloud cover and temperature variation for a specific village—pesticide and fertilizer advice. Local information on weather, soil and crops is provided to the server automatically through a 3G CDMA network.

The mKrishi packet also includes a host of new technologies including soil and weather sensor technology in the farms, interactive voice response (IVR) technology on the handset and voice SMS features in the software to transport voice messages between the farmer and the expert. The programme makes innovative use of the camera in the mobile handset to provide high-resolution pictures of crop images, and software processes these images to bring out patterns to detect plant diseases which can be analysed by the expert. TCS believes mKrishi is the first serious attempt to integrate various technologies and provide crop, soil and location-specific personalized advice to farmers in a local language on a mobile phone. Since the scaling up of mKrishi will depend on the network of local franchisees, operators and experts, TCS is working on developing an eco-partner network including NGOs, agriculture faculty, research scientists from national research labs and farmers' associations. The same technology can serve the needs of the thousands of small fishermen that dot the Indian coasts or thousands of cattle owners who can connect to veterinary hospitals. The potential to scale is huge; in fact any technology deployment in India has to think in terms of scale and implementation in order to cover a large platform.

## Cloud computing

Mobile phones have made rural India accessible and brought into the fold millions of new consumers. Similarly 'software-as-a-service' using cloud computing technologies has made the small and medium business community into an attractive market. In our homes to use electricity we do not need to own the entire power grid—we just pay for the amount of electricity we consume. Siliarly in cloud computing the burden of work shifts from the local computer to the network of computers that make up the cloud. The software resides on the cloud and you pay as you use. The only thing the user's computer needs to be able to run is the cloud computing system's interface software.

From a broader perspective, cloud computing can also be thought of as a business model that enables the customer to get started very quickly with any kind of commoditized service which can be easily configured and defined precisely without getting into long-winded negotiations and discussions. At TCS we have looked at it from both the narrow and broad perspectives, where we think of cloud computing as encompassing a broad range of services including business process services, knowledge process services as well as process development services.

These features make cloud computing suitable for a wide range of activities and customer profiles. For example, small and medium-sized companies which lack an IT infrastructure can tap cloud-based services to support their business operations. TCS is betting big on this technology and has already launched a subscription-based cloud service for small and medium businesses (SMBs) in India that provides SMBs with access to basic IT-based services like accounting and payroll on a pay-per-use basis. This 'IT-as-a-service' model allows SMBs to scale as they grow and pay only for the IT resources they use, without the need to invest in IT infrastructure.

Big enterprise customers can also use cloud services to meet seasonal demand peaks or as part of a strategy to outsource non-core IT operations. Combined with data analytics, cloud computing can help them crunch huge volumes of data in near-real time, providing much faster and more valuable insights into market trends and other variables.

At TCS we offer a platform-based process outsourcing service which runs processes like payroll and business intelligence on our own servers and delivers those services in terms of output to the customer, so the pricing is entirely output-based. The customer gets the amount of pay checks or the number of intelligence reports that they ask for, without having to worry about hardware, software licences etc.

In India cloud computing has the potential to both lower the cost and expand the reach of a wide range of services including e-governance, health and education. For some, the security of a cloud has been a concern and the reason for not moving mission critical applications on the cloud. These concerns are likely to be addressed in a year or two by improving network security. Over time, the growth of mobile cloud and software-as-a-service offerings will enable developers to upload and share data and collaborate in real time on shared files. The cloud developer community will move quickly into open-source and will be using a single Web standard for writing applications that can work on multiple operating systems. India also has the opportunity to lead the way in delivering secure cloud-based services to its citizens via mobile phones and other devices.

## User interfaces

A large proportion of India's PC owners and many of the country's cellphone owners are first-time users of technology and they need a fundamentally different way of interacting with their devices, perhaps through speech- and gesture-based 'sixth sense' technologies. Most new users are not proficient in English and therefore need machine translation and language capabilities built into the technology tools they use.

This is an area where India can and should claim global leadership. Our language processing capabilities are ready for deployment; the Indian Institute of Information Technology (IIIT) in Hyderabad is pioneering this effort. The industry must explore market opportunities to exploit this and explore new applications based on SILKy (speech, image, language, knowledge) interfaces rather than WIMPy (windows, icons, menus and pointing device) interfaces.

One indication of the potential of SILKy interfaces is the success of TCS's computer based functional literacy (CBFL) programme which relies on cognitive capabilities of individuals to associate complex visual patterns representing words in Indian scripts with their meanings as well as their phonetic utterances.

We need to develop standards for authoring on mobile devices for Indian languages. This will require the development and standardization of Indian language semantic Web tools such as WordNet and ontologies to access and ensure interoperability amongst Indian language documents. The content authoring tools, browsers and the various Indian scripts need to be standardized and internationalized. Translation from one Indian language to another is not sufficient. What is required is translation from any international language to any Indian language and vice versa.

The exciting part is that since the technology framework, software architecture and machine learning algorithms are language-independent, they can be easily adapted to alternate environments including the global market. As SILKy interfaces become more comprehensive, there is no reason why they should not eventually become superior to keyboard interfaces, enabling all desktop users to switch to this alternate technology.

## Nanotechnology

Yet another technology that will have a huge global impact in the future is nanotechnology. 'Nanos' in Greek means dwarf; a nanometre is a billionth of a metre, or 1/80,000th of the diameter of a human hair. Nanotechnology is simply the science of the small, actually the ultra-small, and it enables the manipulation of matter at an extremely small level. Today, this field of advanced study has significant impact on all areas of the society and industry. The future world will be defined by how imaginatively we use this technology for the betterment of the human race in a whole range of areas like healthcare and the environment to commercial products in different industries.

The medical significance of nanotechnology is most exciting. It enables researchers to get a better understanding of the basic biochemical and biophysical processes of both healthy and diseased cells. The small size of nanoparticles makes them perfect candidates for transporting active substances to specific regions of the body. 'Stealth coatings' can transform nanoparticles into 'magic bullets' that can attack a specific tumour or a diseased cell. As nanotechnology progresses, doctors can tailor medication to the individual patient based on his/her genetic composition, thus preventing unwanted side effects. As a result, the health system will gravitate to becoming preventive rather than curative.

Nanomaterials are already being used on a commercial scale. Carbon black is used as a reinforcing filler for rubber, while particles of titanium dioxide are used as UV reflectors in sunblock creams. Nanomaterials much lighter than steel are being produced that possess ten times as much strength. Nanomaterials like quantum dots could help solar cells convert more sunlight into electricity because of their unusual electronic properties. Scientists have calculated that this approach could increase the theoretical maximum efficiency of solar cells by about 50 per cent.

Using the Tata supercomputer Eka, we have already simulated the behaviour of gold nanoparticles. Simulation packages which can simulate the properties of any nanostructure given its chemical composition, molecular structure and shape are being developed. This opens doors to the creation of new materials and new processes in medicine.

Nanotechnologies are improving circuit designs as well. The self-assembly process of nanomaterials is enabling electrical signals on chips to flow 35 per cent faster, thereby consuming 15 per cent less energy. Such techniques are moving out of labs and into commercial manufacturing environments. These design innovations have great relevance to India.

From cloud computing to nanotechnology, all of these new frontiers can have a transformational effect on the world. In fact nanotechnology is believed to have the potential to transform life more intensely than the Industrial Revolution did. From the perspective of India we must participate in the research on these technologies; we must embrace these new trends and deploy these technologies in a big way to solve our developmental challenges.

## Hardware focus

While we have done so well on software, we have missed the bus somewhere on hardware. However India should try to recover lost ground and enhance its dominance beyond the software landscape by giving a thrust to its hardware sector. Leadership in both will give us an unparalleled global status. Our electronics sector is at a point of inflexion, just as IT services were a decade ago.

Why should we give the Indian hardware sector a boost? First, currently domestic production is less than 45 per cent of domestic consumption. Based on projections, the Indian market for IT hardware will grow from the present $45 billion to $400 billion by 2020. If we do nothing about it, our import of electronics by 2020 will grow to 16 per cent of our GDP. Most of India's electronics imports are from China and Taiwan, creating a dependency that may be limiting for us in the future.

Also, if we seek to solve poverty, education and employment issues through digital and financial inclusion, we will need millions of low-cost devices including handheld devices, bio-monitoring solutions, micro-payment systems, GIS devices, project monitoring solutions and smart meters. These products must be designed for India's specific needs and clearly our own electronics industry should play a major role in providing these products and solutions. Similarly, low-cost ATMs for the rural sector using biometrics for identification/authentication have already been adopted by large banks such as SBI and ICICI, and offer new opportunities for embedded electronics manufacturers. Mass consumer products with digital chips embedded would require local competencies in both design and fabrication.

India's energy and defence systems need to emphasize self-reliance and the development of indigenous technology and manufacturing capabilities as well, given the strategic nature and scale of such initiatives. That there is a great volatility in global markets was shown in ample measure by the recent economic crisis. Where intellectual capabilities exist, self-reliance should be exercised to its fullest potential.

Given that there is an unquestioned market in the future for IT hardware, poor infrastructure and taxation issues are the two main factors inhibiting both domestic and foreign investments. Because of the challenges, the total return on investment for a manufacturer in India is about 12 per cent, compared to around 34 per cent in China.

While taxation and labour laws need to be overhauled, we also need to engage with industry, entrepreneurs and academia to set up manufacturing clusters for electronics. If we look at how Suzuki's entrance in partnership with Maruti transformed the Indian automotive sector, perhaps we should consider encouraging one big IT hardware player from overseas to enter the Indian market to provide a similar boost.

More generally, we need to develop the entire IT hardware manufacturing value chain from semiconductors and other components to finished electronic products including mobile and handheld devices. Not only will this reduce our import bill, but it will also fuel exports and create employment opportunities for millions.

It is this self-reliance in hardware that is missing in the charter of India's growth. Our IT exports have the potential to offset oil imports, but only if we make progress on both software and hardware. We have the talent and the resources to do this; what we need is the will.

The Tata Group is at the forefront of innovation, a pioneer in the quest for excellence. TCS is no exception. Driving innovation, leveraging technology and creating new business models in new emerging areas is the way we have looked at the future.

While focusing on incremental innovations such as productivity improvements, replicability and quality enhancements on the one hand, we have never been shy of disruptive innovation on the other. Our pioneering the offshore model is a standing example of how we changed the rules of the game. Starting a research unit like TRDDC was another visionary decision made thirty-five years ago— mandating it to address different disciplines including material science was not only unusual but was one of the earliest efforts to explore the pervasiveness of IT in various fields and to create IPR.

When India was ready for IT, we were ready with affordable, appropriate, scalable solutions. Touching the lives of millions of people and making a positive change has been a driving force for us. Our adult literacy initiative or the Ignite programme are examples of what is possible when one questions the basics and looks for a new perspective to a problem.

Underpinning our work has been the effort to push for more with less. We do this in every aspect of our business—we ask ourselves how we can raise the bar by using minimal resources and fewer people. Of course this calls for greater effort and a greater stretch, but to my mind by setting such challenges for ourselves we condition ourselves to think disruptively. One of the challenges I have always shared with my team is: if today you are doing a piece of work with 40,000 people, think of ways of doing it with 4,000. When you begin to think along these lines you will be surprised by how it makes you rethink and question the fundamentals.

As TCS's growth story continues, the expanse of work cannot be directly proportional to the expanse of the workforce. We will need to reinvent and rethink and redesign ourselves. But then this wonderful institution we call TCS has done it before and no doubt we will in the future. There are ample technologies and innovations that make it possible for us to help build a sustainable and inclusive future.

# 8

# TOWARDS TOMORROW'S INDIA

## THE FUTURE OF HEALTHCARE

AS A STUDENT there were three or four things that fascinated me most when I thought about my future career. With my father in the government service, our outlook and thinking led us to believe that the best jobs were in public service, in engineering and medicine, or with the Tatas or Birlas in the private sector. The institutions that were respected most at that time were the All India Institute of Medical Sciences (AIIMS) for medicine, IISc for research, and the IITs for science and technology. Medicine as a career option was certainly one of the considerations for me. As a young boy I was fascinated by the doctors visiting our home, pulling out a stethoscope from their medical kit and scribbling down a list of medicines authoritatively. The respectful treatment they received created a sense of awe in my young and impressionable mind.

Later, when it came to making a choice of subjects for higher studies I chose Science with biology as an option. I was keen to take the pre-university exam for medicine, but that was not to be. But although I was fascinated by the life sciences I would never have been able to manage the surgery part of studying medicine. However, though I could not become a doctor myself, my fascination with the subject remained.

Several years later, after having joined TCS I had the good fortune of meeting with Jack Berdy who owned an IT company called Online Software. He was a client of TCS and I had built a personal relationship with him. Jack believed in following his heart and he decided to sell his IT company to join medical school to become a doctor. We kept in touch and he approached us again for IT-related work for his growing medical practice. This sparked the idea in my mind of the opportunity for IT in healthcare. This was further endorsed when in 1979 I went to the US with my family and found a place to live in Queens. In locating a house we were helped by a relative of Mala's, a doctor doing an internship in the US. He lived close by and we met often. Thanks to him and the many acquaintances with several doctors, I was provided with a peep into the way hospitals functioned. Desperately looking for business, my mind got ticking on opportunities for IT in hospital systems. My innate curiosity in the medical sciences only deepened with time and I felt that the exploration of the use of IT in medicine would be satisfying.

The use of IT in medicine had already begun in a small measure in the US. In the 1980s Burroughs started what they called their hospital management system. In those days computerization had begun to bring in efficiencies in outpatient scheduling, inpatient admission and discharges, scheduling surgeries and tests and integration of the results of these tests. Since we worked with Burroughs we did get significant data conversion and migration work at the Presbyterian Hospital in Dallas in 1986, to help the hospital with upgradations.

More creative work was to follow at the Presbyterian Hospital at Pittsburgh, where the project involved building a three-dimensional model of the heart. Doctors during live cardiac procedures would click a series of x-ray images of the heart using a foot pedal. These images taken on a Siemens imaging computer would then be transferred to a NEXT computer (invented by Steve Jobs). A TCSer who had considerable expertise in imaging having worked in Japan on IBM imaging technologies was specially brought into this project. The work involved capturing the images and modifying them using certain imaging techniques. This 3D model was subsequently used by medical professionals to study the procedure carefully and also to determine the overall heart condition to recommend post-procedure advice to the patients. It also served as a training tool for new medical graduates in procedures like angioplasty.

Our implementation support on these Burroughs systems extended to Europe as well where at Rivierenland Tiel in the Netherlands we implemented and supported the Burroughs system at a regional hospital of around 250 beds and multiple specialities. This work even had an offshore component where work was carried out in Bombay between April and November 1982 for the customization and building of a patient billing system to suit the hospital's specific requirements. In Switzerland we had just established a local partner—TKS-Teknosoft—and in 1984, one of the first assignments in this partnership was with CHUV Hospital at Lausanne, which was a large university hospital with over 500 beds comprising multiple specialities. We helped this large hospital implement and build interfaces for their hospital management system.

Jack Berdy, now CEO of Berdy Medical Systems, New Jersey, had developed the SmartClinic package to computerize the activities in a clinic. Developed in MS Access 97 it had the portability to run on virtually all standard hardware platforms. TCS became the sole marketing partner for SmartClinic in India; we customized SmartClinic for the Indian market and built into the product some features that enabled quick documentation of a physical examination, medication, admission, discharge, pre-operative and post-operative processes. Features such as automated medical history creation and correspondence generation were appreciated and doctors gave us a positive feedback, but eventually TCS did not succeed in selling the volumes that were anticipated. Perhaps the product was ahead of its time for the small and fragmented 'medical clinics' market in India. However, India's leading medical institute AIIMS did consider implementing India's first hospital information system—which was developed by TCS—in the mid-1980s.

So, in those early days. while TCS made a foray into the healthcare sector, we were really doing back-office work and some small hospital projects, mostly in the US and Europe. And so it was for much of the 1990s. In early 2001, in the UK, where TCS always had a very strong presence, the team was responding to a number of tenders from the government. While we knew that we would not be making much headway by just responding to tenders, there were two important benefits in continuing this exercise. First, we got some valuable learning in how to respond to public sector RFIs and RFPs, and second, we developed awareness about ourselves within the government, that we were active in this sector and had an interest in it. Around this time major changes were planned in the UK's National Health Service (NHS) involving information technology. When the formal tender process started, it was one of the largest procurements in the UK, with an estimated spend of about £6 billion. We built a team for the bid, with two plans in place. Plan A was with a PriceWaterhouseCoopers and Fujitsu alliance, while Plan B involved exploring Cerner-like options as a special purpose vehicle. (Cerner Corporation is an international healthcare information technology corporation that specializes in providing complete systems for hospitals and other medical organizations to manage and integrate all electronic medical records, computerized physician order entry and financial information.) We created a small team to focus on Cerner and another to bid along with Fujitsu where TCS was a subcontracting partner. It was a huge effort, involving a number of people in TCS, and I tracked the proposals closely.

In January 2004, I was on my way to Latin America, on my first overseas trip with Ratan Tata. We had to transit through Johannesburg where we had a three-hour wait. It was night by the time we reached Sao Paulo, where I got a call from our UK head giving us the good news that we (the Fujitsu alliance) had won the contract for the NHS southern cluster. (NHS had divided England into five geographic clusters: London, North-East, South, East of England and East Midlands and West Midlands, and North-West.) I was overjoyed to have won such a major and visible deal in the UK. I immediately handed over the phone to Ratan Tata to allow our young UK head to have the privilege of conveying the excellent news to the Chairman himself, which hopefully is one of his memorable moments.

The NHS win was not just a matter of great joy and pride to TCS, but meant a paradigm change. From doing small one-off projects, suddenly we were in the big league in healthcare. We were both competing against and partnering with global top ten IT and consulting organizations including Accenture, IBM, HP, PWC, EDS and Fujitsu. After all the national programme for IT in the United Kingdom was one of the largest IT civil procurements in the world and TCS had the opportunity to be one of the largest suppliers. Changes planned in the NHS were to benefit 13 million patients and some 256,000 NHS staff across seven strategic health authorities, eighty-one primary care trusts, forty-eight hospital trusts, twelve ambulance trusts and 1,938 GP practices, and TCS would provide clinical application implementation and data migration.

The NHS win enabled for us in the UK what the SEGA project had done for us in Switzerland in the securities marketplace, and what the NSE project in India had achieved. More than anything else we would be touching the lives of millions of ordinary people in the UK in a small way. I shared this feeling with Ratan Tata who also agreed that this put TCS on a different plane altogether.

## Bioinformatics

Meanwhile the advances in the fields of molecular biology and genomics in the last six decades saw an explosion in the amount of biological information being made available and gave a new dimension to the study of life science and healthcare. This was made possible once the double helical structure of DNA was deciphered by Crick and Watson in 1953. The new developments in biology have been made possible by the enrichment of the field not only by traditional biologists but also physicists, mathematicians, instrumentation experts, chemists and even computer scientists. A whole new field of bioinformatics has come into being, intertwining the disciplines of genetics and computing.

I saw an opportunity for a new business here for TCS and at the beginning of the new millennium, we decided to understand and gain competence in bioinformatics and eventually make a contribution to the field as well. One of the immediate problems we encountered was the absence of trained people in the field in India.

What we found was a fairly good base of computer scientists and a handful of good biology laboratories in various publicly funded institutions like the Council of Scientific and Industrial Research (CSIR), but the situation in the universities was woeful.

Thus an immediate challenge was to create a suite of software tools that could help in developing bioinformatics capabilities in the universities, in R&D laboratories and in the nascent biotechnology industry. We realized that this would attain the twin goals of developing TCS's capabilities in bioinformatics and also build Indian capabilities in the progress of modern biology aided by computing.

At about the same time the CSIR under the leadership of Dr R.A. Mashelkar had come up with a bold new strategy to identify and encourage futuristic technology development in the country. They named it the New Millennium Indian Technology Leadership Initiative (NMITLI). Besides identifying worthy new ideas to back, the CSIR was also very keen to encourage a cross-pollination between private industry and publicly funded labs. Thus it came up with a public–private partnership (PPP) scheme. TCS did not need a government loan to start the project, but Dr Mashelkar insisted that TCS participate in the PPP to strengthen relationships between the government's R&D labs and the IT industry, leading to larger national knowledge networks in the future.

Towards this end, TCS's Advanced Technology Centre was set up in Hyderabad with a core bioinformatics group. It was a new experiment where we recruited pure biologists and medical doctors and housed them together with computer scientists and programmers to build a team. Nineteen research labs of CSIR collaborated in the project sharing their expertise in biology as well as their understanding of what a biology researcher would look for in such a software package, its requirements and product features.

At that time commercially available software packages would cost almost half a million dollars which most laboratories and universities—and even the smaller biotech companies—could ill afford. Thus the goal was to develop an interdisciplinary team including the biologists of CSIR, where team members would learn from each other and develop a proficiency in bioinformatics—and come up with a software suite at an affordable price.

TCS collaborated with several leading R&D institutions on the project. A team of forty at TCS put in about eighty person-years of work and the result was BioSuite, a product that integrated the functions of macromolecular sequence and structural analysis, chemoinformatics and algorithms for aiding drug discovery. The suite was organized into four major modules and contained seventy-nine different programs, making it one of the few comprehensive suites that caters to a major part of the spectrum of bioinformatics applications.

This unique partnership succeeded in what it had set out to do. It was a proud moment for TCS and for the Indian scientific community at large. The significance of this contribution and its relevance to India was evident from the presence of the President of India, Dr A.P.J. Abdul Kalam, at the formal launch of BioSuite on 14 July 2004 at Hyderabad.

BioSuite ensured that the best available methodology had been adopted for each of the seventy-nine programs, which had been thoroughly evaluated at several stages, leading to the high scientific value of the suite. The package was valuable for high quality academic research, industrial R&D and for teaching purposes, both locally within the country as well as in the international arena.

According to Dr Mashelkar, a reputed US-based company which had a competing product selling for nearly half a million dollars immediately dropped the price to almost 10 per cent of the original after BioSuite was introduced. For R&D institutions in India the suite was given at a fraction of this price and it is now being used by students in several Indian universities. The objective of knowledge networking in public–private partnership mode and creating a software that served a national purpose was thus achieved.

## Sankara Nethralaya

TCS had started its healthcare practice in the 1990s with a vision to advance the quality and efficiency of healthcare delivery through effective use of information technology. Our team had started providing technology solutions to hospitals in India with a focus on data capture to assist administrative activities within the hospitals. It also enabled accounting of key services and links to the financial management of the hospital. After several implementations of hospital IT systems, TCS decided to convert this experience into a hospital management system product which could be deployed in multiple settings with little customization. Soon the focus of the product started shifting from the administrative side of hospital functionality to applications that had direct impact on the quality of healthcare delivery.

A wonderful opportunity presented itself when Sankara Nethralaya—one of India's premier eye hospitals, ranked as one of the best centres for ophthalmic care in Asia—decided to go in for electronic medical records and hospital management systems. TCS was chosen in 1995 as Sankara Nethralaya's partner to deliver on their vision. I had been visiting Sankara Nethralaya for my own eye check-ups and was aware of the good work that they were doing: they cared for 1,200 outpatients and conducted 100 operations every day. The hospital's theatre were equipped with the finest technology in the world, reflecting the commitment of its founder Dr S.S. Badrinath to nothing short of excellence when it came to the care of patients.

On my part, I was keen to deliver a world-class IT system to Sankara Nethralaya. I asked two clinicians, Dr Sumanth Raman, a Chennai-based paediatrician and Dr Arvind Singh, a UK-based vitreoretinal surgeon, to provide clinical leadership to the project. From meetings with the board members of the hospital to nursing and administrative staff, there was a continuous dialogue between the practising clinicians and the technology delivery team to understand the expectations. A small team of programmers actually worked out of a small terrace room in the hospital to reassure the clinicians that the programmers were not far away from the environment for which they were programming. It was a great learning experience for both sides: TCS staff learned the imprecise nature of clinical expectations and the hospital staff learned to convey to the TCS team in understandable terms the complex medical and surgical procedures undertaken in modern eye care. Some of the challenges facing the TCS team included the development of a clinical record that could incorporate freehand drawings of the retina and other anatomical parts of the eye and video clips of operations in real time. These challenges were handled with extreme patience on both sides. Not only was the project implemented successfully, but it was within the originally defined budget. Both teams watched with pride when in 2008 and in 2011, the implementation was recognized by NASSCOM and KPMG respectively with the award for the Best Electronic Medical Record Solution.

I felt that by placing cutting-edge IT at the heart of eye care delivery at Sankara Nethralaya, we had lived up to the vision of Dr Badrinath when he set up this world-class institution. There was a tremendous sense of pride felt by the entire TCS team in having played a role in helping the dedicated clinicians save the sight of those who walked through their doors with so much hope.

Soon TCS saw itself working closely with large healthcare projects in the government sector which began to gain speed over the last decade or so. Recently, for the government of Gujarat, TCS has provided a hospital information system for thirty-one large and medium-sized government hospitals.

Even more ambitious was our work for Tamil Nadu's health systems project. Here the objective was to bring all the health institutions in the state on to a single platform for better operational efficiencies and better delivery of services. In this ambitious project TCS successfully implemented a healthcare management information system at 1,539 primary health centres across the state and implemented the hospital management system in forty-six government hospitals. In the next phase the hospital management system is to be scaled to cover more than 225 government hospitals, thus bringing the entire health department on a single platform. The data flows seamlessly into the hospital management system and also populates Government of India systems like those of the National Rural Health Mission (NRHM). The impact of this truly transformational initiative will be seen over the coming years through vastly improved public delivery of healthcare services.

As part of a philanthropic initiative, when the Tata Group decided to open a new cancer hospital in Kolkata, TCS was proud to deploy its hospital management suite. The key focus of this solution was the newly-developed oncology electronic medical records, integrated with the old hospital management solution. There are plans to further enhance the solution in partnership with global academic and research institutes in the area of clinical analytics and comparative effectiveness research. Today TCS hospital management systems have evolved into a suite of offerings including electronic medical records, laboratory information systems, radiology information systems, clinical decision support systems and business intelligence applications with many of these solutions having a major impact on the quality of healthcare delivery.

In India, the Indian Space Research Organization (ISRO) provides free satellite time for healthcare initiatives. Using a satellite link, a doctor conducting a clinic in a central area such as Sankara Nethralaya can be linked remotely via satellite to either a doctor or a nurse seeing patients in a distant part of the country. The satellite link, which supports both audio and video communications, enables the central clinic to provide outpatient consultations and facilitate follow-ups for patients who have undergone operations and have returned home. This means they do not have to spend time moving to and from the hospital which is often a long distance away.

A similar outreach programme at the Tata Memorial Hospital in Mumbai has succeeded in dramatically reducing the number of 'return visits' that cancer patients need to make—often at great expense and inconvenience—following treatment. As at Sankara Nethralaya, we found that it was important that the link is audio-visual because quite often a consultation is a visual experience. For example, the way a patient walks into the office and the expression on his or her face often gives an indication of how much pain the patient is in. The advantage of the video link is that you can actually see and pick up things which would be missed if it was only an audio feed.

The staff at Sankara Nethralaya found that the only equipment the doctor in the remote clinic needed was a reasonably high resolution camera and the use of practical examining tools. Patient information can be written on a board for transmission and then digitized at the main hospital. That way, before a patient travels to a hospital, all the necessary information is in place. In some cases the patient does not even need to travel to the hospital because they can be seen, treated and dispensed remotely.

The biggest implementation of this system in a modified form has been undertaken by TCS in Tamil Nadu for monitoring AIDS patients. HIV is a very big problem in India mostly because of the stigma related to the disease. However, there are certain problems in treating HIV which only arise in a developing country like India.

When you provide free medication to poor patients, there is a risk that sometimes they will sell the medication rather than take it themselves. The system implemented by TCS in Chennai about four years ago involves small medical units that feed in data from all over Tamil Nadu, a state which has a population of between 75 and 80 million. As a result, the system can keep track of every AIDS or HIV patient in the state, his/her blood values, when he/she was last given medication and how he/she is responding to medication. That way, when somebody walks into a local centre asking for medication, the doctors can immediately check and see when the patient last received a free prescription.

The system has worked very well and we believe the same technology, coupled with individual monitoring of patients, could be used for managing other health and wellness issues such as vaccination and child immunization as well.

While the systems needed to track individuals take time to set up and require the training of medical professionals, once they are operational, they allow large segments of the population to be cared for in a much more effective way. In the systems TCS has implemented, patients are identified by name and by address. In India it is also very common to identify patients with photographs in most cases. There are some privacy issues, but most people are willing to accept the need to store a photograph in the records, if the care they receive as a result improves.

## Heartcare

A lot of sophisticated IT research, both in leading-edge technologies as well as in various domains like healthcare, takes place within TCS's global network of laboratories. One challenge taken up by the TCS team was that of improving the quality of cardiac care. Every year in India, 60 million people suffer heart attacks, 2 million of whom die due to cardiovascular complications. Indians are genetically prone to heart problems and 60 per cent of heart patients worldwide will be in India by 2015—and sadly most of them will be in rural India. Proximity of doctors or cardiac care facilities is a challenge in rural India and commencing treatment as early as possible within the 'golden hour' is critical to increasing survival chances.

What if an affordable smart cardiac device could be developed that would be patient-centric rather than hospital-centric?

Taking up this challenge, TCS came up with a portable cardiac monitoring device with wireless transmission capabilities; this device can store over 10,000 ECGs on a standard 2GB SD card. The USP of this device is its low cost which is under Rs 10,000 ($225)—one-fifth the cost of similar devices abroad. Given the affordability, routine cardiac diagnoses in rural areas becomes possible by making this device available across thousands of healthcare centres without having to make significant investments.

Being portable, the device can be deployed in ambulances and a remote diagnosis can be made by the doctor at the hospital as soon as the patient is picked up by the ambulance. This is enabled through the transmission and central storage capabilities of the device which alerts a predefined mobile number using the GSM/GPRS module and connects to a central server for further analysis. For this unique device a provisional patent has been filed with the freedom to operate (FTO) in the India market.

Treatments, including the life-saving thrombolytic therapy (the use of drugs to break up or dissolve blood clots, which are the main cause of both heart attacks and strokes) which can significantly enhance survival rates in patients, can be administered in the ambulance itself under medical guidance. The multitude of features, its unique transmission capability and the low cost can make this device a game changer in the cardiac device segment and can help save thousands of lives each year.

## Arogyashri

Bringing medical treatment to the people through mobile services or portable devices is one part of the solution for rural India. However, this does not address the needs of those who suffer from ailments that need hospitalization.

India has no nationwide social security scheme. Only 11 per cent of the population has any form of health insurance coverage. About 70 per cent of India's healthcare expenditure is financed out of pocket. Borrowing is the largest source of financing out-of-pocket expenditure, pushing nearly 3.3 per cent of India's population to below the poverty line—defined as those whose annual income is less than Rs 80,000—every year. Poor people who do not have access to good medical care or health facilities have no recourse but to sell their already meagre assets or borrow money to meet medical needs. Often this sets them back financially because surgical operations are expensive, especially in private hospitals which are preferred because of the perception of getting better treatment there. Sometimes an entire lifetime's savings go in the repayment of such a loan.

Arogyashri ('healthcare' in Hindi) is a health insurance scheme for families below the poverty line (BPL) developed by the government of Andhra Pradesh, with whom TCS has partnered to create an IT backbone and infrastructure data management.

Meant for medical treatment for those needing hospitalization for about 1,000 life threatening diseases, Arogyashri enables a completely cash-free treatment costing the exchequer Rs 1,000 crore annually. This state government programme has been a runaway success and its popularity amongst the masses is believed to be a primary reason for the state's chief minister being voted back to power.

Operating in a public–private partnership mode under the Arogyashri Healthcare Trust, the Andhra Pradesh government pays the premium for the beneficiaries, a partnering insurance company takes on the risk, and 440 empanelled hospitals render the services. Acclaimed as one of the best negotiated schemes of the government, it has managed to get on board some of the top private sector hospitals in the state, who, although reluctant at first, today have over 60 per cent of their revenues coming from this scheme.

The modus operandi is simple. Hospitals conduct health camps in rural areas. During patient examinations, if the doctor thinks the patient needs specialized treatment, he/she is given a patient card which can be taken to any of the empanelled hospitals to get treatment. In these hospitals a dedicated person called an Arogyashri Mitra (friend) will assist the patient. TCS has networked all Arogyashri Mitras and their work is captured electronically and performance monitored through key performance indicators (KPIs).

The insurance company runs a 24x7 BPO to get daily data from the Mitras who have direct contact with the patient. A digital system monitors all 5,000 people employed in the programme including doctors, and the extensive use of voice over Internet protocol (VOIP) based communications optimizes costs. Accountability is woven into the system: all patient documents are downloadable and hospitals even have a scorecard. The records of patients' tests are uploaded on a site whose servers are maintained by TCS. Test results get reviewed by three independent doctors online, and only then is a decision on surgery taken, ensuring that no unwarranted surgeries take place.

The scheme has in one stroke democratized healthcare, making the best of healthcare available—that too free of cost—to those who need it most. What must be remembered is that this essential service would not have been possible without the technology backbone that enables collaboration and accountability. To my mind this scheme is an exemplary demonstration of brilliant strategy that leverages the power of IT, making effective implementation possible. The World Health Organization (WHO), I am told, is keen to study the system.

## The future

One of the big challenges for the future is how to improve on and standardize the quality of healthcare provided, harnessing technologies like 3G wireless datalinks to link community health centres to expert doctors and pharmacists in hospitals.

A major step taken by the Indian government towards improving rural healthcare was the launch of the National Rural Health Mission in April 2005. The aim of the Mission is to provide effective healthcare to India's rural population with a focus on eighteen states that have low public health indicators and inadequate infrastructure.

In the past five decades, India has made remarkable improvements in healthcare resulting in doubling of life expectancy at birth, reduction in infant mortality by half and maternal mortality by two-thirds, and the total eradication of smallpox and guinea worm diseases. India's healthcare infrastructure, however, has not kept pace with the economy's growth. The physical infrastructure requires huge upgradations to meet today's healthcare demands, much less those of tomorrow. For instance, India needs 74,150 community health centres for every million of its population, but has less than half that number.

When it comes to healthcare, there are two Indias: the nation that provides high-quality medical care to urban Indians, triggering a growing medical tourism industry, and the other India in which BPL families have limited access to quality healthcare. It is my emphatic belief that this gap can very well be addressed by the use of technology.

In relatively wealthy urban India, medical facilities and doctors are on par with the best in the world. In fact, many of my American friends prefer to consult with expat Indian doctors in the US. According to a recent joint study by the Confederation of Indian Industry (CII) and McKinsey, Indian medical tourism has the potential to grow into a $2 billion industry within the next few years. Medical tourism in India has been growing at 25 to 30 per cent annually and India has the potential to attract 1 million medical tourists each year, which could cumulate to $5 billion to the economy, according to the CII.

The healthcare sector has seen a fair amount of local innovation. The 'do more with less' approach, so deeply ingrained in the Indian psyche, sometimes leads to innovative surgical procedures and patient treatment.

For example, Indian doctors have developed an open heart surgery procedure where the patient remains conscious throughout. Because such 'beating heart' surgery causes little pain and does not require general anaesthesia or blood thinners, patients are back on their feet much faster than usual.

A public hospital in Mumbai that did not have enough incubators regularly advocates keeping premature babies close to mothers' chests, making skin-to-skin contact so that the baby benefits both from the mother's body heat as well as her loving touch. This ingenious method has been highly successful and is being replicated elsewhere in the country.

Some Indian healthcare providers have also experimented with innovative tiered pricing models. For example, Aravind, the world's biggest eye hospital chain, employs a tiered pricing structure that charges wealthier patients more (for example, for fancier meals or air-conditioned rooms), letting the hospital cross-subsidize free care for the poorest.

One of the other key issues we need to address in India is the shortage of doctors. Not surprisingly, it is often difficult to persuade young doctors to set up operations in a relatively remote village—or even in the villages that they originally came from. So in India, some medical colleges require students to sign a 'mission bond' that commits newly qualified doctors to spend two years in a rural area. In practice, however, this is not strictly adhered to.

The shortage of qualified doctors, particularly in rural areas, raises the possibility of introducing different grades of medical providers. For example, perhaps you do not need a qualified doctor at each and every remote centre: trained nurses or health workers equipped with modern technology could provide effective healthcare on a local basis at a much lower cost. Vaccinations, anti-malaria pills and other basic medicine could be dispensed by somebody who is trained for that specific task. Assuming there are wired/wireless broadband links in place, the knowledge and skills of the local healthcare provider, nurse or social worker can be updated on a regular basis.

The same telecommunication links can be used to provide preventive healthcare, for example, giving lectures to the community on the use of clean water and better sanitation facilities.

Of course this type of model requires acceptance at a political level and probably needs to be rolled out in bite-sized chunks because the average Indian politician like politicians elsewhere has a planning horizon till the next election. As a result, huge long-term projects are often difficult for politicians to take on.

These types of projects also need to be 'sold' to the pharmacological industry and equipment manufacturers who could actually make money from these projects. They should be given an opportunity to contribute because in the long term they would benefit immensely. If more medicines are distributed at a rural level, then clearly the companies that are selling the medications are going to benefit. Similarly, telecom companies will ultimately benefit because the communication links needed to support this kind of initiative will generate more traffic and new revenue from an expanding range of services.

There is also a need to encourage private–public partnerships like Arogyashri to address the problems of delivering quality healthcare to rural India and to scale up the possible solutions quickly and effectively.

Interestingly, we are not talking about huge levels of investment. The technology needed to support rural medical centres is not cutting-edge technology, in fact it has often been around for a number of years. For example, we do not need the latest and most expensive microprocessors and arguably you do not even need broadband for all this. Most of the data that would need to be transmitted could be carried on a wireless GSM link or even a copper wire. Broadband and high-speed data connections are only required if you are looking at video, high-resolution images or a lot of data being moved around—and that data is generally moved around within developed areas and not in rural areas.

An example of how technology can address the shortage of doctors and increase access to good healthcare is WebHealthCentre.com, a healthcare portal offering online medical consultation and comprehensive healthcare information, a site that is designed, developed and maintained by TCS. Free online consultation for the various specialities on this site is provided by independent consultants and over three hundred leading doctors attached to premier hospitals. Comprehensive information on various health-related topics has been provided by noted medical professionals. It is perhaps the first multi-institutional online consultation of its kind in India designed to benefit the public at large. The portal has several unique facilities like 'clinic online' where doctors can set up a consultation service on the Internet. Patients can send details of their condition, scans, reports etc. to their consulting doctor. This data is filed away in the patient's name and can be referred to prior to any future consultation. For patients, it gives the security of having accessibility to their doctor, no matter which corner of the world they are in. E-health tools track health parameters; the doctor can have access to specific patient parameters over a period of time. Online laboratory reports allow doctors and patients to view lab reports online. This would prove invaluable in case of a medical emergency. This has been a successful experiment and must be scaled up and replicated to achieve significant impact.

For the Tata Group as a whole and TCS in particular, our healthcare effort has a special significance—it is not just a chance to showcase modern technology but to reduce the suffering of our countrymen, not just to celebrate technical advances in IT but to heal and care for people. We feel privileged to have been given this opportunity.

When I reflect back on all the cutting-edge work that TCS has done in such initiatives which touch the lives of millions of poor Indians in truly remarkable ways, it brings me the greatest of satisfaction.

Poverty and health are interconnected and making good medical services available to all is something we owe to the people and children of this nation. When it comes to dedicated child care facilities, even our most modern cities can be found lacking. For example, the city of Mumbai has only one dedicated paediatric hospital; all other major hospitals have a few paediatric beds or a small separate ward for paediatrics. The 1,000-plus trained paediatricians/surgeons in the city are greatly constrained due to the lack of facilities.

So when I was approached by the Society for Rehabilitation of Crippled Children (SRCC) with a proposal to help raise funds to build Asia's first Tertiary Care Referral Centre for the child and help pioneer healthcare facilities exclusively for children, I immediately took it up as a personal cause. The motto of the Society is: 'No child should go without treatment for want of money' and the model essentially aims to subsidize treatment of the economically weak. It's been a dream of the SRCC team and myself for the past nine years, and we are inching forward. We will reach our goal one day I am sure.

## EDUCATION AND DIGITAL INCLUSION

At the height of Indo–Pak tension post 26/11, I came across an editorial which struck me as ingenious. It said something to the effect that the best way to get back was not with bombs but with books. Pump in aid to start thousands of good schools, teach children science and mathematics and the liberal arts, ignite their minds on the path to intellectual growth, and the rest will take care of itself. That would be my approach, I remember thinking. Amongst my family, education and excelling in studies was the only goal one had to aspire to until you came of age. Intelligence commanded a high premium, hard work was regarded as a virtue and the pursuit of knowledge a life mission. I grew up with these values.

Driving around the city of Mumbai from one meeting to another, seeing young children on the street selling their wares when they should rightfully be in school, bothers me. So I was one of those who welcomed the Right to Education Act being passed as a fundamental right of every Indian in 2009. This brings education to the centrestage: people now have the right to demand access to education.

My wife Mala, who is a high school history teacher, has often shared her experiences and views on our education system with me. Her active interest in the education of the children of our domestics would reveal the struggle faced by the disadvantaged and the poor to obtain a good education. All of this has, over time, sensitized me to some of the main issues in our education system: the lack of good teachers and teacher training facilities, and the extreme shortage of resources in our villages.

At the same time, I was clearly seeing the difference that a well-thought-out training programme and exposure could make to young people within TCS. I was witness to the transformation of youngsters who were 'very raw' when they joined the system and who rose to senior posts within the company over the years. Ignite, TCS's training initiative for science graduates, had exposed me to the extent of transformation that can take place in first-generation learners with the right inputs. In fact, harnessing and managing talent had been institutionalized within TCS, where a fully synchronized system is at work unleashing between 20,000 and 50,000 software professionals each year. Our export-led focus necessitated benchmarking our work and training against the world's best; we had highly demanding customers and the very nature of our business meant that clients would reject those that did not meet the desired competency standards in their projects. Clearly, providing the right opportunity and the right training inputs was the key to nurturing talent.

Apart from TCS, most of the Indian IT companies have been equally successful and the IT industry has created a powerful ecosystem that has helped develop world-class IT professionals. The success of the IT industry has made it one of the most popular career options even in the remotest of villages, where advertisements abound for 'computer training' schools that promise the dream job. However, not everyone can become an IT professional; India needs plumbers and electricians and welders by the millions too. Our school and university system has stoked aspirations towards college degrees at the cost of vocation-led qualifications. Structural deficiencies in the vocationalization of education has left a fragmented system suffering from an image problem. There is a negative perception attached to non-managerial jobs, however skilled they may be. This mindset, coupled with a system that only reinforces the same, ultimately leads to a deficit of skilled people in response to an increasing demand in the industry. Sectors such as retail, pharmaceuticals and healthcare, energy, infrastructure and even the education sector itself, that are now on a high growth trajectory, suffer from a supply–demand imbalance. While there is no shortage of managerial talent at the top, and India can boast of world-class leadership at the helm of its top companies, it is the middle and the bottom layers where the challenge really lies.

This was often the subject of my conversation with the late Prof. C.K. Prahalad, of whom I have been a great admirer. We often discussed the so-called demographic advantage that India held and the critical need for a productive workforce. His masterful lecture on India@75, with the articulation of the need for 500 million skilled people in the workforce by 2020, has become a mission with the Indian government. Clearly our education system—in particular the vocational education system—has not kept pace with industry.

Matching people's aspirations with growing needs of the economy must be a top priority. Outside India's cities ask a villager what he wants for his children and the chances are high that he will vote for a private school education in English for his children: he sees that as a passport for his child to rise above a limiting life. A story narrated by a colleague reveals the aspirations of India's poor. Shoeshine boys, some as young as fifteen years old, are a common sight on the stations for Mumbai's crowded local trains—among the busiest in the world that ferry around the city's vast working population. When one of these boys was asked what he aspired for, pat came the reply, 'I want to be like the man opposite me'— meaning his customer. India's poor are not lacking in talent but in opportunity, and the access to quality education is the first step to empowerment.

## The education system

Globally, India has the largest population (572 million) in the under-24 year age group. The education sector's infrastructure—the largest in the world—comprises a network of about 1 million schools catering to 219 million students and 20,000 higher education institutions serving 11 million students. Public spending on education totals about $30 billion or 3.7 per cent of GDP, while private spending on education totals about $50 billion annually and is expected to grow to $115 billion by 2018. Seven per cent of the schools and 77 per cent of the higher education institutions are private.

While these figures seem impressive in scale, the reality is depressing. Only 5 per cent of India's labour force in the age group 19–24 years is estimated to have acquired formal training. Only 10 per cent of the 300 million children in India between the ages of six and sixteen will pass school and go beyond. Addressing these challenges, the nation's annual budget announced in March 2011 had a 24 per cent higher allocation for the education sector, a target of a 30 per cent gross enrolment ratio (GER) in higher education by 2020, a goal of universalizing access to secondary education and a centrally sponsored scheme of 'vocationalization of secondary education' amongst several other initiatives. But while the government has initiated big reforms in education, the scale of the challenge is too large for the government to handle alone. The participation of the private sector is essential and a public–private partnership model might be a possible solution.

While equity of access to education is an issue in rural areas, our high dropout rates stem from financial pressures on the family where the child is seen as an extra earning hand. Often the quality of education is not engaging enough to hold students back in school, a problem which is compounded by the lack of teachers. There is clearly a vast untapped potential, a potential that must be channelled productively before it becomes a social problem as we are seeing in some parts of the world.

When it comes to governance, education is an item that is on the concurrent list (both a Central and state subject) which makes it a shared responsibility between the Central government and the states. The government at the Centre works towards reinforcing the national and integrated character of education and lays down quality standards. Uniformity at the state level is desirable but not essential. So while logically the education system will greatly benefit from a unified, centrally driven solution to meet the urgency and scale demands of the country, consensus building becomes a critical element of success and often the reason for delay. Often well-conceived plans at the Central level fail due to faulty implementation at the state level; and then again a successful model in one state has limited opportunity for replication across the country or even in other states.

India currently has 480 universities and over 20,000 colleges. In the next ten years, it will need 700 new universities and 35,000 new colleges. There are 5 million teachers in this country today and already we are short of half a million teachers. All of this can be addressed over time; but if we go into a time freeze of say a decade, we will have a severe resource crunch. Transformation across such a wide canvas is a challenge and calls for breakthrough innovation, especially technological, administrative and organizational.

One cannot fix the problem with the same old set of tools. New tools will need to be thought of. These new tools can come in the form of new technologies or new ways of approaching the problem. There is a need to question traditional concepts of a classroom, a need to re-examine who can fit the bill of a 'teacher' and a need to re-examine learning contexts. When faced with a resource crunch you need to find ways to leverage what you have to the fullest. The 'one resource to one beneficiary' model has to be replaced with a one-to-many model. The solution lies in finding ways of how one good teacher could serve the needs of not just one school but all the neighbouring schools, using modern technologies like video links through the Internet. Every educational institution can run several shifts or double up after its normal hours for other purposes. Common educational content can be shared across communities through rural broadband.

Unless we think out of the box to leverage every resource to the fullest, we will never solve the problem. Technology must be a big component of the solution because it can address the three pillars of education: teachers, content and schools. A laptop can bring the school to the student, video-rich digital content can provide an immersive learning experience, and the Internet provides anytime-anywhere learning. Technology empowers students by enabling them to take greater control of their learning and skills acquisition from sources other than the teacher and textbook. Breakthrough technological solutions to address the education gap can come from the private sector; therefore their participation in this sector is critical.

Industry is the 'consumer' of education and training; it is the litmus test for education. The view of industry insiders is that education in our country has not kept pace with industry; the nation needs to play catch-up, and is only now beginning to do so. While our system is not without merit, it has been too inflexible for too long, and has become unable to cope with the demands of a vastly changed knowledge economy.

To become a developed nation by 2030, our economy needs to continue to grow at about 8 per cent per year over the next two decades. Some of this growth will come from greater foreign equity investment and our burgeoning services sector, but the real fuel for growth comes from entrepreneurial activity as we are seeing in developed economies where, according to the World Bank, 51 per cent of GDP contribution is from small and medium enterprises, which are a good measure of entrepreneurial activity. We talk of building a $70 billion IT sector in India; at a moderate estimate that will need over 8,000 new businesses. So while our country needs more entrepreneurs, organizations like TCS need more people with an entrepreneurial spirit. The ability to take risks is an important asset in the dynamic markets of today, especially in the world of IT where agility, first-mover advantage and spotting the next big thing are the mantras of success. With plenty of role models of successful Indian entrepreneurs, I believe we are beginning to break the social stigma associated with failure. I always advise students that if they truly believe in something, they should learn to take risks by observing others. Of course there will be failures, and it is important to learn from them. I remind students that success lies on the far side of failure. This risk-taking ability, an attitude towards experimentation is not something we consciously inculcate within the education and training system— on the contrary we encourage the models of safety, security and success without failure.

Collaboration is yet another value that is largely ignored in the education system in India but is the very essence of a knowledge society. Individual merit is rewarded in schools while industry needs team players and collaborative efforts. Today, companies can't just sell their products to customers any more. Instead, they have to work with their customers in a process of co-creation, where consumers have an ongoing say in the development and eventual success of the products. This phenomenon is responsible for some of the biggest products and services in recent years, such as the iPhone, Facebook and Twitter. If you think of people and their intellect as 'raw materials' that create useful products and services through processes of collaboration, idea exchange and teamwork, then you are defining the workings of a knowledge society. We live in the age of a networked learner rather than an independent learner. So the factory model of education must give way to learning ecosystems, and our education system must reflect these changes.

The increased mobility of people is changing the traditional man–woman roles, demanding new skills from both. We need to consider whether schools should promote programmes in vocational or life skills and whether colleges should have finishing schools specially designed for particular professions—for example, IIT Madras has experimented with an initiative to address the needs of the IT industry.

Learning has become a lifelong necessity. The world is in constant flux, and change is a teaser—we do not know from where it may arise next to confront us. Change is also cruel and unforgiving; it does not spare the weak. We all know of entire businesses that have become obsolete because of disruptive changes. The process of education also needs to encourage the ability to unlearn and relearn continuously. Empowering students to take ownership of their own learning is a value that will serve them well in life. In the world of work, knowledge workers seem to be adept independent and informal learners. Informal learning has no curriculum, is not planned pedagogically but originates accidentally in association with certain stimuli. This concept of informal learning is being used by TCS in the Ignite initiative. The physical environment has been designed to support informal interaction and is a part of a teaching learning strategy.

I also believe that thinking of education only in terms of teachers and a physical faculty is too limiting. The future of learning will be informal and mobile. Mobile learning happens across locations and takes advantage of learning opportunities offered by portable technologies—for instance, delivering training on smartphones and tablet PCs, or providing handheld multimedia guides for visitors to museums and galleries. Over the past ten years mobile learning has grown from a minor research interest to a set of significant projects in schools, workplaces, museums, cities and rural areas around the world.

Multidisciplinary skills are yet another requirement of industry. Situations and problems we confront today demand composite responses and solutions. Making connections between seemingly unrelated subjects is a powerful tool, especially in today's world that makes demands on people to be innovative. Students who grasp the underlying structures of diverse disciplines can use that insight to enhance the quality of their learning. I believe that this varied exposure provides the mind with the stimuli that triggers 'out of the box' or creative thinking. Our schools operate in a linear mode, where subjects compartmentalized into silos are taught with little cross-referencing of underlying principles. This becomes a serious limiting factor in developing a multidisciplinary mindset.

Educational curricula, content and teaching methodologies need to be responsive to these needs even as we address the basic issues in education. Without doubt there is need for closer communication between education, training and industry. We need forums to hear each other's voices, understand each other's concerns and participate jointly in creating solutions.

Today K-12 schools and higher education institutions are required to run as not-for-profit institutions. This, coupled with underfunding, makes a strong case for greater industry and private sector participation. Corporate India needs to look at education and skills development not just as a matter of corporate social responsibility (CSR), but a shared national responsibility.

Further, any capitalist would agree that investing in making millions literate today translates into enabling an emerging middle class tomorrow, a middle class that will consume products and services. By investing in training, corporate India can also create trained manpower for its own businesses. Indian industry faces a potentially large demand–supply gap in the skilled workforce which, if not addressed, could result in serious capacity constraints.

Among the other benefits of greater corporate involvement in education would be an enhanced quality of education and the creation of thought leadership and centres of excellence in the country. Industry could also bring greater project management experience and financial capability to the education sector and potentially operate and manage ailing institutions on a 'for profit' basis.

Technology itself could help improve effective management, improve governance, aid transparency and facilitate collaboration and communication. For example, piloting innovative public–private partnership models can utilize unused capacity in private schools and expanded use could be made of open learning and new technologies, particularly for out-of-school youth and those who want a 'second chance'.

Many companies, both Indian and international, are already taking an active interest in this sector. TCS has focused particularly on the use of IT and telecommunications to improve education and training, and on facilitating the training of the next generation of IT professionals that India, the IT services industry and TCS itself needs.

## TCS and primary education

India's education system is the largest in the world by far. But as the recent 2010 Annual Status of Education Report points out, a large proportion of schools fail to meet the norms and standards required under the Right to Education Act.

One of the fundamental reasons for India's education shortfall is that there is a dire shortage of high quality teachers. Institutions like the Azim Premji Foundation are trying to address the problem by opening teacher training colleges, but it will take time to create a sufficient number of teachers to address the hundreds of millions of students we have.

Another hurdle is that while the need is greatest in rural areas and funds have been made available, many of the better teachers do not want to teach in these areas. In addition, even though there is a lot of free educational content online, most students in rural areas are unable to access it either because the IT and telecom infrastructure required is not available, or because of an unfamiliarity with the English language and western accents.

Even when students can access online education content, most are unable to obtain timely clarification from teachers to resolve questions and doubts related to the course material. A school in Bihar has been using Skype to try and overcome this problem and enable remote 'expert' teachers in urban areas to reach rural students. But this approach cannot scale up to cover a large number of schools because the teachers are already fully engaged in their regular teaching activities and duties. Hub-and-spoke models which capitalize on a single good teacher servicing the need of neighbouring schools by having them connected through IT networks is one model that can be adopted and scaled up.

Today, several attempts are being made to improve online access to educational materials by several different agencies, both government-owned and private. Government initiatives like Gyan Darshan, Doordarshan's educational TV channel, while welcome, lack the communications infrastructure needed to support student–teacher interactivity. Similarly, efforts to provide quality educational materials through projects like Hole-in-the-Wall have limited reach because of the lack of local infrastructure or expertise. We need a lot more of such experiments, and we need the successful ones to be scaled.

## gram-MAITRA

One such effort is being made by TCS, which initiated a rural tele-education idea called gram-MAITRA (Multimedia-based Asynchronous Interactive Remote Teaching) designed to deliver high quality education to primary school students in rural and underprivileged areas.

The gram-MAITRA initiative has four main objectives: first, to engage remote expert teachers through a broadcast-based model; second, to introduce asynchronous interactivity into the process of distance education; third, to increase the reach of each expert teacher, yet retain interactivity; and fourth, to actively involve the local teachers in the process and improve their quality over time.

Gram-MAITRA combines the benefits of DTH (direct-to-home) satellite and Internet technologies to achieve a large geographic footprint and provide interactivity between students and remotely located expert teachers, all at a low cost. The hybrid DTH–Internet model was chosen mainly because the low bandwidth available over traditional fixed telephone lines and most mobile services means it is not possible to guarantee reliable, good quality video streaming over these connections. So, instead, the system uses

DTH broadcast technology to deliver multilingual video lessons and a wired/wireless telecom link to provide Internet connectivity for interactivity, in particular for student–teacher Q&A sessions. The novelty lies in synchronizing the two.

This approach has a number of key advantages over rival systems. Rather than rely on the provision of one laptop per child like some of the other initiatives, TCS's gram-MAITRA makes the far more pragmatic assumption that each classroom can be equipped with a low-cost TV and accessories. It also benefits both the expert teachers, who can be paid extra for developing coursework and hosting the interactive sessions, and the local teachers who improve their skills by taking part.

Lectures are broadcast in multiple languages and students can select their preferred language from the Students' Station. The system does not eliminate the need for local teachers, but assumes they will undertake the role of a local coordinator. This also provides an opportunity for the quality of local teachers to be continuously improved.

The broadcast courseware also includes some questions designed to ensure the active engagement of the student group and the local teacher. For interaction with the remotely located expert teacher, the system provides a lower bandwidth two-way communication channel leveraging TCS's Internet-enabled Home Infotainment Platform (HIP). The HIP is a low-cost device developed by TCS that looks like a set-top box and combines the video output from a DTH set-top box with Internet content accessed via a wired ADSL or a wireless (CDMA/GSM/3G) connection to create a seamless presentation on the TV.

The system allows local teachers to send questions back to the expert teacher on behalf of the student groups. The HIP, which also supports Indian languages, includes a Web browser, an e-mail application, videoconferencing and video chat so it can also be used for face-to-face virtual meetings between students and expert teachers. An SMS feature can be used for voting on course lectures or evaluation.

The expert teachers can answer all received questions in a batch mode so that they can group similar questions raised from different classrooms and answer them together. This asynchronous mode of interactivity makes best use of the expert teacher's time and enables them to reach a larger number of classrooms and students.

So if fully implemented, who would pay for the system and how much would it cost? States would be expected to pay for the system and based on preliminary calculations, TCS estimates the upfront equipment cost per school would be about Rs 17,500 ($375) per classroom. On this basis, a state enrolling 100,000 primary schools in the system would pay an annual subscription of about Rs 140 crore ($30 million).

Like other digital inclusion initiatives, TCS's gram-MAITRA also faces the problem of erratic or non-existent power supplies in rural areas. To address this, and to underscore our commitment to sustainability, we have proposed that the system should be powered by solar cells through a potential partnership with Tata–BP Solar.

## TCS and computer-based functional literacy

At the other end of the education spectrum, India has nearly 200 million adult illiterates who can speak their native language, but are unable to read or write. On a global scale, a little under one-third of the world's non-literate people aged fifteen and above are in India. Statistics reveal a close correlation between literacy and economic development. In fact, literacy is a foundation on which the new knowledge economy is built.

The government's National Literacy Mission (NLM), despite its pioneering work, has met with limited success and at the current literacy growth rate of 1.3 per cent per year, India would need another thirty years or more to reach a literacy rate of 90 per cent—and that is far too long.

India was in dire need of some innovative thinking to achieve a breakthrough in the literacy impasse. The challenge lay in addressing the drawbacks of traditional teaching methods. Initial studies conducted by TCS indicated that conventional teaching methods needed intensive classroom training for around nine to eighteen months to achieve results. This was something that the target population could ill afford, as most adults in India work the whole day. Conventional teaching methods would also require several million instructors. India just didn't have that many.

A TCS project team discovered that developing the capability to write was not a priority. Research showed that writing discouraged adult learners. The reasons ranged from psychological—exercising neuro-motor capabilities was an impediment—to sociological: carrying a slate and chalk to class was a social stigma. In addition, the opportunities for reading far outnumbered those for writing.

The team discovered that it would be easy for adults to develop the ability to read their native language without really knowing how to write it. The entire procedure of teaching an uneducated person to read had to be flexible and reduced to between thirty and forty-five hours, as that was all the time a working adult could afford to spare. Second, TCS would need to leverage technology to make the solution easy to use so that people could learn to read by themselves. Lastly, the solution needed to be so simple that it could be deployed quickly, anytime, anywhere. The other key finding was that that the target population needed to learn to read only around five hundred basic words to meet their daily functional needs.

To meet these requirements, the team came up with an innovative teaching method based on the theory of cognition and the laws of perception. The cognitive process is three-pronged. While reading, cognition takes place (a) directly through the recognition of graphic patterns, (b) indirectly through sound patterns and (c) inferentially through feelings and sensations. The team understood the variables in thought processing that needed to be influenced for optimum understanding, and designed learning modules that introduced and reinforced a pattern in those variables.

Using the primers for adult literacy published by the National Literacy Mission, TCS developed lessons in using 'eclectic methodology', where each new letter of the alphabet is introduced as part of a commonly-used word. A story is woven around a group of words. Pictures, drawings and exercises are used to reinforce what is learnt.

After the lessons were drafted, the presentation medium had to be chosen. Multimedia was the unanimous choice as it could be delivered through a simple computer as infotainment rather than a more traditional lesson. This approach helped minimize the students' fears about the hardware and focus instead on the content;

the TCS team found that the village puppet theatre formed a familiar and comforting metaphor, and used it as the visual theme for the curriculum.

The TCS computer-based functional literacy programme relies on cognitive capabilities of individuals to associate complex visual patterns representing words in Indian scripts with their meanings as well as their phonetic utterances. The initial programme was launched in Beeramguda in Andhra Pradesh in June 2000 and today it is available in Telugu, Tamil, Marathi, Hindi, Bengali, Kannada, Urdu, Gujarati and Swahili. Work on the Arabic and Spanish versions is under way. The programme has spread across Andhra Pradesh, Tamil Nadu, Madhya Pradesh, Maharashtra and Uttar Pradesh, and currently has about 250 active centres; more than 120,000 people have become literate through the programme. Further research includes adding material for teaching writing and arithmetic and fillers on social awareness themes. Efforts are now underway to standardize the technology and offer it to the National Literacy Mission and to agencies to tailor it to more dialects on their own. We are working on adding a number package and a writing package so that the CBFL will be able to support a full literacy programme and full compliance with the NLM primers can be achieved.

The hope for the future of the TCS adult literacy offering is that it should be possible to go well beyond the aims of the NLM, by providing instruction of the language through a local dialect, for example, providing instruction in any Indian language through any other Indian language, including English.

## A business case for education

Using technology to address issues of education has always been a part of TCS's commitment to the community. During outreach programmes with schools TCS professionals have found that schools, for lack of good advice, have invested in computers to teach computing rather than use their capabilities of multimedia to teach mathematics or biology or physics. Visits to schools have shown large computer rooms with thirty of forty computers which would have been served better by a thin client solution. Many such simple observations highlight the need for the optimal use of technology and the need to integrate it into educational processes. Businesses too face a similar challenge when IT is not an integral part of the business strategy.

With increased reform in education and a growing realization that the information and communications technology (ICT) requirements of schools are similar to any other small and medium business where the pay-as-you-use model would work well, TCS launched a solution for schools as part of its SMB business. The selling proposition followed some simple rules. Why should schools own their IT when it could be rented? Why not offer schools customized solutions that can be built as their needs grow, rather than a scaled-down version of a large solution? Viewing the school as an 'enterprise' with its own unique processes and workflows was a new approach to providing an end-to-end IT solution. Addressing all needs of the school right from administrative issues to teaching learning activities makes this a complete solution.

TCS's vision for the education sector is to improve the efficiency of the campus along with enabling collaborative learning in a networked ecosystem. Early successes of this solution endorse the need felt by schools to transition from a tradition-centred classroom to a technology-integrated classroom and adapt to pedagogies which more readily recognize the way young people learn with new technologies.

Admittedly, this is an offering largely for urban schools at present. However, if rural educational interventions are made viable or incentivized for private players, there will be no dearth of organizations that will join the fray. Increasingly for large business houses, doing well is also about doing good. A flourishing private sector in education must be seen not as a threat but as an imperative to meet our national goals.

We must help India's millions get what is their right: the right to quality education. We must enable the light to shine on the shoeshine boy. Children may not have a voice in society—but that's all the more reason why we need to listen to them.

## THE ENVIRONMENT AND SUSTAINABILITY

IN MY FAMILY, like in most other middle-class households in India, we learnt to value and conserve what we had. Not because one could not afford more, but because of deep-rooted values, and gratitude for what we had when there were so many others who were not so privileged. Whether it was switching off a light when you left a room or eating from the same steel plate every day, it was just a part of the everyday need to not be wasteful. My upbringing could best be described as 'simple living'. My family is representative of a larger India; by and large Indians are frugal and industrious— it is part of our culture.

India's ancient culture has been associated with compassion and respect for nature. The cultural landscape of India is one that celebrates nature. Festivals such as Deepavali (the festival of lights) and Janmashtami (marking the birth of Lord Krishna) were celebrated with great reverence at my home and hold pleasant memories for me. Our festivals are mostly timed by phases of the moon or the onset of the harvest season, and suchlike. We have our 'holy' rivers and our ancient 'slokas' (verses) include prayers to the sun, without which there would be no life on earth. Ours is a 'living culture' interwoven into the fabric of life. We have also found a way to weave our culture and traditions into our increasingly modern lives. We feel a oneness with nature and with other living things that we share this planet with; the proverbial cow on the street is representative of that harmony.

India and China are amongst the four ancient civilizations of the world, Mesopotamia and Egypt being the other two. Of these civilizations, only India and China have managed to preserve their 5,000-year-old cultures. In fact, not only have we preserved our culture, but we have even exported some of it to the rest of the world. Amongst our exports to the world is the legacy of our ancient wisdom in the form of yoga and ayurveda. This richness that we inherited could eventually rise to become the currency for our progress, provided we learn to find a delicate balance between tradition and modern life.

We need to find a similar delicate balance when it comes to our environment. There is a vast repository of traditional knowledge in areas such as agricultural practices, seasonal foods and water conservation, and we must find a way to integrate these into modern practices of growth and development. With our economy growing at 8.5 per cent and with the growing needs of over 1 billion Indians, our limited resources of land, water and energy are being greatly strained. Rising dependence on energy, the world over, is driving high-carbon economies. I believe India is uniquely positioned to make the right choices about the path it wishes to take to become a developed economy. Will it follow the carbon-intensive model of the West, or will it carve its own path, the more difficult path of sustainable development?

We are well on our way to becoming the biggest consumers of everything from oil to consumer goods. To fuel this need, huge investments are being made to build transport, energy and industrial infrastructure, to build millions of new homes, and educational and health infrastructure. At this stage, we are best placed to take corrective action for a low-carbon growth model, or, in other words, an economy that has a minimal output of greenhouse gas.

In fact India is already experiencing the adverse effects of climate change. These include the rapid melting of the Himalayan glaciers which feed key rivers of the nation, increased storm activity in the Bay of Bengal resulting in five 'supercyclones' in the last few years, and plummeting agricultural yields due to erratic monsoon rainfall. Warmer temperatures have also increased mosquito and other pest populations in areas where they had never existed before. This has caused outbreaks of vector-borne diseases such as malaria and dengue, as well as an increase in the populations of insects which destroy crops.

Climate change has become an issue of global significance only recently. It drew my attention a little less than a decade ago, as a result of the increasing mentions in global conferences as well as through my interactions with global leaders and TCS customers. It was a concern that leaders had begun to voice. As chair of BASIS (Business Action to Support the Information Society, created by the International Chamber of Commerce and a number of its member companies in 2006 to serve as the voice of global business in the dialogue that has recently emerged on how information and communication technologies can better serve as engines of economic growth and social development) I had the opportunity to participate in forums such as the Organization for Economic Cooperation and Development (OECD), the E-business, Information Technologies and Telecommunication Commission (EBITT) and the Commision on Science and Technology for Development (CSTD) conferences. The rumblings of climate change as a global issue were beginning to be felt at such forums as well. It was obviously building up towards the Copenhagen Climate Conference of 2009.

Climate change and sustainability were of particular interest to me. One lesson we had learnt well in the IT industry was living with a 'resource constraint'. Any crisis almost always results in transformational changes. It forces you to think differently as you adapt to the new situation, and it makes you innovate. The climate change crisis is dramatic and has an air of finality to it, for it threatens our very existence. Our trained eye saw this growing situation as a potential game changing opportunity for IT players like TCS.

Internally, we had already been thinking about mitigation of the environmental impact caused by the growth in IT. We were already looking at solutions to reduce the power consumption of IT equipment, e-cycling, and environmentally friendly buildings. We had put in action some initial energy-saving measures. Many of our facilities had in place sensor-based lighting that senses the level of activity in a room and turn on/off. We rolled out applications to hibernate desktops upon thirty minutes of inactivity. We tried an innovative building design that catered for cooling efficiency and natural lighting. Our security staff was trained to patrol offices at non-working hours to switch off any unwanted lights that were left on. Enterprise-wide campaigns by Maitree, our employee engagement initiative, sensitized employees on green practices that they should adopt as part of their everyday work life, from conserving paper and water to car pooling. In these ways we had been proactively embracing and implementing 'green' measures internally.

However, if we wished to make a big difference we had to look at making the data centres—the nerve centres of our business— energy efficient. Data centres are facilities used to house computer systems and associated components such as telecommunications and storage systems, and these are energy guzzlers. Data centres currently account for nearly 2 per cent of the world's emissions, and are growing at 6 per cent a year. Within a few years, it is estimated that data centres around the world will consume more power than the countries of France, Germany, Canada and Brazil combined. We had to address the challenge of energy-efficient data centres. Towards this, TCS Innovation Laboratories developed new software tools that enabled data centre administrators to monitor the power consumption as well as the thermal conditions in the data centre in real time and use this information to identify inefficiencies in power usage. These inefficiencies can be in the IT equipment itself, for example in idle or underutilized servers, or in the cooling infrastructure. Our tools use computational fluid dynamics (CFD) based modelling to understand the heat distribution in a data centre and prescribe appropriate cooling measures. Through virtualization and consolidation, we were able to release over 170 servers from data centres and they are being used for other purposes, thus avoiding the purchase of new servers. Avoiding new procurement is important considering the emissions associated with the process of manufacturing the equipment. These efforts at data centres have resulted in 79 per cent power savings.

An example of 'green' innovation leadership of the Tata Group is evident in EKA, one of Asia's fastest supercomputers. It has a unique design feature. Normally rows of computer racks have alternating hot and cold aisles; the cold air seeps through perforations in the floor, cooling the blades and coming out as hot air through the hot aisles. In the case of EKA, the racks are arranged in a circle with another concentric circle arrangement for coolers which blow cool air directly onto the blades and into the centre. The resultant hot air is sucked out from the ceiling. This way the cooling is far more efficient, uses less power and the winning point is that the whole setup can fit into a 4000 sq. ft area—a simple but ingenious solution.

TCS Innovation Laboratories is currently developing IT frameworks and tools that help facility managers reduce the carbon footprint ( total set of greenhouse gas (GHG) emissions) of buildings. Our tools offer insights over and beyond what the meters and building management systems provide. Using heat gain models, they are able to benchmark the operational efficiency of buildings very accurately and prescribe 'optimal energy purchase plans' that allow a facility manager to procure cost-effective carbon-free energy for a building. Using these tools ourselves, we were able to reduce the energy bills of our data centres and campus facilities by more than 20 per cent and reduce the company's carbon footprint by 5 per cent. Eleven TCS centres have installed solar water heaters with a total installed capacity of 21,500 litres per day. All new owned facilities have this feature integral to their design. We are also evaluating the possibility of using solar energy for cooking and have installed a 35 KW solar photovoltaic unit at our Bhubaneswar facility at Kalinga Park.

We deliberately brand our facilities using the word 'park', since we believe it symbolizes our commitment to making each of our facilities as green and eco-friendly as possible. Yantra Park in Mumbai can boast of being one of our most environment-friendly facilities with features such as vermicomposting and rainwater harvesting and biogas which helps run the kitchens that service 3,500 employees.

Banyan Park, another TCS facility, is an oasis of green in the middle of Mumbai's concrete jungle. Forty-two bird and fifty-one butterfly species are known to visit and breed at Banyan Park. It is home to Mumbai's largest bat colony and provides a vital ecological service to a vast area of approximately 2,800 sq. km every night. When TCS acquired the site, the challenge was to walk the thin line between conservation and development of the new TCS campus. Based on the biodiversity report, the plans for development of the property were revised three times and the planned capacity was scaled down from 6,000 to 2,000 employees in order to preserve the environment and to maintain adequate open spaces and create a state-of-the-art IT campus in a nature park-like environment. I was deeply involved in this project. When TCS bought this property in 2002 which belonged earlier to Rallis India, another Tata company, the premises housed some beautiful heritage buildings in art deco style. We hired an architect who specialized in heritage restoration not only to restore the old buildings but also to build the new facilities in sync with the existing style. So fond was I of this facility that I often invited people over for breakfast in the elegant verandas that overlook the lush green lawns; often I have even hosted TCS events here to draw people to the facility.

Another facility that I am particularly proud of is at Siruseri in Chennai. Spread over 70 acres, our biggest software development facility is designed to accommodate 25,000 employees. We specially commissioned Carlos Ott, a renowned architect from Latin America, to create a mini city-like facility at Siruseri. I have always been choosy about the architect for our new facilities. I believe that bringing globally renowned architects to India not only helps build world-class facilities but also helps the local Indian architects that work with them to get exposure in best practices. A trait that I learnt from my mentors was the importance of a global mindset and a desire for being world class in everything we do—this is something I feel very strongly about. That is perhaps why we were one of India's first companies to report on our carbon footprint and participate in the carbon disclosure project. In 2008 TCS was one of only two Indian companies that were included in the Dow Jones World Sustainability Index. Our sustainability report has been rated as A+ by the Global Reporting Initiative (GRI), the highest possible rating.

When it came to adopting 'green' practices, we used both a top-down approach—through corporate level policies—and a bottom-up approach, of raising awareness of our employees, to address reductions in carbon footprint. There have been clear targets set and a conscious move towards them. I even remember throwing a challenge to the team to become carbon neutral by 2020. Over the period 2007–08 to 2009–10, the per capita carbon footprint has reduced by about 33 per cent and stands at about 3.25 tonnes of $CO_2$ equivalent per full time employee (FTE), while carbon intensity (measured as the carbon emissions per unit of revenue) stands at 14.62 tonnes of $CO_2$ equivalent for every Rs. 10 million of gross revenue, representing a decline of about 16 per cent during this period. There are very clear targets for 2011 from the previous year, with a 2 per cent decrease in per capita electricity consumption, a 2 per cent increase in green power consumption and a reduction of per capita carbon footprint by 5 per cent.

Having gained considerable experience in becoming 'green' ourselves, we were also struck by the challenge of how we can use IT to mitigate the environmental impact of other industrial, logistical and business processes. Technological solutions for telepresence/telecommuting, GIS for environmental studies, engineering design of industrial processes with computational models for energy efficiency and waste reduction are ways in which IT can help mitigate the problem.

Our own experience of going green, combined with my growing conviction that 'IT for Green' would be the next frontier, led to the acquisition of a company called Nature First. It was a niche company with considerable expertise in conservation which promoted the thought that ecology and economy are two sides of the same coin, a value that we believed in as well. We embraced the view that by focusing on the ecological parameters of land, energy, water, waste, air and carbon (LEWWAC), energy-intensive manufacturing companies can benefit by increasing energy, water and waste efficiencies in their processes.

With this acquisition TCS felt it had enough in house experience and expertise to help other organizations go green. In 2009 we launched a new vertical called Eco Sustainability Services. This new business offering already has a few customers in India as well as overseas and will go a long way in creating eco-corporations for a sustainable future. It is estimated that IT has the potential to reduce carbon emissions by 15 per cent by 2020, which could translate into an economic benefit of $600 billion for those using IT towards low-carbon transition.

'Green IT' or the greening of businesses has the potential to reduce 98 per cent of emissions by improving the efficiency of the core processes of a company including how it deals with its suppliers (the supply chain) and its customers (distribution). An example of a TCS process change is the move to encourage videoconferencing as against having people travel for meetings. The impact of such a move is evident from a recent event where 400 delegates participated through videoconferencing from thirty locations spread across India, the US, Europe and Asia Pacific. Using this technology, TCS saved roughly $50,000 in travel-related costs and about $75,000 overall from just this one event. To enable more such instances, TCS has over 200 videoconferencing units spread across seventy-five offices in thirty cities.

'IT for Green' on the other hand is the use of technology to enable products and services to serve the needs of environment and sustainability businesses. For example, to help protect biodiversity, TCS has developed a GIS-based forest management system called GeoVun ('vun' means forest). GIS and satellite imagery can be effectively used to monitor, protect and enhance forest cover. Intelligent systems such as wind forecasting, sun-tracking and smart grids ensure that existing renewable technologies are being used at the optimal and most efficient levels.

I believe that TCS as one of the world's top ten IT services players is playing a leadership role in the area of sustainability. Far-sighted business leaders in India who have global ambitions are recognizing that transition to a low-carbon model makes immense business sense in the long term. In fact in the region, Indian companies are way ahead in disclosing their carbon emissions and setting performance targets for mitigation of greenhouse gas emissions. Forty-four Indian companies responded to the Carbon Disclosure Project in 2010.

New technologies have helped us learn more sophisticated ways of making steel or aluminium or electricity, but they have also depleted natural resources, forests, oil reserves, clean air and water at a faster rate. We are already using 30 per cent more resources than the earth can replenish each year. These limited resources will need to meet the needs of 9 billion global citizens by 2050. Today the responsibility of technology is to reverse this trend. We still need sophisticated ways of making steel or aluminium, but we will need to look at greener fuels rather than a traditional coal-based plant; we will need to examine every business process and consciously examine ways to make it less carbon-intensive. Sustainable agriculture is yet another aspect worth following actively. Traditional methods of farming that use large amounts of water, fertilizers and seeds are being replaced by a more sustainable strategy of diversified cropping patterns. If scaled up, this strategy could significantly lower greenhouse gas emissions from agriculture.

Clearly economy and ecology are becoming converging issues. The climate change challenge is affecting policy-making bodies of governments and driving large corporations to go 'green'. As the movement snowballs, it will eventually envelop smaller businesses and citizens as a whole.

When the Japanese government introduced its 'top runner' programme which aims to raise fuel efficiency standards for automobiles and energy conservation standards for electronic appliances, Japanese automakers made significant progress on hybrid technology and companies like Toyota and Honda took leadership in the hybrid vehicles space. As is evident, governments can be a key enabler in creating a regulatory environment that pushes the desired behaviour.

As a responsible nation India has agreed to cut carbon intensity (the amount of carbon by weight emitted per unit of energy consumed) by between 20 and 25 per cent from the 2005 levels by 2020. India's National Action Plan on climate change and energy security identifies eight missions for focused policy interventions: solar energy, energy efficiency, sustainable habitat, water, Himalayan ecosystems, sustainable agriculture, strategic knowledge for climate change and a 'green' India. Each of the missions are to move ahead in public, private and people partnerships which aim to bring the Central and state governments, businesses, civil society and community organizations to work together. Translating this into action on the ground will be our toughest challenge in the years to come.

To give these plans teeth, the government would have to establish legislation aligned with the policies and plans. It would need to reward adopters of climate change strategies while severely penalizing those who do not comply. This is the kind of challenge that will result in leapfrogging technologies, indigenous research and creative solutions. Indigenous and creative technologies are the critical elements here because in India cost and local adaptiveness of technologies are important for mass adoption.

What I find most exciting is the opportunity for innovation. I am convinced that the need for green technologies will be the driving force for future innovation. Scientists and technologists have a new responsibility in today's changed world. New inventions will be judged by how eco-friendly they are; people will need to develop new skills and capabilities for a greener world. Maybe we will need to borrow from our ancient wisdom and customs and blend them with our new world advances in science and information technology as we strive to look for solutions to these problems. The TCS research team at TRDDC did exactly this decades ago when it developed a water filter made of rice husk ash which is known to have water purifying properties—a precursor of the Tata Swach.

At a national level innovation centres for building technological capabilities to combat climate change and mainstreaming climate-friendly technologies before 2020 to make them actionable in the next few years are being undertaken. With a focus on solar energy and the goal of the National Solar Mission to target 20,000 MW of power by 2022, many of our world-renowned educational institutions such as the IITs are working on photovoltaic cells and solar thermal systems to be integrated in a microgrid. IIT Bombay has tied up with Applied Materials on new energy-related initiatives including the fabrication of next-generation solar cells. India's first integrated bioenergy centre has been set up at IIT Kharagpur; its focus is to advance the use of renewable energy in rural India.

Solar technology is currently prohibitively expensive. But having said that, there are examples of villages being lit by solar energy, using LEDs to provide up to forty hours of light on a single solar charge. This was made possible as a result of a partnership between NGOs in India and the US. Most importantly it is an affordable device, something of great significance to the rural poor. Should the cost of solar power fall to the level of coal-fired power, market forces could help solar energy expand to reach a larger scale. There is absolutely no doubt in my mind that IT will be a key enabler in this transformation, and TCS would like to be at the forefront of this opportunity.

To accelerate the embracing of greener measures by both government and industry, there is a need to change the evaluation model we use currently. Our economic valuation model has always been productivity-driven. This business-as-usual approach, if followed, will eventually damage economic growth through ecological depletion; hence the threat is as much economic as it is ecological.

The global debate on the role of developing versus developed nations in taking responsibility for future carbon reductions is a tricky one. In India, one of the key challenges in tackling climate change is the limited financial support available from the developed nations to support sustainable development and the need for 'climate justice'—the balance between emissions and the vulnerability of the developing world to climate change.

Industrialized countries, which account for 20 per cent of the world's population and contribute 70 to 80 per cent of current emissions, need to take responsibility and commit to greenhouse gas emission reduction targets. I believe that there needs to be compensatory mechanisms including funding and technology transfer from developed nations to help developing nations with their mitigation and adaptation strategies. It has been estimated that such mitigation and adaptation strategies could cost between $20,000 billion and $100,000 billion by 2030.

I believe that we should build economic sustainability by driving ecological competitiveness through the six forces: land, energy, waste, water, air and carbon. Corporations should be measured over and above their financial performance, on ecological quantitative parameters related to land and biodiversity management, energy security, water neutrality, waste management, air quality and carbon neutrality. Companies should contribute to the ecological betterment of the industry and community and finally, they should strive for new technologies within their field that optimize resource allocations and low-carbon options.

The alternatives to the current unsustainable growth path we are on will emerge out of disruptive thinking, disruptive technologies, disruptive models, and above all, disruptive action. This disruption is the sustainable innovation agenda for business.

Green valuation will be a catalyst to drive this paradigm shift. Ecological parameters must become part of the standard valuation-and-reward model. That in turn means that countries and companies can drive their valuations much higher if they are ecologically neutral or positive, but that valuations will be negatively impacted if neutrality is not maintained. Economies like Norway, the Maldives, Germany, Costa Rica and Guyana are already leading the way and the European Union is taking leadership in this and defining a quantifiable ecological framework for its member countries.

TCS itself has begun adopting the 'green valuation' model. Meanwhile we have underscored our commitment to sustainable business by creating the world's most energy-efficient data centres. TCS already has three Leadership in Energy and Environmental Design (LEED) certified facilities across India.

As an IT engineer, one is trained to constantly keep an eye and ear open to applications of technology in new emerging areas. TCS's thinking has been conditioned to challenge ourselves to look for ways to do things faster, at lesser costs and in sustainable ways. This works like a self-imposed 'efficiency driver'. TCS's brand tagline and driving spirit of 'Experience Certainty' helps reinforce this behaviour further. It ensure that our values, strategy, behaviour and implementation are all in sync. For us in IT, we have learned to be proactive. Action on the ground has never waited for government policies; it has happened in spite of the government— the policies have invariably followed. Leadership in sustainability can be achieved by implementing action on the ground and not waiting on policy; we should do it because it is our collective responsibility.

An an ancient Indian proverb says: 'We do not inherit the earth from our ancestors; we borrow it from our children.' While our proverbs may be ancient, they are just as relevant today as they were before. We must indeed return what we have borrowed, and we must return it in a better state than it was.

# EPILOGUE

I WOKE UP on 6 October 2009 with a sense of great excitement. It was my sixty-fifth birthday and the day of my so-called retirement from the position of CEO and MD of Tata Consultancy Services. It was also my first day in my new life, a new beginning.

I had decided several months ago that on 6 October I would officially vacate my office and welcome Chandra into it. My staff had ensured that we had cleared the premises of all our belongings the evening before, leaving only the official papers for the next CEO's staff. It was neat, clean and precisely planned.

At 10 a.m., I reached TCS House and walked up to my second-floor office. I took in a sweeping view of the paintings on the office wall, the now empty desk and the view of Azad Maidan (a public park) and the large gulmohar tree whose branches almost touched the glass windows. It was a beautiful office where I had spent some great moments—and now it was to have a new resident.

It was here that we gathered that day, the entire corporate team of TCS including Chandra, Maha, Jayant and Phiroz. There were speeches to be made, cakes to be cut and photographs to be taken. I spoke briefly about TCS, Chandra as the new CEO and the future looking bright. Chandra made what can be technically called his first speech as CEO. I was quite matter-of-fact throughout the brief ceremony, not letting emotions run high; if they did we all tried not to show it.

By 12 noon my office members and I left for Banyan Park where we had decided to have a temporary office until my office at Bombay House, the Tata headquarters, was ready. I had several meetings planned for the day and that's how I wanted my new life to begin.

As I drove to Banyan Park in the suburbs of Mumbai, I found my thirty-seven-year-long journey at TCS flashing before my eyes. Looking back I was proud of the institution we had all built together, the people who inspired me, who supported me from the time I started as a programmer in TCS to the time I reached its highest echelons as CEO and MD.

I felt fortunate to have witnessed and been a part of the great transformation of the global and Indian IT industry with TCS playing an important role in it. I had seen technologies come and then fade away, losing the battle to the next wave. I had been a part of the globalization that has swept our world. I had seen new markets emerge. I had witnessed young people join TCS and rise to become leaders in their own right, some starting their own companies which are doing well today.

The early frustrations seemed such a long, long time ago, when we were struggling at TCS wondering what were the technologies to embrace, the deep introspection on whether we should move away from IBM 1401s and ICL 1903s and leapfrog to next-generation computing.

Between 1972 and 1974, when the future was still hazy, with the challenges of dealing with government processes, export restrictions and the difficulties in getting foreign exchange, the odds seemed against us. I remember thinking for a moment whether I had made the right decision to come back to India, whether I would live to regret my decision to have left a good job at NCR in the US and also the promise of a green card.

As it happened, 1974 was a turning point, when it was decided that TCS would take on the latest generation Burroughs computers imported to India. But our optimism was shortlived for in 1978 Tata Burroughs was formed and again TCS's very existence was in question.

I recalled those trying times when TCS finally decided to go on its own, retain its own identity without being tied to any hardware provider—and my dilemma of whether to shift to Tata Burroughs or stay back with TCS. Again I decided on staying back without worrying about the future. We were by then too high on our passion of creating something of value and this drove the opportunity for TCS and for myself as an individual.

I realized at that moment of reflection that I had never in my life opted for the safer, well-trodden path. All my decisions were fraught with risk. Sometimes the choice was not my own, like in 1979 when I was sent to set up the US office as its first Resident Manager. When I asked Kohli, my mentor and well-wisher, why he chose me, it was most reassuring to hear him say that it was because he trusted me and had confidence in me. Our US presence was a turning point that created a TCS beach head for the future. The hard work of the next two decades and the journey of excellence that we pursued finally brought me in 1996 to the position of CEO.

I remembered wearing the CEO's mantle with some trepidation, for it meant that now I was the last person on the decision-making pyramid. I remember the 'lonely at the top' feeling, the sinking feeling. But at that very moment of self-doubt, I realized that this was an opportunity to choose a different model of empowerment and create leaders in large numbers for TCS.

Things were happening so fast then that I really had very little time for myself or the family and soon enough we were ready for the IPO in 2004—a great moment for TCS and for me, since I was at the centre of it all. If I was busy before, I became even busier now. I became the public face of TCS even though I was wary of facing the media; with time I became increasingly comfortable with journalists. And finally I had come to this day in October 2009 when I felt I was leaving a great business behind.

That day, I felt confident that I handed over the baton to a team that was right for TCS; the organization had its head and heart in the right place. Governance had never been stronger, the commitment to society and the activities around it were well embedded into the organizational DNA, TCS possessed enormous depth as far as technology capability was concerned, and there was a hunger for innovation that drove R&D capabilities.

I was very keen that the transition to Chandra as CEO should be as smooth as possible. I had been grooming the second line of TCS's leadership for several years, but once I had made firm my recommendation on my successor, I was completely confident that he was the right person for TCS's future.

I wanted the organization and the next-in-line leadership to align with Chandra. I knew he was different from me and that people would take a bit of time to adjust to the new CEO, and I felt I must do everything to smoothen the way for him. In my interactions with the leadership team towards the last few months of my tenure as CEO and MD, I made it clear that I backed Chandra and his decisions fully.

I looked out of the car window—I had almost reached my Banyan Park office. The drive to the suburbs had been a whole life's flashback for me. I felt a sense of relief; it felt good to be where I was now. I stepped out of the car into the new life that awaited me.

I was looking forward to having more time to focus on things I care about most—health and wellness projects especially for children, education and training, mentoring young professionals, sustainability and climate change issues and so on. I was starting life all over again, starting on something new just like I had done as a young man in 1972. That was the year I had got married as well. I recalled my wife Mala's constant joking about TCS being my first wife. Today as I started my second life the same thoughts came back to me—but this time around, I promised to give more time to the family.

I felt life had come full circle for me. I had a team around me that felt passionately about the issues I cared about. I felt we could begin recreating once again, recreate something new, touching many more people's lives on a larger scale, not restricting ourselves to a single organization but on a larger canvas.

Whether it is in the sector of education, health or climate change, the scale of the problem is huge. I draw strength from the TCS experience that taught me to think deep, tackle complexity by breaking it into manageable components, build prototypes, learn and refine and then scale. My thoughts are consumed by how we must influence the youth to create the next generation of professionals who must think of problems very differently from our approach forty years or even ten years ago. That is the future and that is what is exciting about building the future. The timeframes are compressed now—you don't have to wait for forty years for change because there is a model, an experience, a learning that can definitely be applied. TCS cleared the forest, created a path for others to tread on. TCS's story is meant to be an inspiration. That's why it needed to be told. In recounting it, if in a small way I can influence the thinking of people, that would mean the most to me.

Today there is a larger vision that consumes me. I have chosen to be in public service—being invited by the prime minister to be his Adviser on Skill Development was an offer I could not refuse. This endeavour is hugely exciting and challenging at the same time. Even after a career spanning forty years, I still feel the same level of excitement about what I do—contributing to the creation of a demographic dividend by skilling millions of Indian youth.

Each morning I get up wanting to make a difference, wanting to influence something, wanting to try out something, wanting to interact with different people on different aspects, challenge myself and challenge the people I work with.

'*A CEO should be judged not just by what he built but more importantly by what he leaves behind for his successor to build upon*'

–S. Ramadorai

# APPENDIX I

## IN THEIR EYES

I AM A strong believer in sharing my experiences with my colleagues and helping them in their professional growth. However rather than advising people I prefer to spend time with them informally—at their own homes with their families or at my home, or even while driving from one meeting to another—which helps people unwind. Here are some experiences they have had with me that they remember . . .

### N. Chandrasekaran, who succeeded me as CEO, TCS

My earliest interaction with Ram was when I handled a complex assignment for a financial trust services corporation in the US during 1993. When I completed this successfully, Ram and Mr Kohli were invited to the US to receive the best project award by the client. During that meeting the client spoke about me and that registered in Ram's mind.

Ram then assigned me to another complex project in the UK for a company that later became one of TCS's largest clients. In September 1996 Ram had just taken over as CEO of TCS. I happened to be in Mumbai during a client visit. During a break in the meeting Ram said in his typical soft-spoken manner, 'I want you to work in my office.'

When one is with Ram one has to be extremely attentive; a mere nod or a word, or the lack of one can have deep meaning. The importance of this was not lost on me. I told him that I was willing and would confirm after discussing with my wife Lalitha who was back in the UK at the time. After winding up my project responsibilities, I came back to India in January 1997 and reported to Ram in his office.

Ram provided me with every opportunity to grow emotionally and professionally. After my assignment in his office, I was asked to take over the operations at SEEPZ which serviced some our most important clients. This was a big jump for me and I did not want to disappoint Ram. In addition to running the SEEPZ operations, I was also responsible for getting new business. I continued to be in close touch with Ram and he provided me with a lot of latitude and guidance which allowed me to grow and learn. I used to discuss every major initiative with Ram through a routine of daily phone calls which we continued even when one of us was travelling. That way we were both always continuously updated with all key developments across the company even as we expanded manifold.

As TCS neared the end of the 'Y2K decade' Ram and I discussed the need to realign TCS to participate in the growing market for package solution implementations. In those days TCS's strength was in custom developing bespoke applications for every client requirement. Ram and I discussed this and felt that we needed to develop strategic alliances with product vendors of ERP, the supply chain, and solutions like CRM. The idea was to use these solutions and build applications around them, and thus was born the concept of eBusiness for TCS. Here too I had complete support from Ram and soon this became a business worth half a billion dollars. This proved to be a watershed for TCS—not only did we successfully shrug off the tag of being a Y2K vendor, but it also gave us the confidence to start various new service lines and grow them into substantial businesses.

## S. Mahalingam, CFO, TCS

Ram is one of the most intense persons you will come across. He focuses on the issues in hand, sets his own target and relentlessly pursues it. When he went to the US as Resident Manager in 1979, he had to create completely new contacts and try to get work on non-Burroughs systems as well. I have seen first-hand how he developed contacts at American Express, Producers Cotton (a company in Fresno, California) etc. and converted them to major assignments. Subsequently I have seen this again as we developed major relationships at GE and other companies. He not only created new business contacts, but also introduced them to other TCS managers, thus making them a TCS contact rather than a personal one.

Ram is technologically up to date and hands-on. He bought an Apple IIe for personal use in 1980 (this was before the PC era) and figured out the hardware and software capabilities for himself, as a technical person would.

Ram transformed TCS from a centrally controlled organization to a decentralized organization. He went about it in a methodical manner. He changed the organizational culture to a participative one, engaging Prof. Ghemawat in 2000 to weld together a leadership team which would debate strategies and competitive positioning and work towards improving efficiency. If TCS has great leadership bandwidth now, it is these programmes that we have to thank for it.

Ram is a fighter. When TCS became a publicly listed company, the perception was that it was not an aggressive company. Ram not only fought in the marketplace, but also set about changing the perception with opinion-makers, financial analysts and portfolio managers, and also within the Tata Group.

Ram genuinely cares for people. There are any number of instances where he has gone the extra mile to take care of a person. He actually took my son—who was just about a year and a half old and couldn't travel unaccompanied—to Chennai on a flight with him. I didn't even have to ask him.

## Nina Screwvala, Global Head – TCS Maitree

Mr Ramadorai's approach and philosophy to mentoring has always been oriented towards achieving sustained development and impacting self-growth. This he attained, albeit in a non-structured manner, by triggering personal introspection.

As far back as I can recollect, his developmental feedback inputs, though very candid, never generated any negative or demotivating sentiments since they were always given spontaneously and with unflinching sincerity of purpose. Indeed, mistakes and errors of judgment were never seen as occasions for recriminations but instead encouraged to be perceived as learning opportunities. His silent way of making individuals be aware of and realize their potential was invariably through a combination of measures like empowerment and allocation of responsibility for diverse and challenging assignments, while at the same time providing behind-the-scenes support and ongoing reassurance through his projected conviction in one's abilities.

At the early stage of my mentee relationship with Mr Ramadorai, I functioned in the role of his personal assistant. However, at no stage did my mentor even remotely allow me to feel that my job was relatively unimportant or that it had any constraints in terms of giving innovative suggestions or constructive feedback, all of which channelized my work style towards a more progressive and proactive approach.

In the subsequent years of my association with TCS Maitree, the brain child of Mrs Mala Ramadorai, he provided the optimum blend of visionary direction, inspiration and top-level support while conferring levels of flexibility and freedom to pursue his overall direction and interact within the group and with industry counterparts, at the same time constantly keeping a latent mentoring eye open to provide guidance, directional inputs and support.

## N. Venkatram, Partner, Deloitte Haskins and Sells

I first met with Mr Ramadorai (Ram) in March 2001, and our interactions increased over time as the pressures built up on the TCS IPO. I recall being urgently summoned to Banyan Park on Saturday 6 March 2004 for a review meeting with the bankers and lawyers. In that meeting, an important decision was taken on the deadlines and deliverables for audit after a fairly stressful exchange between the merchant bankers and the auditors. Ram understood our viewpoint and supported our position on the dates, despite the pressures to hurry up on the listing process. In the middle of this difficult discussion on the IPO timelines relating to the financial statements, we also took a break to cut a cake that was wheeled in, since it was my birthday.

This captures my impression of Ram: a quiet person with a steely resolve, willing to listen to the other person's viewpoint with objectivity and understanding, and then taking the call—and personally, a person who has affection for those he values and trusts.

## Girija Pande, Chairman, TCS Asia Pacific

Ram has been a great mentor, especially to a person like me who was completely new to TCS. Having spent over two decades in banking in Asia it was with some trepidation that I accepted his offer to create an APAC business for TCS out of Singapore. I remember telling him that I had been a 'user' of technology rather than a provider. His response was: 'We have enough techies—we need some businesspeople to create this new business.' That encouraged me.

It was difficult initially but Ram was available whenever I needed him, and most of my conversations with him over the phone were around 5 a.m.! I learnt IT by talking to him or when I took him to meet customers where he would come alive with his vision for TCS and the technology industry. I am sure I made many mistakes as within a decade TCS APAC grew from a small scale of 250 associates to over 10,000 that we have now in thirteen countries, but it was always an encouraging voice at the end of the phone that kept me going. Very often Ram's underplayed style of 'invisible' mentoring was just what I needed.

Ram has been a friend, philosopher and guide to me in my TCS journey and his managerial style and vision will always guide me.

## S.D. Haridas, who retired in 2007 as Vice President, TCS

All I needed to do was to watch Ram closely to learn from his meticulous planning, the ability to brainstorm under tough situations, his calmness under pressure, his listening skills and grilling methods when objectives were not met.

In 1983–84, Ram and I were visiting a particularly difficult client on the west coast of the US. We had been providing important technical support on system software to this client, which was also a major account for TCS, accounting for almost 10 per cent of our revenue. The client's outstanding with us were mounting, even as we were repeatedly told that the 'cheque was in the mail'. While the situation was delicate, Ram was prepared to take a tough stand—even pull the plug, if needed. His strategy worked, and we were able to get some payments cleared before leaving the place after the meeting.

Ram has been a hard negotiator who remains calm, and is able to take calculated risks if needed. This was a great learning experience for me on how to negotiate in tough situations.

During Ram's quarterly visit to the US, we used to often walk the streets of New York in the late evening, sometimes in hostile weather. We would be looking up at the jungle of skyscrapers, discussing ways and means of making inroads into major corporate accounts like Chase, AT&T, IBM, Tandem, HP etc. He was relentless in the pursuit of his objectives 24x7, and I often wondered if he got much sleep during his visits. He was always eager to make cold calls, explore tie-ups with local associates to widen the net for business, and develop niche products as part of a broader strategy to get referrals. It was a great learning for me in terms of developing marketing and relationship building skills.

## Harish Menon, who worked as my Executive Assistant from 1999 to 2003

It was in the early 2000s that I worked with Ram as his Executive Assistant. He has been my mentor and guide over the years, and I have derived so much value from his mentorship. One incident that stays particularly strongly with me, gave me a glimpse into his amazing ability to stay grounded and real.

One evening we were at an official event at the Mayfair Room in Worli, Mumbai, not far from where he lived. After the event formalities were done, we moved together to the buffet dinner service. Evidently tired of the rich, predictable fare at such events, Ram whispered to me, 'Do you really want to eat this stuff?'

I guessed something was on his mind, so I asked him what it was.

'What do you say to some simple, wholesome food which I have waiting at my home?' he said.

'Sure,' I replied.

Since this important dining decision had been made, we bid a quick farewell to the event organizers and stepped outside the venue.

'I have just taken delivery of a Tata Indica,' I said to him. It was a newly-launched car from the Tata stable, and had been provided to me by the company a couple of days earlier.

'Really? Let's ride in it then, I have never taken a ride in one,' he said. So we did—my driver under some mental stress that he was unexpectedly chauffeuring TCS's CEO.

Soon we got to Ram's home, where he quickly changed into his comfortable South Indian veshti. We sat together at the kitchen table and shared a simple meal of rice, sambar, vegetables and curd, while trading old TCS stories, personal experiences and business points of view. After the meal, he took his plate over to the kitchen sink for a quick hand-rinse, and then put the rest of the dishes away. I naturally followed suit, quite amazed by this simple home ritual which, quite clearly, was a personal habit with him.

We then spent some time watching sports on the TV before I bid Ram goodbye and headed home.

I learnt later that since his wife Mala was away from the city, his cook had prepared dinner that evening and kept it for him, which he was keen not to waste. For me it was a lesson in personal humility and simplicity of approach in life, regardless of one's many achievements and professional stature. Here was the powerful head of a billion-dollar global corporation, who considered no task too humble to be undertaken by himself.

## Rajani Deshpande, wife of Kiran Deshpande, ex-TCSer

Ram used to visit our home in the US often. Soon, I got to be very comfortable with him, not as my husband's boss, but as a dear friend. During his trips, he was often over for dinner, since he preferred a home-cooked meal and a homely atmosphere to a hotel room. Whenever he stayed with us, I was struck by his simplicity and his friendly manner.

I was particularly touched when he visited Dallas the very day my first son was born in January 1987. Ram and Mr Kohli were in Dallas on that day. He dropped by at the hospital later in the day, and sat next to me, apologizing for the fact that he had to pull my husband away the day I had my baby. His attention was so touching and sincere that it took my pain away.

Ram would always get us nice gifts when he visited. We had great times whenever we were together, be it in India or in the US. I have wonderful memories of him.

## Satya Hegde, Senior Vice President and General Counsel, TCS

In early 2004, I was hired as Senior Vice President and General Counsel of TCS, and had the privilege of being a direct report of Mr Ramadorai and working closely with him over five years. From top to bottom in the organization, many people referred to him as 'Ram'—a mark of his accessibility to everyone, and his ability to simultaneously generate a sense of respect, affection and closeness. However, I have never been able to address Mr Ramadorai as Ram—for me he was 'Sir' in the first instance and 'Sir' always! I have pride in stating that whatever the legal organization—and me personally—have been able to achieve in TCS is owed entirely to the foresight, vision, statesmanship and mentoring of Mr Ramadorai and his unending energy to motivate and drive us to success.

In many organizations, the in-house legal department is not a darling, largely because of the lack of a sense of involvement by lawyers in the business objectives. When I joined TCS as its General Counsel, I asked Mr Ramadorai about my responsibilities, authority and powers in TCS. He just laughed for a while! Then he became serious and said, 'What I want is a legal department that is "involved" in the business and the success of the company. We will need a robust legal process that should protect the company and support business growth. You have to charter and define what is needed to achieve those objectives.'

After that encounter, he silently monitored several things. Suddenly, the legal department started becoming visible at all levels; processes started taking shape with responsibility and accountability defined. The demand, the drive, the guidance and unconditional support provided at a personal level by Mr Ramadorai were what shaped the definition of the role, responsibility, powers and authority of the legal organization of TCS. That is why the in-house legal department is viewed quite differently in TCS.

## Henry Monzano, CEO of Comicrom, which was acquired by TCS in 2005

I had the opportunity to work with Ram for almost five years, and I would say that in those years he mentored me to convert myself from an entrepreneur who TCS acquired a company from to a top executive with responsibility for Latin America.

Ram played a very important role in guiding me. Most importantly he taught me the TCS culture, dedication and focus on the client, and the importance of giving them a good service. I realized that if we had a better understanding of our clients' business this in the end translated into more business for TCS and increased efficiency for the client.

I will say that I learnt about the importance of making and honouring commitments, aspiring to do quality work, and having the desire to undertake challenges, from Ram. I will also always respect one of the most important values he has: honesty.

## Girish Ramachandran, Director of TCS Europe till 2009

Every time I meet Mr Ramadorai, the first thing he asks is about my wife and our little son. It is remarkable that he meets so many people every day, but still remembers and makes it a point to ask after everyone.

I still remember a few months after I had moved into Europe, I had to receive Mr Ramadorai at the airport and then drive him to his hotel. I was nervous and started sharing the agenda for the day hurriedly as soon as he had got into the car. Mr Ramadorai heard my entire narration patiently, after which he told me to focus on the most important meetings and inform him what should be accomplished during his visit to the country. He coached me to focus on a few important things, and this left an indelible mark on me.

He is one person who I have found can have a conversation about anything in the world. He reads through all the newspapers he can get his hands on and encourages everyone to take up interests other than work, such as music, travel, movies etc. I still remember the speech he gave when he got his professorship at Nyenrode University, one of the best speeches I have ever heard. He spoke so eloquently that the audience was spellbound and amazed at his extent of knowledge about the globalized world.

I was fortunate to be with Mr Ramadorai the day his name was announced for the Padma Bhushan. We were in Germany that day, opening our new office in Frankfurt and celebrating by enjoying a folk performance from Kerala. It had been snowing continuously and we were in a fix, because we had to reach Davos early next morning. I worked out alternate options of getting there, but Mr Ramadorai had his own plans. He told me immediately after the performance ended that we would take a car and drive up to Davos. Such was the determination of this person that we drove through the snow and reached Davos by 3 a.m.

When we purchased TCS's Banyan Park premises, I was invited to see the campus along with Mr Ramadorai and Chandra on a Sunday morning. There was a large administration team waiting to receive us and show us around the campus. As we were walking through the campus, Mr Ramadorai spotted some trash on the road and, true to his nature, picked it up himself and threw it in the dustbin. What more can I say?

## Ravi Viswanathan, Head of TCS's Global Telecom Business Unit

My first real meeting with Mr Ramadorai was in 1993 when I was selected to do a study for a GE Lighting company in Gujarat. Over the weekend my colleague Rahul and I worked hard on the presentation and, having had it reviewed by Maha, took the late evening flight to Mumbai. The next morning, we met Mr Ramadorai at 8 a.m. at his office on the eleventh floor of Air-India building. He was warm but we felt a bit uneasy in the environment. His desk had a lot of papers, magazines and files heaped on it. Anyway, we produced the entire deck of about eighty slides and walked him through the slides one by one. Even as he was listening to us he was busy clearing some files. At one point I paused so that he could finish what he was doing. He looked up and asked me to carry on.

After we had presented four or five more slides, he finished his file work and suddenly looked at us and said that he was not comfortable with the message in the previous chart as it was not in sync with what we were saying in an earlier slide. I was amazed at the fact that he had not only been listening to us, but was assimilating what we were saying even as he was multitasking. I was amazed at the sharpness and clarity with which he guided us through the presentation. The next morning Rahul and I left for Gujarat awestruck by Ram's ability to quickly abstract the scope of the project and our response.

I did not really have an opportunity to work for Mr Ramadorai as I went to Europe in 1994. In 1996 I happened to be in Mumbai when the announcement of his taking over as the CEO of TCS made the news. I asked for an appointment with Melanie—then Mr Ramadorai's secretary—and she said that I had to wait as there was a long line of people (naturally). My turn came at 7 p.m. and I gave him an overview of the operations in my territory. I told him about the key customers, the revenue, the projects in the pipeline and the opportunities in the area and also requested him to visit Scandinavia. He was warm, asked a lot of questions and wished me luck. He also asked me if there were anything that he needed to know, to which I said no.

At that time there was a very troublesome project with a bank in Scandinavia and they were threatening to take legal action. Although I was sure that we had done no wrong and that the bank was intimidating us, I chose not to mention this to Mr Ramadorai as I didn't want him to have a bad impression of me or the region on day one.

At about 8.30 p.m. I came back to the eleventh floor to pick up my tickets from the travel desk; as I was going towards the lift, Mr Ramadorai was walking towards the lift too and he looked at me and smiled. He then said, 'Why are you not giving me the bad news about the region?' I was surprised that he knew about it and the thirty-second ride in the lift to the ground floor took forever as he asked details about what went wrong in the engagement. As he waited for his car, he said 'Ravi, never let the bad news come from any other channel than you.'

This was an invaluable lesson in leadership for me, something I uphold even today. I also advise people saying the same thing: Let the good news come from any other channel but the 'not so good' news has to come from within and not externally.

During my last days in Scandinavia, Mr Ramadorai would call me almost every day without fail to follow up on this tricky engagement which was getting ugly with the board member writing to the CEO. Sometimes he would call at 9 p.m. India time and then again at 9 am. India time to ask about the situation and if we were addressing it effectively. I used to get worked up while this was happening, but I realized later that one had to be on top of the tough situation all the time. He was not only well informed but also guided us through the whole negotiation process.

In Mumbai when I was working in his office along with Ananth, Mr Ramadorai called us for a meeting one day at 8 p.m. just as he was leaving for home. Ananth and I were working on his inputs for the executive committee meeting later that week. While we discussed the meeting, he also asked me to follow up on a burning issue in Delhi, review a large customer engagement in Chennai with respect to staffing and billing and also look at staffing a critical engagement in Bangalore by following up with the Regional Manager.

Ananth and I worked till 2 a.m. on the presentation slides and met Mr Ramadorai at his house; we were going to drive with him in the car while discussing the slides. After going through the slides, as the car reached Haji Ali, he turned to me and asked me about the Delhi situation and if I had reviewed the program. He also asked me if I had spoken to the Bangalore Regional Manager on staffing and how many we had staffed last night, and then about the Chennai program. These were days when cellphones were not as popular as they are today and it was almost impossible to reach anyone after they left work. I told him that I was going to be in Delhi the next day and in Chennai on Friday and would send him a report over the weekend. He said that he needed the report immediately and chided me for wanting to do everything by myself. Then he said something that I have not forgotten to this day: 'A leader's ability is judged by how he get things done.' This is a lesson that has stayed with me ever since—getting things done is the key dimension which differentiates leaders.

In one of the business review meetings during one of the bad quarters, the review just did not go well and I was incredibly sapped of all motivation and felt a little low on self-confidence. I had a dinner meeting with colleagues and was just out of sorts, which was showing. Midway through the dinner Mr Ramadorai called and spoke about the review and asked what had gone wrong during the quarter, and I explained. He was in Germany on that day and said, 'Let us learn from what happened—let us look forward. I have a lot of confidence in you.' The short call that he made got my blood pumping again. It was almost as if he had sensed sitting in Germany that my morale was down and that he needed to talk to me and give me a pep talk.

In spite of his busy schedules I was amazed at how Mr Ramadorai would find time to come to Chennai to attend Mala's concerts. He is at once a corporate achiever of the highest order and the true family man—something I have not been able to get to balance in my own life. To say that the last fifteen years in TCS transformed me is an understatement. I benefited immensely and am thankful to Mr Ramadorai for having taken me under his wing at a crucial time in my career.

## Anita Rajan, who joined TCS as my Executive Assistant in 2002 and continues to work with me

I joined TCS with some trepidation in 2002; it was a big career move, vastly different from what I was doing earlier in Research and Training, and meant working directly with the CEO. When things had been worked out, Mr Ramadorai asked me how I felt about joining TCS and I honesty answered: 'A bit nervous.' He promptly put me at ease by saying that it's always good to be a little nervous before something important, as that brings out the best in a person. When I asked him about a brief on my role he said he wanted me to be a 'change agent'. I thought deeply about this and realized that what he was really saying was, 'I want you to do things differently and bring a fresh perspective.' It was a very empowering thought; it conveyed an implicit sense of trust and was a big motivator to make a difference.

Working with Mr Ramadorai I realized that what you leave unsaid can be even more powerful than what is explicitly said. He uses silence very effectively. In office, my morning papers will often include articles marked by Mr Ramadorai as 'interesting read'; often I feel guilty that it should really be the other way round! He has a voracious appetite for new ideas, new perspectives, new theories and new technology developments; this innate curiosity to know more also makes him a great listener with people. What is admirable is that he loves to share this learning with others by mailing or marking good articles and suggesting good books for others to read, thus helping his colleagues expand their own horizons.

He will shoot ten different things at you at the same time, all of which need attention—and will expect nothing short of excellence. It pushes you to raise the bar and figure out how to get things done in the most efficient way. What makes you take up the challenge is the fact that he leads by example—he will never ask for something that he would not have done himself.

In the nine years I have worked with him, one of the first people to wish me on my birthday are Mr Ramadorai and Mala; no matter where he is in the world, he will call. That says a lot about him: he values relationships and invests in them, be it with a customer or a colleague. He is a standing example of the mantra: 'Successful businesses are built by investing in relationships with the people behind them.'

# APPENDIX II

## MILESTONES

1965  Creation of the Tata Computer Centre which is set up in Nirmal building at Nariman Point, Bombay

1965  TCS starts data centre operations with rented IBM 1401 computers in Nirmal building

1968  TCS incorporated as a separate entity (Shops and Establishment Act certificate)

1969  F.C. Kohli joins TCS as General Manager

1969  ICL 1903 computer purchased and installed in Nirmal building

1971  TCS's first overseas programming assignment (in Iran)

1972  S. Ramadorai joins TCS

1973  Foreign Exchange Regulation Act (FERA) passed by the Indian government

1974  F.C. Kohli takes over as Director in Charge of TCS after P.M. Agarwala's premature demise

1974  S. Ramadorai put in charge of computer maintenance and support

1974    TCS imports the first Burroughs machine (the B1728) into India

1974    TCS signs agreement with Burroughs to provide software expertise and market Burroughs computers in India

1974    TCS does its first software export project out of India for Burroughs

1975    Nationwide Emergency imposed by Indira Gandhi's government

1976    TCS imports its first large mainframe computer, the Burroughs B6748, for software exports

1976    Burroughs Hardware Centre of Excellence created in Bombay

1976    TCS goes beyond programming and begins hardware installation, support and maintenance work for sophisticated Burroughs range of computers for Indian customers

1977    Emergency lifted; Indira Gandhi's Congress government voted out of power

1977    TCS opens an office in the UK

1977    F.C. Kohli is made Director of Tata Industries

1978    Tata Burroughs Limited incorporated and TCS decides to go on its own

1979    First non-Burroughs contract in the US with American Express

1979    First TCS office in the US, S. Ramadorai made first Resident Manager in the US to build TCS footprint

1979    TCS signs an important contract with IGIC, New York

1979    First contract in the US with American Express

1980    Congress government headed by Indira Gandhi is voted back to power

1981    TCS awarded WTSL banking system project

1981    TCS imports its first IBM mainframe (370/158) at SEEPZ, Bombay to set up an ODC for the WTSL project

1981    TCS's R&D centre TRDDC set up in Pune

1981    TCS wins first software export award from the Government of India

1984    Indira Gandhi assassinated; her son Rajiv Gandhi becomes prime minister

1985    TCS sets up an office in Switzerland

1986    Tandem Hardware Centre of Excellence created in Bombay

1987    IBM Hardware Centre of Excellence created in Madras

1988    TCS sets up an IBM centre in Madras with a 3090/150E large mainframe

1989    TCS is awarded the SEGA contract in Switzerland on a turnkey basis

1991    Economic liberalization initiated in India by Prime Minister P.V. Narasimha Rao and Finance Minister Manmohan Singh

1991    TCS crosses the Rs 100 crore turnover mark with 3,000 employees

1992    DEC Hardware Centre of Excellence created in Calcutta

1992    Formal launch of the Software Quality Group in TCS

1992    TCS sets up an office in Japan

1993    TCS obtains ISO 9000 certification

1993    TCS wins the National Stock Exchange contract

1994    F.C. Kohli is appointed Director of Tata Sons, becomes Deputy Chairman of TCS

1994    IEEE documentation standards adopted at TCS

1995    Nani Palkhivala retires as Chairman, TCS; Ratan Tata takes over

1995    HP Hardware Centre of Excellence created in Mumbai

1995    TCS sets up a GE delivery centre at SEEPZ, Mumbai

1995    TCS sets up Nortel Switch at Borivali near Mumbai to do software projects for Bell Northern

1996    Dematerialization of paper in India; TCS awarded NSDL project, completes it in record time

1996    First CMM assessment from SEI for TCS Chennai at Level 5

1996    First engine-related design project for GE Aircraft Engines

1996    First software factory in Chennai for Y2K remediation

1996    S. Ramadorai becomes CEO of TCS

1997    First Global Development Centre set up at Sholinganallur in Chennai

1998    TCS revenues cross Rs 1,000 crore

1998    A world-class campus designed by Frank Glyn set up at Sholinganallur

1998    NDA government led by BJP comes to power; Atal Bihari Vajpayee becomes prime minister

2001    TCS acquires CMC, a government-owned hardware and software company

2001    A world-class campus designed by Mario Botta set up at Noida

2001    TCS sets up operations in Hungary

2002    S. Ramadorai wins CNBC Asia Pacific's Asian Business Leader of the Year Award

2002    Launch of Maitree, TCS's employee engagement initiative

2002    TCS opens an office in Latin America

2002   TCS sets up its China operations

2003   TCS revenues cross $1 billion

2003   TCS implements a single global digital platform, Ultimatix

2003   A world-class campus designed by Mario Botta set up at Hyderabad

2004   TCS receives the JRD QV Award

2004   For the first time, all TCS centres are assessed at CMMi and PCMM Level 5, making TCS the first organization in the world to achieve this

2004   Integrated Quality Management Standards (iQMS) are published as reverse knowledge transfer to SEI

2004   UPA government headed by the Congress comes to power; Manmohan Singh becomes prime minister

2004   TCS goes public: the TCS IPO is the largest till then in India, raising more than $1 billion and incorporating 1.1 million shareholders

2004   S. Ramadorai is appointed CEO and MD of Tata Consultancy Services Ltd

2004   TCS signs the National Health Service, UK contract

2004   S. Ramadorai wins the *Business India* Businessman of the Year Award

2005   TCS acquires Comicrom, a Chile-based banking BPO organization

2005   TCS acquires the services arm of Pearl, a pension funds management company in the UK designated as Diligenta

2005   TCS acquires FNS in Australia, a banking product company enlarged to TCS Bancs today

2005   Tata Infotech Ltd (the erstwhile Tata Burroughs) is merged with TCS

2006    CTO organization set up to drive innovation and R&D

2006    ISO 2000 certification for TCS

2006    Connectivity and distributed digitized framework for the entire Enterprise Management set up to bring in efficiencies in internal IT and communications infrastructure

2006    Brand launch of the 'Experience Certainty' campaign

2006    Launch of Ignite

2006    Padma Bhushan conferred on S. Ramadorai

2007    The number of TCS employees crosses 100,000

2007    TCS House, TCS's new headquarters in Mumbai, inaugurated formally

2008    TCS acquires eServe, back-office operations of Citi

2008    TCS realizes its vision of becoming a Top Ten global player on multiple parameters

2008    TCS revenues cross $5 billion and profits cross $1 billion

2008    A world-class campus designed by Carlos Ott and Carlos Ponce de Leon set up at Siruseri in Chennai

2008    TCS opens its largest North American facility in Cincinnati, Ohio, employing over 1,000 locals

2009    TCS revenues cross $6 billion with 144,000 employees

2009    S. Ramadorai is awarded the CBE

2009    S. Ramadorai retires as CEO and MD of TCS and is appointed Vice Chairman, TCS

2009    N. Chandrasekaran becomes the new TCS CEO

# INDEX

d'une série de seaux en plastique, quelques objets métalliques (un bac à glace, un moule à gâteau) faisant office de cymbales. Le rythme était insistant, joyeux. Je ne pus m'empêcher de penser qu'il était plus éloquent et plus honnête que tout ce que Lowery venait de nous dire – plus proche de la vraie pulsation de la ville.

Et inévitablement, Kelly et moi nous éloignâmes en marchant à ce rythme.

— Qu'est-ce que vous concluez de tout cela, Ben Truman ?

— Des conneries.

— Exactement. Vous êtes mon prix d'excellence. C'était des conneries pure sucre. Maintenant pourquoi Lowery ne tient-il pas à ce que nous fourrions notre nez dans l'affaire Trudell ?

— Parce qu'il a un secret à garder.

— Je dirais que c'est une très bonne théorie. Peut-être est-il temps que nous rendions une nouvelle visite à Julio Vega. Il en sait plus qu'il ne nous en a confié.

Nous l'ignorions, mais il était déjà trop tard. Julio Vega était mort.

## 48.

Vega se balançait dans la cuisine de sa minuscule maison au bout d'une rallonge électrique enroulée autour d'un lustre. Un nœud coulant derrière l'oreille lui maintenait la tête baissée. Devant, la rallonge se perdait dans les plis gras de son cou. La chaise sur laquelle il avait grimpé gisait sur le flanc.

Kelly posa le dos de sa main contre celle de Vega. Ce léger contact fit tourner un peu le corps avant qu'il ne s'immobilise de nouveau sous le nœud coulant.

— Froid, dit-il.

Kelly avertit qui de droit. La criminelle de Boston et une équipe de la police d'État ne tarderaient pas à débarquer. Même les suicides sont considérés comme des « morts non naturelles » et doivent être instruits.

La mort de Julio Vega n'aurait pu être plus naturelle, pourtant. C'était la conclusion logique d'une décennie de honte, de récriminations et d'exil. C'était le seul moyen pour Vega de rembourser sa dette. C'était également son seul moyen d'échapper à une révision de l'affaire Trudell. Une nouvelle salve de questions pour expliquer la dernière victime en date : comment la descente dans la planque à la porte rouge aurait-elle pu mener dix ans plus tard à la mort de Bob Danziger ? L'état même du cadavre de Vega soulignait ce que son suicide avait de naturel. Rien des restes criblés de balles et gonflés de gaz de Danziger et de Ratleff, non, il avait l'air de dormir. Sa tête penchée, son menton sur son omoplate, ses paupières entrouvertes, ses doigts recourbés, même son nombril dénudé par son sweat-

shirt, chaque détail suggérait l'humanité du cadavre de Vega. Quoi que la police pût en dire, c'était tout sauf une mort non naturelle. La mort avait naturalisé Julio Vega.

Mais les cadavres doivent être examinés comme des saucisses et les spécialistes arrivèrent : flics en uniforme, inspecteurs, photographes, techniciens médico-légaux. Un fourgon noir du bureau du légiste attendait d'emporter le cadavre. Des flics qui avaient connu Vega se déplacèrent aussi, dont Martin Gittens.

— Je savais que cela finirait par arriver, soupira-t-il. C'est cruel ce qu'ils ont fait à Julio.

Gittens souffrait manifestement. Au milieu des années 1980, Vega et Trudell avaient été ses protégés. Il les avait alimentés en renseignements, leur avait apporté sa crédibilité dans la rue, les avait aidés à faire leur trou. Longtemps Gittens resta à l'écart, silencieux. Je faillis m'approcher de lui avant de me raviser. Mes rapports avec lui étaient déjà assez fragiles comme ça.

Kelly prit un des inspecteurs à part pour lui demander ce qu'ils pensaient.

— C'est un suicide. Nous nous contentons de mettre les points sur les *i*.

Et, pendant ce temps, le corps continuait à se balancer au bout de sa rallonge. Il n'était pas question de le détacher tant qu'on ne l'aurait pas photographié, tâche retardée par le fait que les services techniques ne savaient pas où donner de la tête ce matin-là.

Une fois l'activité autour du corps un peu calmée, Kelly et moi nous plantâmes en dessous. Je m'efforçai de suivre le regard de Kelly pour voir ce qui le fascinait autant. De près, Vega me rappelait un parachutiste coincé dans un arbre.

— Regardez les marques de ligature, Ben Truman.

Deux zébrures entaillaient le cou là où la rallonge s'était enfoncée dans la chair. La plus grande des deux allait d'une oreille à l'autre, au-dessus de la pomme d'Adam. La rallonge était incrustée dans cette zébrure et, au-dessus, on voyait une tache de lividité, la rougeur du sang coincé par la pression de la corde. Au-dessus de cette zébrure, on en distinguait une seconde, plus petite. La rallonge avait en fait entaillé la peau à plusieurs endroits et le sang avait perlé et séché sur sa longueur.

On notait également une lividité autour de cette seconde zébrure, moins distincte.

Je lâchai un grognement incertain.

Kelly me toisa avec une expression désapprobatrice.

— Vous remarquez quelque chose d'inhabituel ?

Il semblait agacé d'être obligé de souligner quelque chose d'aussi évident, comme s'il s'adressait à un enfant obtus.

— Je ne sais pas. C'est mon premier pendu.

— Eh bien, moi, non. Et je n'ai jamais vu personne se pendre deux fois.

Nous attendîmes dans l'atmosphère anémique de la maison que l'on décroche Vega et qu'on l'allonge sur un brancard. On le fourra dans le sac avec la rallonge électrique encore nouée autour de son cou tel un foulard. Elle lui rentrait trop dans la chair pour qu'on puisse la retirer sans abîmer la peau.

Caroline arriva. Elle me tendit une feuille rose de message téléphonique avec un numéro mais pas de nom.

— Pourquoi n'as-tu pas noté le nom ? Je ne connais pas ce numéro.

— Parce que c'est celui de Max Beck.

# 49.

Les colverts du jardin public ne tenaient pas en place. De la petite île au milieu de l'étang où ils étaient rassemblés s'élevait une vraie cacophonie. Les mâles notamment avec leur cou vert chatoyant semblaient à cran. Ils se fonçaient dessus, en braillant et en battant l'eau de leurs ailes.

Max Beck les observait. Assis sur un banc sous un saule pleureur, il mordait distraitement dans un sandwich. Il avait coincé l'emballage en papier sous une cuisse pour l'empêcher de s'envoler. Il paraissait s'être débarrassé de son personnage de Défenseur des méprisés, avec sa rectitude et sa combativité frimeuses, pour le poser tel un manteau sur le banc à côté de lui. Là, près de la mare aux canards, il devenait ordinaire – un fonctionnaire approchant la cinquantaine, obèse, avec des boucles poivre et sel battant au vent.

— Maître Beck ?

Il sursauta.

— Oui ? Oh, chef Truman, merci d'être venu. (Il se leva d'un bond et me fit une place à côté de lui.) Asseyez-vous. Vous voulez un sandwich ? Je vous en ai pris un au thon.

Je saisis le sandwich et le fis tourner dans ma main.

— Ça va. Cela ne va pas vous transformer en avocat de la défense.

Je m'assis.

— Vous déjeunez souvent ici ?

— Non. Généralement je ne déjeune pas. On dirait que je n'ai jamais le temps. Ou je suis au tribunal ou je m'y rends. De

toute façon il faut que je me surveille. (Il se tapota le ventre.) J'ai choisi cet endroit parce que je pensais que nous y serions plus tranquilles.

Les canards se remirent à brailler.

— Quelque chose les tracasse, dit Beck.

— Il commence à faire froid. Ils ont hâte de partir.

Je déballai mon sandwich et nous mangeâmes tous les deux en silence. Une étiquette délicate s'applique aux rendez-vous à l'heure du déjeuner. Elle requiert des interruptions de conversation pour mâcher et elle impose d'éviter d'interroger quelqu'un qui vient juste de fourrer une bouchée de sandwich au thon dans sa bouche. De sorte que Max Beck et moi – une drôle de paire qui ne savait pas trop comment s'aborder – nous contentâmes de nous sustenter pendant un moment.

— Quelqu'un sait que vous êtes ici, chef Truman ?

— Non. Au téléphone, vous avez dit que c'était confidentiel. En outre, ce n'est pas vraiment un truc dont j'irais me vanter auprès de mes copains flics.

— Vos copains flics m'ont classé dans les méchants.

— Ils pensent que vous êtes un adorateur du diable.

Beck sourit. Passer pour un adorateur du diable ne paraissait pas le troubler.

— Alors, merci d'être venu. Nous ferons vite, avant qu'on ne vous voie. Généralement je fais appel à un procureur pour organiser ça. Mon client veut se livrer.

— Qu'il se livre.

— C'est là qu'on en vient au point inhabituel. Il veut se livrer à vous.

— À moi ? Pourquoi moi ?

— Il vous fait confiance.

— Il ne devrait pas. Votre client vous a-t-il dit qu'il s'est introduit dans ma chambre la nuit dernière avec un de ses gros bras et qu'il m'a collé un flingue contre la tempe ?

Beck secoua la tête.

— Je ne suis peut-être pas le meilleur flic pour Harold aujourd'hui.

— Je vois. Mais vous n'avez pas porté plainte, n'est-ce pas ?

Je ne répondis pas.

— Harold dit que vous l'avez aidé à récupérer sa fille.

— Ce n'était rien.

— C'était important pour lui. Chef Truman, la police de Boston remue ciel et terre pour retrouver mon client. Il ne faut pas qu'ils réussissent. Vous comprenez ça ?

— Je crois qu'il faut qu'ils le retrouvent. Il y a un mandat contre lui.

— Certes. Ce que je voulais dire, c'est qu'il ne faut pas que Harold soit placé sous leur responsabilité, qu'il disparaisse dans une cellule quelque part ou se retrouve dans une impasse obscure avec à ses trousses un groupe de flics blancs armés. Ce n'est pas une question de légalité.

La généralisation me hérissa. Moi aussi j'étais un flic blanc armé.

— C'est vous qui parlez ou votre client ?

— Mon client et moi parlons d'une même voix.

— Ah. C'est l'aspect adoration du diable.

Beck fronça les sourcils. Il rompit un bout de pain, le jeta par terre, et les canards se ruèrent dessus.

— Mon client m'a prié de vous faire une proposition. Il dit être disposé à se rendre à cause du mandat mais à deux conditions seulement : il ne se livrera qu'à vous et seulement à la condition qu'on l'emmène immédiatement dans le Maine pour y être jugé. Un procès ne lui fait pas peur. Mais il ne veut pas que Boston le garde à vue, ni pour une journée, ni pour une heure. Comme il est très déterminé, il faudrait que cela se passe ainsi.

— Sinon ?

— Sinon, la police de Boston peut continuer à le chercher et quand elle le trouvera, Harold ne se rendra pas. Il y aura de la casse.

— Harold, probablement.

— Oui. Harold, probablement. Cela vous rassure, chef Truman ?

— Bien sûr que non. Vous êtes toujours aussi cynique à propos des flics ?

— Certains, oui.

— Eh bien vous ne me connaissez pas. Je ne mérite pas cette réflexion.

— Non, vous avez raison. Excusez-moi. Mon client a le sentiment d'être en danger avec certains éléments de la police de Boston, c'est tout ce que je voulais dire. Attendez que je vous montre quelque chose.

Beck posa son sandwich et s'essuya les mains sur ses cuisses. Il tira de sa serviette une lettre sur papier à en-tête du procureur général, de trois ou quatre pages, à interligne simple. Le mot CONFIDENTIEL en barrait le sommet. On lisait sur la ligne de l'objet : *Accord entre l'État et Harold Ellison Braxton.*

— Passez au verso, suggéra Beck.

Trois procureurs avaient signé la lettre, le ministre de la Justice, le procureur général Andrew Lowery et le substitut Robert M. Danziger.

— Harold m'a demandé de vous montrer ça. Vous savez ce que c'est, chef Truman ? C'est une lettre de coopération. Signée par Bob Danziger. Saviez-vous que Harold travaillait avec Danziger ?

— Non.

— Vous ne trouvez pas étrange que Harold aille assassiner un procureur qui vient juste de lui offrir l'immunité ? Regardez ça. (Il ouvrit la lettre à la deuxième page :) « *Faire jouer l'immunité* pour le témoignage de Harold en ce qui concerne les événements du 16-17 août, la nuit où Artie Trudell a été tué. » Vous savez ce que cela signifie ?

— Oui, cela signifie qu'ils ne peuvent utiliser contre lui tout ce qu'il leur révèle, à moins que l'État ne puisse démontrer qu'ils disposaient d'une source indépendante pour le renseignement. Ils peuvent toujours l'inculper de meurtre, mais ils ne peuvent pas se servir de ses propres paroles pour ce faire.

Je parcourus la lettre qui ne précisait pas le crime sur lequel Bob Danziger enquêtait. Mais c'était évident.

— Mon Dieu, Danziger a retourné Braxton. Il s'en servait pour rouvrir l'affaire Trudell.

— Oui. Et je vais vous dire ce que signifie aussi cette lettre. Elle signifie que Bob Danziger ne pensait pas que Harold ait tué Artie Trudell. On n'accorde pas l'immunité à un tueur de flic, même une immunité aussi limitée que celle-ci.

— Je ne comprends pas. Si Harold n'a pas tué Artie Trudell, que pourrait-il connaître de l'affaire ?

— Chef Truman, Harold entretient des rapports très complexes avec la police. Il n'a rien du monstre qu'ils veulent en faire. Il a aidé de nombreux inspecteurs, dont votre ami Martin Gittens.

— Braxton a joué les indics pour Gittens ?

— Joue. Braxton joue les indics pour Gittens.

— Je ne le crois pas.

— Demandez à Gittens. Ils fréquentent les Flats depuis longtemps tous les deux, en coexistant plutôt bien. Je ne dis pas qu'ils sont amis. C'est une relation d'affaires : un échange de valeurs. Gittens obtient des renseignements, Harold obtient (il chercha le mot) de la marge de manœuvre.

— De la marge de manœuvre. Cela veut dire que Gittens l'a protégé. Je n'y crois pas.

— Pas protégé. Il aide juste Harold à ne pas s'attirer d'ennuis. Si une descente est prévue, Gittens lui filera le tuyau, c'est tout. Ce n'est pas si inhabituel. Espionnage et contre-espionnage.

Beck dut remarquer que tout cela me démontait parce qu'il se tut pour me laisser le temps de digérer. En attendant, il lança des bouts de pain par terre. En prenant soin de les jeter à la portée d'un petit chardonneret avant que les énormes colverts ne viennent le chasser.

— Comprenez ce que je vous dis, chef Truman. Martin Gittens est un bon flic. Il fait ce qu'il a à faire. Il prend l'information là où il la trouve. Il travaille sur des affaires de stupéfiants, et les seuls à détenir des renseignements sur le commerce de la drogue en font partie. (Il haussa les épaules.) En fait, je l'aime bien pour un flic.

— Gittens a-t-il protégé Braxton dans l'affaire Trudell ?

— Il l'a averti de la descente, oui. Voilà pourquoi Harold n'était pas là. Mais après cela, Gittens a joué franc jeu. Quand il a pensé que Harold était le tireur, il l'a pourchassé avec plus de hargne que quiconque. C'est Gittens qui a trouvé l'arme du crime, rappelez-vous.

— Avec les empreintes de Braxton dessus.

— Ces empreintes ont été plantées.

— Oh, allons !

— Écoutez, on peut relever des empreintes. Il suffit d'un bout de Scotch et d'un peu de savoir-faire. Nous avions un technicien médico-légal prêt à témoigner que ces empreintes y avaient été placées, probablement par un flic s'efforçant d'étayer une affaire fragile.

— Alors Braxton était Raul ?

Autre haussement d'épaules théâtral.

— Qui sait.

— Bon, pourquoi Danziger avait-il besoin de Braxton ? De quoi allait-il témoigner ?

— Juste que Gittens lui avait filé le tuyau pour la descente. C'est tout ce qu'il sait. (Beck m'enveloppa d'un regard presque sincère.) Chef Truman, Harold n'a pas tué Bob Danziger. Je ne dis pas que c'est un ange, mais il n'est pas coupable de ça.

— Comment puis-je en être sûr ?

— Parce que Danziger le savait. Danziger savait que Harold n'avait pas tué Trudell. C'est la raison pour laquelle il lui a accordé l'immunité. Découvrez ce que Danziger avait entre les mains, ce qu'il savait.

— L'ennui, c'est que je ne peux plus lui demander, hein ?

— Il devait tenir quelque chose, une preuve, un témoin, quelque chose. Mon client vous fait confiance. Il veut que vous lui fassiez confiance aussi. Il ne vous demande pas d'être son ami, d'approuver tout ce qu'il fait, juste de lui faire confiance. Permettez-lui de se livrer.

Je jetai le reste de mon sandwich aux canards qui se précipitèrent dessus.

— D'accord, comment on procède ?

— Nous choisissons un endroit en dehors de la ville, en dehors de la juridiction de la police de Boston. Harold se livrera volontairement à vous. De là vous l'emmènerez directement dans le Maine pour qu'il y soit jugé.

— À sa place, je ne tiendrais pas tant que ça à un procès.

— Chef Truman, à sa place, à l'heure qu'il est, le procès serait le cadet de vos soucis.

# 50.

Battery Point est une langue de terre qui avance dans le port de Boston au sud-est de Mission Flats. Elle n'abrite qu'un petit parc qui permet surtout aux voitures de faire demi-tour. Une plaque explique que jadis on y avait posté des canons anglais pour garder le sud de la ville. Un muret entoure le poste d'observation ; derrière, la terre se transforme rapidement en marécages. Si vous franchissiez ce muret, vous vous retrouveriez dans l'eau jusqu'à la taille. Quelques pas de plus et vous seriez submergé. Le terrain est inconstructible et trop éloigné du centre de la ville pour donner envie à des promoteurs de le combler, comme ils l'ont fait à Back Bay. C'est ainsi qu'il a pratiquement été préservé dans son état d'origine. En fait, si on ignore les intrusions modernes – les avions décollant de Logan, un champ de réservoirs d'essence, les ordures dans l'herbe – on a une idée de l'aspect de l'endroit à l'époque où les premiers Anglais ont débarqué. Luxuriant et fertile ; rocheux, glacial et terrifiant aussi. Une Nouvelle-Angleterre adaptée à la vision puritaine enthousiaste d'une communauté sans péché, une théocratie chrétienne intégriste, une anti-Amérique. Un nouveau monde. Ils doivent être passés à côté de ces marécages. Si vous vous étiez tenu à cet endroit quatre cents ans plus tôt, vous les auriez vus, ces proto-Américains en quête d'un meilleur accostage.

Gittens me fit poireauter un bon moment. Lorsqu'il arriva enfin, nous grimpâmes sur le muret pour contempler la ligne de

gratte-ciel de la ville au nord. Le vent venant du port gonflait nos vestes. Je croisai les bras pour me protéger du froid.

— Quel endroit ! dit-il.

— J'ai pensé que nous ferions mieux de discuter en privé.

— Oh ?

— J'ai des renseignements à propos de l'affaire Trudell.

— Bon Dieu, vous êtes encore là-dessus ?

— Martin, cela ne vous préoccupe pas que tous ceux ayant un lien avec l'affaire soient morts ? D'abord Trudell, puis Danziger et maintenant Vega.

— Vega ? Il s'est suicidé.

— Non. Il y avait deux séries de traces de ligature et on ne peut pas se pendre deux fois. Vega a été assassiné. Quelqu'un s'est organisé pour que cela passe pour un suicide. Vega a dû se débattre, il a dû s'échapper la première fois, si bien que l'assassin a été obligé de recommencer.

— Vous vous prenez pour Nancy Drew ? (Gittens était agacé.) Vous compliquez trop les choses. Oubliez Vega, oubliez Trudell. Braxton a descendu Danziger parce que Danziger était un procureur. Vous pigez pas ça ?

— Et Trudell ?

— Quoi, Trudell ?

— Qui l'a tué ?

— Ben, c'était peut-être le second tueur planqué sur le tertre, comme à Dallas.

— Je suis sérieux, Martin.

— D'accord. Braxton l'a tué. C'est ce que vous voulez entendre ?

— Impossible.

— Impossible ? Pourquoi ? Parce que Braxton est un chic type ?

— Non. Parce qu'il n'était pas là. Braxton était au courant pour la descente. Vous l'aviez averti.

Pendant un instant le seul bruit fut le murmure du vent dans mes oreilles.

— C'est une belle connerie et ne vous avisez pas de le répéter à quelqu'un. On se moque de vous, Ben. Je n'ai pas averti Braxton. Qui vous a dit ça ?

— Danziger. C'était dans son dossier, et il y a pire. Danziger

356

avait accordé l'immunité à Braxton. Il s'apprêtait à le faire témoigner à ce sujet ; à convoquer un grand jury.

— Faux.

— Vrai. Voici la lettre de coopération. Au minimum, cela explique pourquoi Braxton se trouvait dans le Maine. Il n'était pas là pour tuer Danziger ; mais pour le rencontrer. Il allait être le témoin clé de Danziger.

Gittens examina la lettre sans commenter, le visage dénué d'expression.

— Martin, Danziger savait.

— Il savait quoi ?

— Il savait que Braxton était votre indic. Il savait que vous le protégiez.

— Mais c'est faux. Écoutez, est-ce que j'ai obtenu des infos de Braxton ? Et comment ! Est-ce que je lui ai donné quelque chose en échange ? Absolument. C'est comme ça que ça marche. C'est mon boulot. Cela ne fait pas de Braxton « mon indic ».

— Vous lui avez filé le tuyau pour la descente au cours de laquelle Artie est mort ?

— Bien sûr que non !

— L'avez-vous jamais protégé ?

— Non. Pas au sens où vous l'entendez.

— Braxton était-il Raul ?

— Non. Et ne vous avisez pas d'écrire dans un rapport que vous avez même posé cette question.

Je tiquai, soudain peu sûr de moi.

— Ben, écoutez-moi bien : Brax-ton-a-tué-Trudell... Affaire classée.

— Cela ne tient pas debout. Si Harold a été rencardé à propos de la descente, pourquoi se serait-il encore trouvé dans l'appartement à l'arrivée de Trudell ?

— Harold ? Qu'est-ce que cela veut dire ? Est-ce que vous tenez tout cela de Braxton ?

— Pourquoi a-t-il laissé l'arme, Martin ? Braxton est bien trop malin pour abandonner l'arme du crime avec ses empreintes dessus. Pourquoi aurait-il fait ça ?

— Pourquoi ? Parce que dans la réalité, les choses foirent, c'est tout. Pourquoi était-il dans l'appartement ? Comment je le saurais, bordel ? Peut-être qu'il a dû y retourner pour récupérer

quelque chose. Peut-être qu'il pensait partir plus tôt mais qu'il a été retardé. S'il a été averti – et dans les Flats, qui sait, peut-être est-ce le cas – peut-être que l'équipe de la descente a débarqué plus tôt qu'il ne le pensait. Il a merdé. Et une fois piégé à l'intérieur, il a dû tirer pour protéger sa fuite parce c'est tout ce qu'il sait faire. Quelle alternative avait-il ? Négocier ? Il s'appelle pas Henry Kissinger.

— Et l'arme ? Pourquoi a-t-il abandonné l'arme ?

— Parce qu'il est humain. Parce qu'il était stressé et qu'il a commis une erreur. Oui, il est malin, mais les malins commettent des crimes imparfaitement. Cela se produit tout le temps. C'est comme ça qu'ils se font gauler. Bon Dieu, Ben, c'est ça l'essence du meurtre. Ce n'est pas du calcul, c'est de l'hystérie.

— Et Raul ?

— Vous voulez bien oublier Raul ! Raul n'a jamais compté. Je vous l'ai dit, il n'y avait pas de Raul et en même temps il y en avait des milliers. Cela ne change rien.

Il posa un pied sur le muret et regarda dans la direction de l'aéroport sur la rive opposée.

— Tous les mystères n'ont pas de solution claire et nette. Le monde est moins ordonné que ça. Des gens s'impliquent et ils (il eut un geste d'exaspération) et ils compliquent tout. Ils agissent pour des raisons qu'ils ne comprennent pas. Ils agissent sans putains de raisons. Je sais que c'est votre premier meurtre et que vous voulez tout éclaircir. Mais parfois c'est impossible parce qu'on ne comprend jamais vraiment les autres. On ne peut pas comprendre pourquoi ils font ce qu'ils font. Il faut accepter cette part de mystère, Ben. Les gens sont mystérieux, le monde aussi. On ne peut pas tout savoir. On n'est pas censé tout savoir. Nous ne sommes pas dans un livre d'histoire. Mais dans le réel. Un endroit d'où la perfection est absente.

J'eus alors la certitude que Gittens était le flic idéal pour Mission Flats. Fait pour les terrains accidentés, avec le tempérament adapté à cet endroit chaotique, sans bornes. Quand les règles ne fonctionnaient pas, il leur tordait le cou. Quand les faits ne correspondaient pas, *idem*. Et généralement c'était nécessaire – voire préférable. Sans des êtres comme Gittens, le système se gripperait. Mais toute cette complexité le rendait plus difficile à percer que Franny. Je bluffais quand je prétendais que mes renseignements sortaient des dossiers de Danziger. En

fait, ils venaient de Vega, Braxton et Beck. J'avais bluffé, mais Gittens n'avait pas révélé son jeu. Contrairement à Franny, Martin Gittens ne trahissait rien. Il était indigné qu'on puisse suggérer qu'il ait commis une erreur – et coupable ou non, qui ne le serait pas ?

— Qu'est-ce que vous avez l'intention de faire de toutes ces... théories à propos de l'affaire Trudell ?

— Je ne suis pas sûr. J'ignore toujours qui était le tueur. Pour ce que j'en sais, c'était peut-être Braxton après tout. Tout le reste est juste – ce doit être les règles du jeu par ici.

Gittens déchira la lettre de coopération et en jeta les bouts dans l'eau. Certains se coincèrent dans les roseaux, finirent par couler. Ce geste me choqua, mais quand Gittens reprit la parole, sa voix était si rassurante que je compris qu'il avait déchiré le document pour mon bien. Certains secrets devaient rester secrets.

— Bon, faites attention. Il y a des gens qui ne veulent pas qu'on rouvre l'affaire. Des gens importants.

— C'est ce que j'ai entendu dire. Mais que puis-je faire ? Je ne peux pas m'arrêter comme ça.

— Savoir quand s'arrêter fait partie du boulot, Ben. Nous ne sommes pas censés répondre à toutes les questions, nous ne sommes pas censés suivre chaque piste jusqu'à l'infini. On n'a pas le temps. Notre boulot est de résoudre l'affaire qui se présente, puis de passer à la suivante. À un moment ou à un autre, il faut savoir tirer un trait.

# 51.

Gittens avait raison, bien sûr. Des mystères perdurent toujours. Tout meurtre renferme une centaine de minuscules énigmes – que faisait la victime à cet endroit ? Pourquoi a-t-elle crié (ou non) ? Pourquoi le tueur a-t-il abandonné l'arme ? Pourquoi s'est-il attardé sur les lieux ? On peut passer sa journée à écraser ces moucherons, sans que cela serve à rien. Les homicides, avec leur violence aléatoire et leur absence de témoin oculaire, engendrent des mystères. La plupart sont insignifiants et les enquêteurs apprennent à vivre avec. Une affaire est « élucidée » quand le fait essentiel – l'identité du tueur – est établi. On ne réunit pas tous les suspects dans un salon pour permettre au fin limier d'exposer une solution immaculée et imparable. Gittens avait raison : le monde est moins ordonné que ça.

J'étais donc prêt, après ma conversation avec Gittens, à accepter un peu d'incertitude. Si Artie Trudell était préoccupé dans les semaines précédant sa mort, nous n'en connaîtrions probablement jamais la cause, et il n'y avait pas de raison de penser que c'était important. Frank Fasulo et l'affaire du Kilmarnock ; Raul, la porte rouge et le meurtre Trudell ; le tueur qui avait bougé le corps de Danziger pour chercher quelque chose – selon toute probabilité, personne ne saurait jamais la vérité à leur sujet et peut-être que cela n'avait aucune importance. L'assassinat de Danziger était résolu. Toutes les preuves désignaient Braxton, toutes. Le reste n'était que du bruit de fond – des rumeurs, des cancans et des tuyaux. Il me fallait l'accepter.

Mais il restait un mystère, un de ces moucherons que je ne pouvais m'empêcher de chasser. Franny Boyle était le seul témoin qui n'avait toujours rien dit. Je laissai Gittens et fonçai dans le centre pour le voir.

Je me garai dans Union Street, passai devant Faneuil Hall et la statue de Samuel Adams, l'hôtel de ville avec ses imposantes géométries de béton et m'engageai sur City Hall Plaza.

Ce n'est une place que de nom. C'est trop vaste et vide pour être une place. En fait, la City Hall Plaza est un vide. Une ouverture nue et battue par les vents grande comme quatre ou cinq terrains de football entièrement carrelée de briques rouges. Ce n'est pas un lieu où l'on s'attarde. C'est un endroit où l'on presse le pas pour arriver plus vite de l'autre côté.

Et c'est précisément ce que j'étais en train de faire, presser le pas pour rejoindre Cambridge Street. Je songeais à Gittens – l'avais-je injustement jugé ? – et à l'histoire de cet endroit, à l'urbaniste fou qui avait décidé cinquante ans plus tôt de raser au bulldozer le vieux Scollay Square pour le remplacer par ce flipper monochrome, je me disais notamment que le bombardier Harris avait fait preuve de moins de minutie pour raser Dresde tout en me félicitant de la pertinence de cette remarque, me disant que je trouverais peut-être l'occasion de la répéter à Caroline, histoire de l'impressionner – bref, des pensées diverses et variées se bousculaient dans ma tête.

Quand un petit bout de brique explosa à mes pieds comme une mine terrestre.

Je crus d'abord que quelqu'un avait jeté un caillou ou qu'un bloc de pierre était tombé d'un immeuble. Mais il n'y avait personne autour de moi et le bâtiment le plus proche se trouvait à cinquante mètres.

J'entendis un sifflement, puis un fantôme abattit un marteau sur mon triceps gauche. Mon bras se redressa tout seul. La manche de ma veste était déchirée et du sang coulait. Une douleur sourde envahit mon muscle – mon muscle –, une douleur qui ne surgit qu'avec retard, après ce premier instant incroyable.

Ce ne fut que lorsqu'une troisième balle souleva un autre nuage de poussière de brique que je me rendis à l'évidence : on me tirait dessus.

Mon cerveau se vida. Plus une seule pensée, rien que le besoin primal, fuir.

Je partis en courant. D'abord en direction de Cambridge Street, pour m'éloigner des tirs. Mais le seul abri sur ce foutu plateau était l'entrée du métro, un bunker de brique rouge derrière moi. Je virai donc et fonçai par là, bien que cela me ramenât droit vers le tireur.

Des gens allaient et venaient autour de l'entrée du métro. Des avocats et des secrétaires, des employés de bureau à la fin d'une longue journée. Ils se retournèrent en me voyant courir. Ils n'avaient pas remarqué les coups de feu. Il n'y avait pas eu de détonation pour les alerter. La petite foule m'observa – un homme arrivant sur eux au pas de course, le bras en sang, une vision étrange mais rien d'alarmant. Un yuppie en costume eut un sourire hésitant comme s'il s'agissait d'une blague.

En courant, je tirai mon pistolet de son étui et l'armai. Une bêtise de film d'action que j'aurais mieux fait d'éviter. Je ne savais pas du tout d'où venaient les tirs et, de toute façon, comment aurais-je pu riposter avec autant de monde autour ?

L'ironie voulut que ce soit mon arme qui provoque un mouvement de panique.

Il y eut un hurlement. Les gens refluèrent dans l'entrée du métro, puis quand le hall fut plein et qu'ils ne purent franchir les tourniquets, ils jaillirent à l'extérieur et s'éparpillèrent en criant.

Je ne pris la peine ni de montrer mon insigne ni d'annoncer que j'étais flic. Je courus.

Arrivé près de l'entrée du métro, je m'accroupis contre le mur. Mon bras palpitait à présent, ma manche de chemise était lourde de sang.

Au guichet, l'employé se plaqua contre le mur du fond. Il ne quittait pas mon arme des yeux, la bouche ouverte en un O parfait.

— Ça va, je suis flic, lui lançai-je.

— Vous voulez que j'appelle les flics ?

— Non ! Pas de flics.

Je me pressai le bras pour endiguer le sang et examinai les possibilités. Qui me tirerait dessus ? Braxton ? Une autre racaille ? Gittens ? Après tout, je l'avais froissé quelques minutes plus tôt avec des questions sur l'affaire Trudell. Mais aucune de ces

hypothèses ne tenait debout. Braxton avait fait de moi son confident. Et pour ce que j'en savais, Gittens était toujours dans les Flats. En l'absence d'explication, la paranoïa s'installa.

Je m'approchai du guichet et tentai d'engager une transaction ordinaire, comme si les événements des soixante secondes précédentes ne s'étaient jamais produits.

— Un jeton, s'il vous plaît. (Je cherchai un dollar dans ma poche, en vain.) Bon Dieu, je n'ai pas de liquide. Désolé.

L'employé me regardait bouche bée. Toujours collé au mur du fond.

— Ça va, vieux, m'assura-t-il, vous pouvez passer.

## 52

Le temps que j'arrive à l'Unité des enquêtes spéciales, mon bras me faisait moins mal, mais ma manche et ma main gauches étaient couvertes de sang. Quand j'apparus sur le seuil de son bureau, Caroline sursauta.

— Ben ! Oh mon Dieu, que t'est-il arrivé ?

— Je crois qu'on m'a tiré dessus.

— Tu crois ?

— Oui. C'est la première fois.

Elle courut chercher une trousse d'urgence, puis nous nous installâmes sur son canapé pour qu'elle nettoie la blessure à l'alcool. Elle m'ordonna de retirer ma veste et ma chemise ensanglantée. Je portais toujours le T-shirt de la veille, quand elle était venue dans ma chambre d'hôtel. Si elle le remarqua, elle n'en souffla mot.

— Elle t'a juste éraflé, dit-elle, probablement pour m'apaiser.

— Elle m'a éraflé ? Je me suis fait tirer dessus.

— D'accord, mais pas exactement. C'est une égratignure.

— Pardon, mais j'avais l'impression que lorsqu'une balle te touchait, cela signifiait qu'on t'avait tiré dessus.

— D'accord, Ben, tu t'es fait tirer dessus. Je voulais dire que tu vas bien.

— Caroline, arrête ce truc.

— Quoi ?

— Cette manie que tu as de toujours vouloir avoir le dernier mot.

— Je viens d'admettre que tu t'es fait tirer dessus. Je suis d'accord avec toi.

— Je sais, mais c'était dans ta façon de le dire.

Elle fronça les sourcils.

— Désolée. J'essayais juste de t'aider. Tu as raison, tu t'es fait tirer dessus. (Elle lâcha la gaze dans la trousse de première urgence.) Je suis de ton côté, Ben. Tu le sais. (Elle me regarda droit dans les yeux jusqu'à ce que je le reconnaisse – elle était sans aucun doute de mon côté.) Ne l'oublie pas.

— Désolé, j'ai un peu flippé.

Nous nous embrassâmes, sans raison particulière sinon que quelque chose nous y poussa et je compris – pour la première fois – que si difficile qu'il fût d'être proche de Caroline Kelly, elle faisait partie de ces êtres sélectifs et férocement loyaux qui, une fois qu'ils vous ont accepté, ne vous lâcheront jamais dans les moments les plus difficiles. Ces gens-là ont peu de relations et de nombreux amis. Ils sont avares de leur affection parce que cela leur coûte énormément de la donner complètement, mais une fois qu'ils l'ont accordée, ils ne reviennent jamais dessus. Avec un peu de chance, on en croise un ou deux dans une vie.

D'un tiroir, Caroline sortit un sweat-shirt et me le lança. Ce sweat qui portait le logo de la police de Boston et le slogan, LA PREMIÈRE POLICE DE L'AMÉRIQUE, s'ornait de quelques-uns de ses cheveux noirs.

— Merci.

— Ce n'est rien. J'en donne un à tous ceux qui débarquent avec une blessure par balle.

J'enfilai mon sweat-shirt quand Caroline décrocha le téléphone.

— Qu'est-ce que tu fais ?

— J'appelle la police.

— Non.

— Oh, chef Truman, ne sois pas ridicule. Il faut qu'on le signale.

— Certainement pas.

Elle raccrocha.

— Tu donnes dans la paranoïa. Pourquoi quelqu'un voudrait te tirer dessus ?

— Peut-être qu'ils n'aiment pas les ploucs.

— Tu n'es pas un plouc.

Elle dit cela d'un ton dédaigneux, des fois que je prenne ça pour un compliment.

— C'est l'affaire Trudell. Quelqu'un ne tient pas à me voir tourner autour. Est-ce que Franny est là ? Il faut que je lui parle. Il est le seul qui reste et il ment depuis le début.

— Il est dans son bureau.

Je me levai.

— Attends, fit Caroline en reprenant son téléphone.

— J'ai dit pas de flics.

— J'appelle mon père.

— Bien. D'accord. Fais-le venir ici.

— Ben, puis-je faire une autre suggestion ? Appelle Kurth. Franny ne tentera rien si Kurth est là. Il n'oserait pas.

— Bon Dieu, Caroline. Tu ne crois pas que ce type est un peu...

— Je sais, il est un peu bizarre. Mais, Ben, s'il existe un flic à qui tu peux faire confiance, c'est bien lui.

# 53.

Franny semblait nous attendre. En quelques heures, il avait subi une horrible transformation. Affalé derrière son bureau, il avait l'air épuisé, malade et désespérément triste. Il avait même dû pleurer – son visage luisait de perles de sueur semblables à des larmes – mais la tendresse était si éloignée de sa personnalité que je me dis qu'il devait simplement être ivre, ce qui était le cas.

Il ne broncha pas quand nous nous présentâmes à sa porte. Il nous regarda chacun à notre tour : Caroline, John Kelly, Kurth et moi.

— On dirait que toute la bande est là, dit-il. (Il avait une bouteille de bière coincée entre les cuisses. Il la prit pour boire une gorgée.) Vous en voulez ? Mais n'en dites rien au patron, je ne veux pas perdre mon augmentation. (Puis une ombre passa sur son visage et il arrêta les blagues. La bravade exigeait trop d'efforts et, en cet instant, pourquoi s'embêter ?) Je me demandais combien de temps cela vous prendrait.

— Franny, lui dis-je, voulez-vous un avocat ?

— Encore cette histoire d'avocat. Non, Opie, je n'ai pas besoin d'avocat. (Ses yeux se posèrent sur le mur derrière moi.) Je vous ai déjà raconté mon premier homicide, Opie ? C'était à l'époque où nous avions de vrais gangsters, les types du North End, pas ces gamins asiatiques. De vrais parrains. La victime, on l'a trouvée enchaînée à un pilier sous la jetée près du Red Falcon Terminal, sur le front de mer. Ils l'ont ligotée au pilier sous la jetée à marée basse et ils l'ont laissée là à attendre la marée.

C'est la vieille école, mec. Nous n'avons jamais élucidé cette affaire. Personne ne voulait parler. Bordel... je ne l'aurais pas ouverte non plus. (Il s'avachit encore dans son fauteuil.) Je pense tout le temps à ce type : enchaîné, regardant l'eau monter. Rien à faire. Qu'à la regarder monter. Il essuya une larme invisible sur sa joue et me contempla comme si j'étais très loin.

Je me détournai de ce visage.

Sur son bureau trônait la photo accrochée au mur de Danziger, l'Unité des enquêtes spéciales à la moitié des années 1980 – les substituts Bob Danziger et Franny Boyle, les inspecteurs Artie Trudell, Julio Vega, Martin Gittens, environ une douzaine d'autres, accolés, respirant l'assurance. L'équipage du bombardier réuni sur le tarmac avant le vol dont il ne reviendra pas.

— Franny, Bob Danziger vous a demandé votre aide, n'est-ce pas ? Vous étiez l'un des seuls témoins encore là, vous et Julio Vega. Danziger voulait retrouver le tueur d'Artie Trudell.

Silence.

— Vous a-t-il demandé de l'aider, Franny ? Ou s'apprêtait-il à vous envoyer un mandat de comparution ?

— Il n'avait pas besoin de mandat, marmonna Franny. Il m'a dit que je le devais à Artie. Cela suffisait, après tout ce temps. En fait, Danziger ne savait pas dans quoi il s'engageait avant qu'on ne commence à parler. Maintenant il le sait. (Ses yeux dérivaient de gauche à droite comme s'il assistait à un match de badminton organisé derrière moi.) Peut-être que je finirai pareil. Ce sera toujours mieux que ça.

Je devrais souligner que, d'après Caroline, à son époque Franny Boyle était l'avocat le plus redouté, éloquent et charismatique de Boston. Il n'excellait pas dans les subtilités du droit et, sur ordre du procureur général, il n'était pas autorisé à intervenir pour le jugement d'un délit grave sans être flanqué d'un confrère, prêt à le remettre sur le droit chemin s'il commençait à aller trop loin dans la rhétorique de prétoire. Mais on mesure le talent d'un avocat à ses succès et Francis X. Boyle ne cessait de les accumuler, au point que cela devint chez lui une fierté perverse quand on put prouver par la suite qu'il avait en fait condamné des innocents. L'innocence de l'accusé, selon lui, relevait simplement un peu la barre.

Ce soir-là – le soleil venait de se coucher, et le bureau de Franny resta plongé dans la pénombre jusqu'à ce que quelqu'un

allume les néons au plafond – nous eûmes un aperçu du don de Franny lorsqu'il reprit suffisamment ses esprits pour raconter l'histoire du meurtre de Bob Danziger, une histoire qui remontait à vingt ans. Les rares règles légales que je connaisse, Franny les outrepassa en livrant son récit. Il entra dans la tête des personnages, cita des ouï-dire et des rumeurs, ajouta des faits qu'il ne pouvait pas connaître, il déforma même peut-être quelques preuves. Il était comme toujours, pour citer les termes de Caroline, « un pourvoi en attente ». Mais c'était un sacré conteur. Il devait avoir été un avocat drôlement doué parce que, aussi ivre et brisé fût-il, il savait raconter une histoire. Il vous la faisait vivre.

*Frankie Fasulo est obligé de se cramponner. Il faut qu'il entoure la poutre en I de son bras gauche et qu'il la serre contre ses côtes, sinon le vent qui souffle sur Tobin Bridge va le soulever du garde-fou sur lequel il se tient debout et le faire passer par-dessus bord, et cela n'aura pas d'importance, cela fera pas une putain de différence qu'il ait ou non les couilles de sauter. Putain de vent ! Il y a quelque chose derrière lui, une présence. Le vent est vivant, comme dans un récit biblique – comme Dieu apparaissant aux juifs sous la forme d'une petite tornade ou d'une tempête de sable. C'est vrai, ce putain de vent force contre son dos, son cul, l'arrière de ses jambes. Il essaie de le faire tomber par-dessus bord. Il veut le voir passer par-dessus bord. Alors Fasulo serre la poutre en I contre lui. C'est douloureux de s'accrocher à ce truc parce qu'il n'a pas de gants et que l'acier est glacial, merde, si froid qu'il lui pique les mains comme un courant électrique et il sent le froid à travers sa veste, qui se résume à une veste de l'armée merdique vert olive avec un symbole de paix sur l'épaule. Il l'a fauchée sur un banc de la station de trams sur St. James Ave, profitant de ce que ce connard de hippy avait le dos tourné. Quelque part un connard de hippy se les gèle en se demandant où est passée sa putain de veste de l'armée merdique avec son symbole de paix et, même perché comme il est, Frankie Fasulo ne l'oublie pas. Ha ! Pas étonnant que ces salopards de viets nous aient foutus hors du Vietnam : ces putains de vestes de l'armée protègent pas du froid ! Fasulo essaie de regarder droit devant lui, vers – c'est quoi, ça, bordel ? – Chelsea, Charlestown, une putain de banlieue tout illuminée avec la ligne des gratte-ciel de Boston au fond. C'est beau. Il en est conscient : c'est salement beau, les mecs. Il tente d'admirer la vue mais il n'arrive pas à empêcher ses yeux de fixer l'obscurité sous ses pieds, la surface de*

*l'eau où se reflètent des petits points de lumière de la ville. D'ailleurs à quelle distance elle est cette surface ? Un bon kilomètre, non ? – ça représente combien un kilomètre de toute façon ? Est-ce qu'un pont peut être haut d'un kilomètre ? C'est trop. Il ne peut pas. Il ne peut pas lâcher cette poutre en I, avancer d'un pas et tomber, tomber, tomber. Mais il ne peut pas reculer non plus.*

*On est le 20 mars 1977 à quatre heures six du matin.*

— *Je peux pas ! hurle Fasulo mais les vents ici sont si forts que peut-être on ne l'entend pas, alors il crie de nouveau : je peux pas, bordel !*

— *À toi de voir, Frankie, dit la voix derrière lui, frimeuse et cool parce que c'est pas le cul de ce mec qui est debout sur la rambarde à un kilomètre ou je ne sais quoi au-dessus de cette putain de Mystic River.*

*Putain, les jambes de Fasulo tremblent si fort qu'elles vont le faire glisser du petit garde-fou sur lequel il se tient. Il va foncer en tremblant jusqu'à ces eaux noires. Mais il fait si froid, bordel, qu'il n'arrive pas à contrôler ses muscles. Ou peut-être qu'ils ont la trouille, ses muscles. Peut-être qu'ils pètent de trouille comme le reste.*

— *Je descends !*

— *À toi de voir, Frankie.*

— *Qu'est-ce qui se passe si je descends ?*

*Pas de réponse.*

— *J'ai dit : qu'est-ce qui se passe si je descends ?*

— *Comme je l'ai dit, Frankie, tu récolteras un peu de ce que tu as donné. Mais attends, Frankie, je vais te proposer un marché. Rien que pour prouver que je suis pas un mauvais bougre. Je t'obligerai pas à me sucer la queue, qu'est-ce que t'en dis ? Je te ferai pas tout ce que tu as fait à ce flic, Frankie, tu vois ?*

— *Je n'ai pas...*

— *T'as pas quoi, Frankie ? Allons, qu'est-ce que t'as pas fait ?*

— *Je ne l'ai pas fait !*

— *T'avise pas de mentir, Frankie ! T'avise pas de faire ça.*

— *D'accord, d'accord, d'accord, je l'ai fait ! Je l'ai fait ! Il était pas censé être là ! Nous voulions juste le blé. Il aurait pas dû rentrer comme ça ! Qu'est-ce qu'on pouvait faire ?*

— *J'en ai marre de ces conneries, Frankie. Tu descends de ce truc du côté que tu veux, j'en ai rien à branler. Mais ferme-la, d'accord ? Je te donne le choix, Frankie. C'est plus que tu n'en as accordé à ce flic. Ce flic était mon ami, Frankie, tu savais ça ? Tu connais même pas son nom, hein ? Tu savais que c'était mon ami ?*

— *Je ne savais pas.*

— Eh bien t'aurais dû le savoir avant de lui foutre ta bite dans la bouche, Frankie.

— Je savais... pas !

Fasulo regarde de nouveau en bas. Peut-être que ça sera pas si terrible. Pas si terrible après tout. Plein de types sont morts en construisant le Tobin Bridge, c'est ce que tout le monde dit. Ils sont tombés, peut-être, point barre. Certains sont même tombés dans le béton frais et ils sont intégrés au pont, c'est pas ce qu'on raconte ? C'est pas vrai ? Ou est-ce qu'on dit ça de tous les putains de ponts ? Ça doit pas être si terrible de tomber, hein ? Qui c'est ce putain de flic ? Comment il m'a trouvé, bordel ? Quelqu'un a cafté, un enculé de fumier, et je vais le buter ce fumier, sauf que je vais pas le buter cet enfoiré de merde parce que jamais je vais sortir de ce PUTAIN DE BORDEL DE PONT...

— Allons, Frankie, on a pas toute la nuit. Qu'est-ce que tu choisis ?

— Je peux pas !

— Mais si. Viens pas me dire que tu peux pas.

— Je peux pas.

— Alors le fais pas. Descends.

— Quoi ? Vous voulez dire que c'est fini ?

— Ouais, allez, Frankie. Descends.

Mais le flic ponctue son offre en armant son flingue et ce son – métallique, précis, usiné – s'enfonce directement dans le tympan de Frank Fasulo comme si l'arme était juste à côté de lui.

— Allez, Frankie. À toi de voir. Tu veux que je le fasse ou tu veux le faire toi-même ?

— C'est pas juste !

— Viens pas me parler de justice, Frankie. C'est juste, crois-moi.

Une profonde inspiration – l'odeur du froid, son goût sur la langue comme du mercure – et Fasulo se penche légèrement en avant, suffisamment pour commencer à perdre son équilibre, commencer à tourner autour de la poutre au creux de son coude gauche, à tourner autour de la poutre comme si c'était un lampadaire et il va en faire le tour, et un pas de plus et il n'y a plus rien sous ses pieds et le vent le retient, il flotte, en suspens juste un instant...

il vole...

et puis il ne vole plus, il tombe

et il tombe et il tombe

et ce n'est pas si terrible finalement, pas désagréable du tout – il a le temps de penser, de vivre la sensation – le vent souffle fort et lui picote les oreilles et les joues comme des aiguilles... et il lui remonte le pantalon

*sur ses tibias et il sent le froid sur ses mollets... et ses cheveux qui lui fouettent les yeux... et son corps se met à faire la roue... et le vent commence à tirer sur son manteau...*

*et sur le pont Martin Gittens – en civil – le visage serein et beau remet soigneusement le cran de sûreté et range son Beretta dans son étui parce que c'est fini à présent et il fallait que cela finisse comme ça – personne n'avait besoin de lui dire quoi faire...*

*sauf que son équipier, le grand rouquin avec sa face de lune – un visage comme une grosse boule de pâte, aime à dire Gittens, un visage qu'ils pourraient utiliser comme sac de première base à Fenway, comme il aime à le dire –, Artie Trudell fixe avec sa face de lune l'endroit où Frank Fasulo le violeur de flic et le tueur de flic est passé par-dessus bord, le fixe comme si un vent miraculeux allait rattraper Frank Fasulo et le rejeter sur le pont.*

— Kurth, vous notez tout cela ?

Kurth opina du chef. Il griffonnait furieusement sur un bloc-notes, en s'efforçant de suivre Franny. Il ne devait pas essayer de tout copier mot à mot. Mais...

— Vous voulez que je revienne en arrière et que je répète, vous le dites.

— Ne vous inquiétez pas pour moi, Franny. Continuez.

— Je ne veux pas que vous ratiez quoi que ce soit. Ceux qui entendent cette histoire, ils ont tendance à pas être là le jour du procès.

Il nous regarda tous méchamment pour bien se faire comprendre : le prix pour le spectacle de cette danse macabre était que, tôt ou tard, n'importe lequel d'entre nous pourrait être forcé de sortir du public pour participer.

*Dix ans. C'est le temps qu'il a fallu à Artie Trudell pour cesser de supporter le souvenir de Frank Fasulo passant par-dessus bord à Tobin Bridge. Dix ans qu'il revient régulièrement en pensée à ce pont. Dix ans qu'il ne cesse de voir Fasulo debout sur le garde-fou, serrant cette poutre et hurlant pour se faire entendre malgré le vent « Je peux pas ! » – puis le pas en avant... non, il n'a pas avancé, pas au début... il s'est penché, Artie Trudell s'en souvient distinctement... il s'est penché comme un plongeur qui avance légèrement le torse, gîtant, prolongeant l'instant de contrepoids, sentant l'attraction de la gravité qui s'accélère quand le plongeur cède – Artie sent cet instant fatal de déséquilibre, quand le*

poids du corps commence à bouger non en avant mais vers le bas... il la sent, cette perte irréversible d'équilibre. Puis Fasulo est parti en vrille – oh, cette horrible rotation de son corps, ce demi-tour vers la gauche parce que sa main s'agrippe encore à la poutre en I... le tournoiement, si proche de celui d'un plongeur, qui suggérait que Fasulo ne pouvait pas lâcher, qu'il n'avait pas décidé de sauter mais qu'il tombait ou se faisait pousser – pousser par Gittens – pas Artie, Gittens – puis la main qui glisse de la poutre et Fasulo qui disparaît par-dessus bord. Artie Trudell avait été incapable de bouger, bien sûr. Il ne parvenait même pas à détourner les yeux de l'endroit où Fasulo était passé par-dessus bord. Alors Trudell n'a pas vu la chute libre, mais cela ne lui a pas épargné des visions de cette chute. Non, cela n'a réussi qu'à déchaîner son imagination qui s'est mise à multiplier les images de chutes vertigineuses infinies – tombant et tournoyant dans le vide noir du froid et des étoiles... la vitesse et la terreur d'une telle pureté, et l'impact... Trudell ne parvient jamais vraiment à l'instant de l'impact. Il se réveille ou il cesse tout simplement de repasser la scène avant que Frank Fasulo ne s'écrase dans l'eau.

Dix ans de ça.

Ce n'était pas si difficile au début. D'abord, il y eut une période de choc quand toute l'affaire parut irréelle. Le souvenir était trop vif, trop grand, comme un film. Trudell l'enfonça dans le trou sombre où il conservait ses autres cauchemars. Il le « refoula », comme des observateurs le diraient plus tard.

Et quand cela se mettait à remonter du trou, Trudell allait voir Gittens – à qui d'autre pouvait-il présenter sa conscience coupable de meurtrier ? Et Gittens l'apaisait. Gittens avait une vision d'ensemble, lui. Gittens lui rappelait ce que Fasulo avait fait. Viol, meurtre. Et pas seulement ceux du flic du Kilmarnock, aussi terribles fussent-ils. Frank Fasulo était le mal incarné, disait Gittens. Fasulo avait récolté ce qu'il méritait et qui sait combien d'autres vies avaient été sauvées grâce à ça. Martin Gittens dormait comme un nouveau-né, prétendait-il, du sommeil du juste. Ces petites séances servaient un moment. Elles calmaient Trudell et elles lui permirent de faire son boulot, ses patrouilles, d'abord comme simple flic, puis comme inspecteur des stupéfiants dans les Flats, la zone chaude, où tout le monde rêvait d'être nommé. C'est là qu'Artie Trudell se trouve maintenant. Les stupéfiants de la zone A-3 – Mission Flats. « Le petit Beyrouth », comme l'appellent les flics et qui pourrait dire que ce n'est pas pire que le vrai Beyrouth en cet été de canicule de 1987 ? Et Gittens ne l'a-t-il pas soutenu ? Ne lui a-t-il pas facilité les choses ? Même Julio Vega – qui semble en connaître plus long en

matière de politique du service que le divisionnaire lui-même – même Vega sait que Gittens est un homme de confiance. Donc si Gittens dit que c'était la chose à faire, ce doit être vrai. Point barre.

Mais en cet été 1987, Frank Fasulo s'est mis à ramper de nouveau dans la conscience de Trudell, cette fois d'une manière différente et surprenante. Trudell n'emprunte plus le Tobin Bridge depuis longtemps. Maintenant les rares fois où il doit se rendre sur la North Shore, il fait le long détour par la Route 128, le périphérique autour de Boston. Quelques minutes supplémentaires de conduite, ce n'est pas cher payé pour éviter les cauchemars que fait surgir la traversée de Tobin Bridge. Mais il est un autre pont que Trudell est obligé de traverser, un qu'il ne peut éviter. Il s'agit du Sagamore Bridge, l'un des deux ponts qui séparent le Massachusetts du Cape Cod. Le Sagamore est un pont élevé, bien plus élégant que le Tobin, un projet des grands travaux des années 1930 qui enjambe le Cape Cod Canal. Et, par manque de chance, les beaux-parents d'Artie Trudell possèdent justement une maison à Dennis. Et sa femme insiste pour aller au Cap, pour les enfants. Trudell réussit à échapper à la plupart de ces expéditions. Il accumule les affectations, les tours de garde et encombre tant et si bien son emploi du temps qu'il n'a pas une minute pour des voyages au Cape Cod. Désolé, chérie. Mais il y a trop de week-ends à éviter et elle finit par lui dire : « Est-ce que tu veux me faire croire que tu ne peux pas prendre un seul jour de congé, Artie ? Pas un ? Serais-tu le seul flic de Boston ? » Alors Artie Trudell – qui n'a jamais aimé les bagarres, tout géant qu'il soit – est obligé d'affronter le Sagamore Bridge. Deux fois par voyage, une fois à l'aller, une fois au retour. Ces traversées provoquent une sorte d'angoisse que Trudell a du mal à expliquer. Il vérifie même dans le dictionnaire des névroses, la bible du dingue qu'il se sent devenir. Le nom exact est la géphyrophobie, la peur de traverser des ponts, et l'angoisse de Trudell n'est rien par comparaison avec certains des cas cités. Il y a des gens qui en souffrent tellement qu'ils ne peuvent même pas s'approcher d'un pont. L'angoisse de Trudell ne ressemble en rien à cela. Mais elle est bien réelle. Il devient irritable, distrait, il transpire à grosses gouttes, surtout quand les embouteillages du Cap l'immobilisent sur le pont pendant quinze à vingt minutes d'affilée. Il redoute le chemin du retour et il ne trouve pas le sommeil la nuit précédente. Là, l'été 1987, c'est devenu pire, bien pire, parce que chaque traversée fait surgir des souvenirs de Frank Fasulo. Chaque voyage dans le Cap pour voir ses foutus beaux-parents, chaque traversée de ce putain de Sagamore Bridge déclenchent une nouvelle crise de cauchemars, de suées nocturnes et d'inquiétudes. Et de visions : Frank

Fasulo basculant en avant tel un arbre coupé. Fasulo tournant autour de la poutre du pont comme Gene Kelly autour du lampadaire dans Singin' in the Rain. Fasulo plongeant à une vitesse vertigineuse... En juillet, Trudell ferme à peine l'œil et sa culpabilité et son épuisement ont commencé à s'alimenter l'un l'autre. Artie Trudell sent qu'il se vide littéralement.

Et, un jour, il comprend la vérité : il a commis un meurtre. La révélation ne lui tombe pas dessus comme un éclair. Non, un jour elle est là tout simplement et Trudell ne sait pas trop quand elle est arrivée. Peut-être a-t-elle toujours été là et avait-il choisi de ne pas la voir. Mais la voilà, la vérité indéniable – Artie Trudell est un assassin. Ou un complice, ou un conspirateur ou un acolyte, quel que soit le terme que les avocats choisiront d'employer. Le terme technique n'a pas vraiment d'importance. Quel que soit le nom adopté par les juristes, Trudell sait que la description la plus véridique est la plus simple : ASSASSIN. Il sait en tout cas qu'il ne peut plus vivre avec ce secret.

On est le lundi 3 août 1987, deux semaines avant la descente dans l'appartement à la porte rouge.

— Je vais voir Franny, annonce Trudell.

Gittens ne réagit pas. Il voit le visage d'Artie Trudell devant lui et il sait qu'Artie est au bout du rouleau. Il a une tête de déterré. Les yeux cernés de rouge, le teint blafard. Gittens ne veut pas lui foutre la trouille.

— Je ne sais pas quoi faire d'autre, Martin. Nous avons tué ce type.

— Chut ! Parle pas si fort, mon grand.

Ils se trouvent dans le vestiaire du commissariat de la zone A-3, un sous-sol en parpaing qui ressemble jusqu'à l'odeur à un vestiaire de gymnase de lycée. Au sol, du béton peint. Des néons qui bourdonnent au-dessus de leurs têtes. Il est onze heures du soir et la salle est vide. Cela n'empêche pas Gittens et Trudell de se comporter comme dans une foule. Assis face à face sur des bancs, penchés l'un vers l'autre, ils murmurent. On est dans l'A-3, au Silence ! Hôpital. On règle ses propres problèmes ici – et quiconque regarde Artie Trudell comprend qu'il y a un très gros problème.

— Martin, je ne sais pas quoi faire. (Trudell se serre la tête à deux mains comme s'il pouvait en chasser l'idée de l'homme ASSASSINÉ.) Je ne sais pas quoi faire.

Gittens l'attrape par les poignets.

— Allez, Artie, arrête ça.

— Bon Dieu, Martin.

— Quoi, Artie ?

— J'ai été un vrai putain d'enfant de chœur !

— Eh bien, ça m'étonnerait qu'on te réengage.

— Je suis un assassin. Nous l'avons assassiné.

— Non. Nous avons déjà discuté de tout cela. Ce n'était pas un meurtre, Artie. Tu sais ce qui allait arriver à ce type ? Il allait se faire choper et passer le reste de sa vie à Walpole. Point barre. Il était déjà mort. On ne tue pas quelqu'un qui est déjà mort.

— Je ne le crois pas.

— Artie, si nous n'avions pas agi, ce type serait toujours vivant aujourd'hui. Est-ce que ce serait juste, après tout ce qu'il a fait ? Il obtiendrait peut-être même une remise de peine, Artie, songe un peu à ça. Son avocat dirait qu'il était complètement défoncé à la coke et il s'en sortirait avec un second degré et cela fait seulement quinze ans à tirer avant une remise de peine. Tu aimerais voir ça, Artie ? Tu aimerais voir Fasulo de retour dans les rues pendant que le flic qu'il a descendu se fait bouffer par les vers ? Ce ne serait pas juste, non ? Ce flic est mort et il ne ressuscitera pas.

— J'ai l'impression d'être mort moi aussi.

Sentant Trudell au bord des larmes, Gittens cesse d'expliquer et se contente de l'apaiser.

— Chut ! Allons, arrête ces conneries. Artie, il faut que tu te reprennes.

— Je vais demander à Franny ce que je dois faire.

— C'est une erreur.

— Je m'en fous.

— Là tu te trompes, Artie. Que va dire Franny à ton avis ? Tu crois que tu peux aller voir un procureur, lui avouer un meurtre et t'en tirer ? Pense à la situation dans laquelle tu le mets. Ne fais pas ça à Franny. Il sera obligé de le signaler. Ils nous coffreront tous les deux. Ils pourront pas faire autrement.

— Je m'en fous maintenant.

— Vraiment ? Tu veux être un assassin ?

— Nous lui dirons que c'était, comme on dit, dans le feu de la passion.

— Artie, Andrew Lowery en aura rien à foutre du feu de la passion. Le jury non plus. Ils nous rateront pas. De toute façon, c'était pas le feu de la passion ; nous avons attendu plus d'une semaine. Et tu sais ? C'est ce qu'on appelle un meurtre au premier degré, mon pote. Prison à vie sans remise de peine. Tu veux te retrouver à Walpole à vie ?

376

*C'est ça que tu veux ? Tu as une femme et deux gosses. Comment tu vas*
*aller à Walpole à vie ?*

   *Trudell ne répond pas.*

   — *Il faut que tu te reprennes, mon vieux, tu m'entends ? Remets-*
*toi les idées en place. Nous n'avons assassiné personne.*

   — *Je n'ai assassiné personne, le corrige Trudell.*

*Air mauvais de Gittens.*

   — *J'étais juste planté là. C'était toi qui tenais le flingue.*

*Air mauvais de Gittens.*

   — *Je n'ai rien fait. C'est tout ce que je dis, Martin.*

*Air mauvais de Gittens.*

*Trudell bat de nouveau en retraite.*

   — *C'est tout ce que je dis.*

   — *Écoute, Artie, parle pas comme ça. C'est pas la bonne façon de*
*penser. Il faut que nous nous tenions les coudes sur ce coup-là.*

*Pas de réaction.*

   — *Artie, promets-moi que tu ne feras rien avant de m'avoir*
*consulté, d'accord ? Tu peux me donner ta parole ? Tu me promets que*
*tu ne diras rien ni à Franny ni à personne avant que nous en discutions*
*de nouveau ? C'est tout ce que je te demande. Tu peux me donner ta*
*parole ?*

   *Trudell fait non de la tête avant d'opiner.*

   — *Oui. Je crois. Mais pas éternellement, Martin, tu m'entends ?*
*Ça ne peut pas durer éternellement. Je ne peux pas. Je pète les plombs,*
*moi.*

   *Gittens étudie la grosse tête éléphantesque de Trudell.*

   — *D'accord, mon grand. On en reste là, d'accord ? Nous trouve-*
*rons une solution. Ne fais rien de stupide, d'accord ? Donne-moi un peu*
*de temps pour trouver une solution.*


   — Il est venu vous voir, Franny ?
   — Oui.
   — Et ?
   — Il m'a tout raconté, comme je viens de le faire. Il était
un assassin et que devait-il faire ? (Franny se tripota les joues
avec ses doigts grassouillets.) Je ne savais pas trop. J'avais besoin
de temps pour y réfléchir. On n'inculpe pas comme ça un flic
d'assassinat. J'ai dit à Artie qu'il avait bien fait de venir me voir.
Mais au fond, je n'étais pas sûr qu'il ait bien fait. Je n'étais pas
sûr de vouloir être au courant. C'est vrai, Artie avait raison : il

était un assassin. Nous aurions pu le poursuivre, bien entendu. Donc cet ami vient me demander de l'aide et qu'est-ce que je devais faire ? Je n'en savais rien. Je lui ai dit que j'allais réfléchir et que je le recontacterais, mais qu'il devrait prendre un avocat de son côté. En définitive, ce serait au procureur, à Lowery, de décider s'il fallait inculper les deux ou juste Gittens. C'était l'affaire de Lowery. On pouvait peut-être trouver un arrangement pour Artie, mais ils étaient tous les deux sur ce pont. Je ne savais pas quoi faire. (Ses yeux se posèrent de nouveau sur la photo.) J'hésitais.

*Artie Trudell a le sentiment que quelque chose ne va pas. Un malaise croissant au sujet de cette descente. Il n'arrive pas à mettre le doigt dessus. Rien ne cloche manifestement. L'enquête, le mandat, la montée d'adrénaline quand l'équipe attend devant la porte rouge – Julio Vega et lui ont franchi une cinquantaine de portes comme celle-là, voire une centaine, voire plus. Là – le 17 août 1987 à deux heures vingt-six – les guerres du crack font rage dans les Flats depuis si longtemps que les descentes de ce genre sont de la routine. Mais l'ombre de Harold Braxton et de son gang violent n'est pas la source du malaise de Trudell. Trudell a déjà frappé le Mission Posse, après tout. Dans les Flats, on retombe toujours sur le Mission Posse. En plus, Braxton est un homme d'affaires. Il ne va pas lutter pour protéger cet endroit. Il ne laissera aucun de ses précieux gorilles dans l'appartement pour le défendre. Braxton va le sacrifier et passer à autre chose. C'est comme ça que ça marche avec les planques du gang : les flics coupent un bras, un autre repousse ; une jambe, une autre repousse. Et ainsi de suite, éternellement, amen. Non, ce ne sont pas les risques habituels qui mettent Artie Trudell à cran ce soir. C'est quelque chose de naissant et d'indicible. Le genre de pressentiment indéfinissable qui incite les gens à refuser de monter dans des avions ou à tendre l'oreille pour écouter des pas. Quelque chose dans l'air.*

*Peut-être que c'est tout le reste. Ces parasites qui occupent la tête de Trudell tous les jours maintenant, ce bruit de fond qui en est venu à obscurcir toute autre pensée : Frank Fasulo, géphyrophobie, le Sagamore Bridge. ASSASSIN. Bien sûr Gittens va trouver une issue. Gittens l'aide encore à préserver les apparences. C'est Gittens, après tout, qui a organisé cette descente en filant à Trudell et à Vega le tuyau de Raul. Est-ce que Gittens n'a pas toujours protégé la carrière de Trudell depuis que*

*Vega et lui sont aux stupéfiants ? Gittens n'a-t-il pas toujours trouvé une solution ?...*

Stop ! Il faut que Trudell fasse taire ce torrent de pensées. Pendant les dix minutes suivantes, il faut qu'il les tienne à distance. Après la descente, il pourra revenir à son obsession, mais pour l'instant il n'y a de place que pour une pensée – franchir cette porte et rentrer chez soi vivant. C'est l'instant du risque suprême pour n'importe quel flic, et Artie Trudell le sait. Les parasites pourraient provoquer sa mort. Ou est-ce là ce que souhaite Artie ?

Ce n'est probablement rien d'autre que la chaleur qui trouble le grand policier. L'air est visqueux. Irrespirable. Même les murs sont humides. Trudell n'est pas bâti pour ce type de chaleur. Ses vêtements sont à tordre. Il a le visage en sueur. Les couilles en sueur. Les paumes en sueur. La sueur lui coule dans la raie des fesses. Qu'on en finisse, se dit-il. Qu'on en finisse et qu'on rentre au commissariat où il y a l'air conditionné.

Vega et lui se tiennent des deux côtés de la porte, le dos plaqué au mur. Vega désigne la porte rouge d'un signe de tête et regarde Trudell : mauvaise porte, Artie. Mauvais plan.

Trudell réussit à sourire. C'était lui l'insouciant dans le temps. Le grand môme. Il retrouve un peu de sa vieille espièglerie pour sourire et gonfler ses biceps. Pas de problème, JV. Ils ont pas construit une porte assez solide.

Les flics de l'équipe sont nerveux. C'est dangereux d'attendre ici. Il faut y aller ou annuler. Ils peuvent pas rester assis là avec leur bite dans les mains. Trudell sent leur nervosité. Tout le monde sait que Vega et lui n'ont encore jamais dirigé de descente. Tout le monde observe pour voir quel genre de meneurs vont se révéler ces deux-là.

Vega donne le signal.

Trudell se plante devant la porte, soulève le bélier noir et en saisit les deux poignées. Le tuyau rempli de béton est incroyablement lourd, même pour lui. On dirait une torpille qu'il s'apprêterait à fourrer dans un canon.

Vega compte : cinq doigts, quatre, trois, deux – à un, il désigne Trudell.

Boom !

Le bélier heurte la porte. Le palier vibre.

— Allez, le grand, marmonne Vega.

Boom !

La sueur coule sur le visage de Trudell mais il n'a pas de main

*libre pour l'essuyer. Elle lui coule dans les yeux. Elle pique un peu. Il respire profondément. Acharne-toi sur un point ! Frappe au même endroit jusqu'à ce que ça cède ! Il trouve un point sur la porte rouge, à la hauteur de l'épaule. Trudell se concentre sur ce point...*

*où une fissure a commencé à se former...*

*un nouveau coup ici...*

*un craquement...*

*et de l'autre côté de la porte, le même craquement...*

*dans l'appartement, la même petite fissure dans le bois...*

*et c'est exactement à cet endroit que Martin Gittens attend avec un fusil – un fusil à pompe Mossberg 500 –, le canon à quelques centimètres de la porte rouge.*

*Gittens porte de délicats gants de coton blanc, des gants de bijoutier, pour éviter d'abîmer les empreintes déjà présentes sur le fusil. Ce sont les empreintes de Braxton, bien sûr ; le fusil a été saisi neuf mois avant. Gittens sera obligé de recharger entre deux coups. Cela veut dire qu'il aura le temps de tirer une fois, peut-être deux. Puis il faudra qu'il se fasse la malle.*

*Il vise ce point faible, la fissure dans la porte. C'est là qu'on tient le bélier, et quinze centimètres plus haut – non, plus haut encore, parce que Artie Trudell est tellement grand –, vingt centimètres au-dessus du point d'impact. Boom ! La porte tremble de nouveau et tout l'immeuble frémit. Sous les pieds de Gittens, le sol bouge.*

*Gittens lève le fusil pour viser la tête d'Artie Trudell – profonde inspiration, lente expiration – et il presse la détente.*

— Je l'ai soupçonné dès le début, dit Franny. Je n'en étais pas sûr, mais j'avais mes soupçons. Artie m'avait dit ce que Gittens avait fait à Fasulo. Et puis Gittens qui débarque si vite à l'appartement cette nuit-là et qui se plante devant la porte sans hésiter... j'avais mes doutes. Mais j'ai fermé ma gueule parce que tout laissait encore penser que Braxton était le coupable. Maintenant je suis certain. Vega est mort, et je suis certain. Gittens a descendu Artie. Je le sais, c'est tout.

— Et Raul ? Qui était Raul ?

Franny haussa les épaules.

— Peut-être qu'il y avait un Raul, peut-être pas. Peut-être que Gittens a obtenu un tuyau d'un indic et qu'il s'en est servi pour piéger Artie. Je pense que Raul n'existait pas – Gittens était Raul. Mais quelle différence ça fait ? Gittens est celui qui a

tiré, c'est tout ce qui compte. Qui sait, peut-être que Braxton était Raul. Toutes ces années, Gittens a eu cet indic qui savait tout dans les Flats et toutes ces années Braxton a réussi à se tirer de pratiquement tout. C'est sûr que ça donne l'impression que quelqu'un le protégeait. Mais je ne sais pas. Nous ne connaîtrons jamais la vérité au sujet de Raul.

— Mais vous avez témoigné au procès, vous en avez attesté. Vous avez déclaré que toute l'histoire à propos de Raul était la vérité.

— Chef Truman, je suis un avocat. Je n'y étais pas. Je ne sais que ce que me disent mes témoins.

— Conneries. (John Kelly qui avait écouté tout le récit en silence cracha pratiquement ce mot au visage de Franny.) Gittens a menti, et vous avez joué le jeu. Vous saviez que quelque chose clochait, mais il était plus facile de poursuivre Braxton que de chercher à savoir ce que Gittens mijotait vraiment.

John Kelly dardait sur Franny un regard méprisant, comme si c'était lui, Kelly, et non Braxton la victime de la lâcheté et des mensonges de Franny.

— Je...

Franny se tut. Le petit sursaut de sang-froid et de vitalité qui lui avait permis de raconter son histoire avait disparu. Éteint. Malgré tout son brio et son talent, Franny Boyle n'avait connu qu'une vie incessante de reflux depuis 1987. Il devait avoir eu l'impression de s'éloigner de cette époque, porté par le courant.

— Si vous avez besoin que je témoigne, lança Franny à la cantonade, je le ferai. J'ai dit la même chose à Danziger.

— Vous voulez qu'on arrête Gittens ? demanda Kurth à Caroline.

Elle fit non de la tête.

— Nous avons trois meurtres et aucune preuve. Il ne reste plus personne de ceux qui étaient sur ce pont la nuit où Fasulo a été tué. Avec la mort de Vega, personne ne peut nous livrer un récit de première main de la nuit où est mort Trudell. Et personne n'était dans ce bungalow quand Danziger a été tué. Trois meurtres, zéro témoin. Je dirais que l'inspecteur Gittens a su ne pas laisser de traces.

— Nous avons un témoin, intervins-je. Harold Braxton.

# 54.

Chelsea, Massachusetts, juste en dehors des limites de la ville de Boston, six heures trente-quatre du matin.

Nous les attendions dans un parking désert. À trente mètres au-dessus de nous le Tobin Bridge, son exosquelette de poutres en I dominé par sa colonne vertébrale, une route surélevée. Dick Ginoux était avec nous, ayant ramené la Bronco de Versailles la veille au soir. Il battait la semelle dans le froid, l'air légèrement perplexe dans son uniforme et sous son chapeau de Smokey l'Ours. Kelly arborait son habituel manteau en flanelle, mais ce matin il avait épinglé sa petite étoile à six branches sur sa poche de poitrine : AGENT, POSTE DE POLICE DE VERSAILLES. Il jouait gaiement de sa matraque en sifflant tout bas « I'm Looking Over a Four-Leaf Clover ». Il était difficile de dire si sa nonchalance était une volonté délibérée de m'aider à garder mon calme ou si Kelly se sentait réellement blasé. Pour ma part, je m'efforçais de réprimer un sourire shooté à l'adrénaline. La scène me rappelait un échange d'espions dans un roman de la Guerre froide. Dans la Bronco, je trouvai ma veste du poste de police de Versailles, avec son petit *Chef Truman* brodé dessus.

Nous ne parlions guère. Le ciel était gris cendre, l'air d'un froid intense pour novembre. Pendant longtemps les seuls bruits furent celui de la circulation sur le pont loin au-dessus de nos têtes, le sifflement de Kelly et le souffle du mouvement de sa matraque.

Bien entendu, Dick se mit à chanter doucement à son tour,

*I'm looking over, a four-leaf clover, that i've overlooked befo-o-ore. The first is for sunshine, the sec-cund for rain...*

— Dick.

— *The third for my ba-by that lives down the lane.*

— Dick !

— Oh ! laissez-le chanter, chef, me conseilla Kelly. Il n'y a rien de mieux à faire.

— Allez, Ben, insista Dick. *I'm lookin' oh-ver, a four-leaf clohver, that a oh-ver-looked be-fo-o-ore.*

Et incroyablement Kelly se mit lui aussi à chanter – horriblement. C'était comme de voir un oncle bien-aimé se lancer dans une danse endiablée à un mariage. On ne savait pas s'il fallait rire ou détourner le regard. *There's no use explainin', the one ree-main-in', is sum-one that I a-do-o-o-ore !* Allez, Ben Truman.

Je cédai et gémis avec eux pour le couplet final.

Kelly me gratifia d'un hochement de tête approbateur.

Il était près de sept heures quand la Mercedes noire de Beck pénétra dans le parking. La voiture s'arrêta devant nous, et Beck et Braxton en descendirent. Braxton portait un sweat-shirt à capuchon trop grand sous une veste en cuir Avirex. Il nous jeta un regard mauvais.

J'avançai d'un pas mais Kelly m'attrapa le poignet.

— Vous êtes le responsable ici. Laissez-moi me charger de ça.

Kelly palpa Braxton en lui récitant la litanie habituelle :

— Harold Braxton, vous êtes arrêté pour le meurtre de Robert Danziger. Vous avez le droit de garder le silence. Vous avez le droit de vous faire assister d'un avocat à tous les interrogatoires. Vous avez le droit...

Braxton se tenait les bras tendus, me regardant d'un sale œil, détestant la procédure et m'en voulant de ne pas l'en dispenser. Avec son regard furieux, il semblait proclamer qu'il ne se soumettait pas, pas vraiment, pas dans son cœur. Il ne reconnaissait ni notre autorité ni sa propre impuissance.

Kelly lui baissa les bras pour le menotter dans le dos.

— Chef Truman, dit Beck, est-il nécessaire qu'il fasse tout le voyage du Maine avec les bras dans le dos ? Pourquoi ne pas le menotter par-devant ? C'est un long trajet.

Braxton baissa les yeux. Il refusait de participer à un plaidoyer de clémence.

J'acquiesçai. Kelly menotta Braxton devant, puis le conduisit à l'arrière de la Bronco. Nous vivions l'arrestation dont tous les flics de la ville rêvaient, mais sans y prendre aucun plaisir.

— La mise en accusation aura lieu demain matin, dis-je d'une voix sourde.

Beck hocha la tête et tourna les talons.

Je levai un dernier regard vers le pont – le pont dont Frank Fasulo avait sauté vingt ans avant. Toute cette carcasse à nu, ces kilomètres de poutres. Un de ces endroits laids où la sous-structure d'une ville se révèle. Dépôts ferroviaires, usines, bouches d'égout – nous les voyons et cela nous rappelle les complexités cachées. Comme si on avait dépecé la ville pour en révéler le squelette, les veines, les systèmes secrets. J'en avais ma dose de tout cela.

— C'est fait, dis-je à Kelly, Dick et moi-même. Rentrons à la maison.

## 55.

Je n'avais été absent de Versailles que dix-sept jours, mais j'avais l'impression d'être parti plus loin et plus longtemps. Je rentrai avec cette sensation particulière qui accompagne la fin d'un long périple : l'agréable tension entre le sentiment d'être revenu au foyer et d'être ailleurs en même temps, quand on se sent un étranger sous son propre toit. On remarque des détails. On trouve une certaine beauté à une rue, un parc ou un immeuble, que l'on n'avait jamais discerné avant. C'est le choc du connu, le même sursaut qui s'empare de vous quand vous voyez votre femme ou votre amant à un coin de rue et, qu'une seconde, vous les voyez avec des yeux d'inconnu. Vous vous dites : *Elle est ravissante. J'avais oublié à quel point.* Versailles me paraissait profondément belle, même les quartiers qui ne le sont pas du tout.

Derrière les collines, des cumulo-nimbus arrivaient de l'ouest. Apparemment nous aurions droit à une pluie froide hivernale. La saison des feuillages était terminée, les touristes partis. C'était l'heure de l'hiver, l'heure de la première apparition du « froid mordant ».

Un groupe de mômes jouait au foot sur le champ communal, sans se soucier des nuages d'orage.

Dans Central Street, Jimmy Lownes et Phil Lamphier traînaient devant l'Owl, cigarette au bec, et jetaient des coups d'œil vers le ciel. Jimmy nous adressa un petit signe en levant deux doigts, une Marlboro coincée entre ses phalanges. Il ne tarderait

pas à répandre le bruit que j'étais rentré avec un jeune Noir en état d'arrestation et toute la ville serait au courant avant le dîner.

Au poste, nous conduisîmes Braxton dans la cellule. Si j'avais des doutes à propos de sa culpabilité, Braxton n'en restait pas moins en état d'arrestation pour meurtre. Il fallait respecter les règles.

Puis Kelly, Dick Ginoux et moi nous attardâmes un moment à la porte du poste.

— Bon Dieu, fit Dick. Il va tomber des trombes d'eau.

— Tu devrais rentrer chez toi, Dick, te reposer un peu. Je reste avec lui.

— Non, chef...

— Ça va, Dick. Ça ira.

Il me jaugea du regard.

— Très bien, Ben. Si tu le dis.

— Merci d'avoir gardé la maison pendant mon absence.

Dick détourna les yeux.

— Je passerai voir si tout va bien plus tard.

Avant de s'éloigner, il adressa à Kelly un petit signe de la main qui ressemblait à un salut.

— Officier Kelly.

— Officier Ginoux.

Kelly émit un soupir las.

— Bien, on dirait que vous avez réussi à rentrer au bercail, Ben Truman.

— On dirait, oui.

— Vous voulez que je prenne le premier tour de garde ?

— Non, monsieur Kelly, je pense qu'il est temps que vous rentriez aussi chez vous.

— Chez moi ?

— Vous êtes en retraite, vous vous souvenez ?

— Ah, ça. Bien.

— Il n'y a plus rien à faire ici. C'est l'affaire de Boston maintenant. Ils vont coincer Gittens, si ce n'est pas déjà fait. Là, c'est juste un tour de garde. Nous inculperons Braxton demain matin, puis les flics de l'État l'embarqueront jusqu'au procès. Vraiment, rentrez chez vous. Ça ira.

— Vous allez vous en tirer avec lui ?

— Oui. J'ai vu pire.

Kelly grogna. Il sortit sa matraque de son manteau.

— Prenez ça. Au cas où il déconnerait.

— Je ne peux pas prendre ça.

— Bien sûr que si. Qu'est-ce que je suis censé faire avec ? Je suis en retraite.

— Vous êtes sûr ?

— Prenez-la, Ben Truman.

Je la pris.

— Bon, fit Kelly, comme soulagé d'être enfin débarrassé de ce petit bâton. Parfait.

Il resta planté là un instant, l'air de ne pas trop savoir quoi faire.

— Je passerai vous voir bientôt, pour vous tenir au courant.

— J'aimerais assez.

Kelly rejoignit sa voiture et se plia pour rentrer dedans comme un faucheux se faufilant dans une fissure. Il descendit sa vitre.

— C'est dommage, vous savez. Vous auriez fait un excellent professeur.

— Qui a dit que cela n'arrivera pas ?

Il eut un petit sourire entendu, puis désigna de la tête la matraque dans ma main.

— N'allez pas vous blesser avec ce truc.

De retour dans le poste, je tirai une chaise en travers de la porte de la pièce de derrière et posai les pieds sur le chambranle. La matraque était lourde sur mes genoux.

— Plus rien que vous et moi, hein, chef Truman, dit Braxton.


En fin d'après-midi, les cumolo-nimbus arrivèrent. La pluie frappa les vitres du poste avec un bruit de caisse claire.

Vers quatre heures je demandai à Braxton ce qu'il voulait pour le dîner. Il avait à peine ouvert la bouche pendant les quatre heures écoulées depuis notre retour de Boston après cinq heures de route.

— Je prendrai un homard.

— Vous pensez à un autre Maine. Essayez encore.

— Steak.

— Steak ? Pourquoi pas un burger ou un sandwich ?

— Je vous l'ai dit : steak.

— D'accord. Steak.

Quand l'Owl livra le repas, je l'apportai derrière et déver-

rouillai la cellule. Comme il n'y avait pas la place pour s'asseoir dans le petit couloir, je tirai ma chaise dans la cellule en face de Braxton assis sur la couchette. Son steak était gris et creux au milieu comme un oreiller récemment abandonné. Il en prit une bouchée et grimaça.

— C'est quoi, ce truc, de l'orignal ou quoi ?

— Ouais, j'aurais probablement dû vous prévenir à propos du steak.

Il continua en silence. Mon dîner était meilleur, un sandwich à la dinde. Je lui proposai d'échanger mais il refusa d'un geste.

— Tu ne crains pas que je me tire ? fit-il en désignant la porte ouverte.

— Non. Où iriez-vous ? Vous êtes dans un trou paumé. En outre, pour l'instant l'endroit probablement le plus sûr pour vous reste cette cellule.

— Peut-être que c'est aussi plus sûr pour toi.

Une conversation pleine de non-dits. Braxton n'avait pas assassiné Bob Danziger. Il le savait, bien entendu, et en partageant mon repas avec lui, je lui faisais comprendre que je le savais aussi. Tous mes commentaires polis étaient porteurs du même message. Que voulez-vous pour le dîner ? Et comment est le steak ? Et le reste était censé faire passer le message suivant : je sais que vous n'avez pas tué Danziger.

— Gittens vient, vous savez, dit Braxton.

— Je m'en doutais.

— Qu'est-ce que tu vas faire ?

— Je ne sais pas.

— Tu ferais bien d'y réfléchir, chef True-Man, parce que Gittens est déjà en route, je te le jure.

— Qu'est-ce que vous feriez, Harold, à ma place ?

— Je ne suis pas à ta place, mec.

— Mais dans ce cas et que Gittens vienne ?

— Je convoquerais mes nègres.

Il se servait du terme avec aisance. Il n'avait aucune signification politique pour lui.

— Je ne peux pas faire ça.

— Tu as des flics. Appelle-les.

— Ce n'est pas si simple.

— Pourquoi pas ?

— Parce que. (Je repérai un endroit poussiéreux par terre.) Ça ne marche pas comme ça.

— Et le grand type ? Appelle-le.

— Kelly ? Non, impossible.

Braxton acquiesça – non parce qu'il comprenait, mais parce qu'il n'avait pas envie de gaspiller sa salive avec un con de flic qui refusait de l'écouter.

— Tu veux que j'appelle les miens, que je les fasse venir ici ? On te couvrira si tu veux.

— Non, Harold. Non, merci.


Le téléphone sonna. Il était près de cinq heures ; la nuit tombait. Le poste de police gémissait sous le vent et la pluie. Je sus avant de décrocher que c'était Martin Gittens.

— Ben ? Il faut qu'on parle, Ben.

— Martin. Qu'on parle de quoi ? Il y a un mandat contre vous. Où êtes-vous ?

— J'ai enquêté. J'ai un truc à vous montrer. De nouvelles preuves.

— De quoi s'agit-il ?

— Oh, je crois que vous devriez le voir vous-même.

Je ne répondis pas. Il y eut un silence sur la ligne.

— Ben, reprit Gittens s'exprimant avec lenteur et patience, Ben, tout ira bien. Mais il faut que nous gardions notre sang-froid. Sang-froid et réflexion. Vous en êtes capable, Ben ?

— Oui. (Ma voix eut un raté. Je m'éclaircis la gorge.) Oui, Martin, j'en suis capable.

— Je le sais. Je vous ai observé, Ben. Vous gardez votre sang-froid depuis un moment, hein ? Réfléchissez maintenant. C'est votre décision : voulez-vous me rencontrer et voir ce que j'ai ou préférez-vous que je parte ?

— Je vous rencontrerai.

Dans la cellule derrière moi, Braxton me lança :

— Le fais pas, mec. N'y va pas.

— Bonne décision. Et si nous nous retrouvions près du lac ? Nous pourrons parler là-bas.

— Le lac ?

— Oui, Ben. Le bungalow de Danziger. Ça vous convient ? Ou est-ce que cela vous ennuie ?

— Non, cela ne m'ennuie pas.

— Bon. Il faut que nous travaillions ensemble, vous et moi. Nous nous ressemblons beaucoup, vous savez.

— Non, c'est faux.

Après un silence, Gittens reprit :

— Venez seul.

Le temps que j'arrive au lac, la lumière était d'une phosphorescence menaçante. La pluie avait cessé et les surfaces luisaient. Avec le recul, je suppose que cet éclat n'était que la lueur de la lune glissant entre les nuages qui avaient commencé à se disperser. Mais là, la lumière nocturne paraissait légèrement miraculeuse. Elle semblait émaner du lac lui-même, jaillir de l'eau pour éclairer le ciel.

À travers le pare-brise, je vis Gittens planté dans le sable compact près de l'eau. Il contemplait le lac, vêtu d'un treillis impeccable et d'un ciré jaune avec un nom de créateur au dos.

À côté de lui se trouvait mon père.

Braxton, assis dans le siège du passager, demanda :

— T'es sûr de vouloir faire ça ?

— Je n'ai pas le choix. C'est mon père qui est avec Gittens.

— Très bien. Je te couvrirai. (Me voyant hésiter, il haussa les épaules.) C'est comme ça.

Ce n'était pas très clair, mais il semblait estimer que la formule expliquait toute la situation.

Braxton et moi descendîmes de la Bronco, et Braxton resta à côté pendant que je rejoignais Gittens et mon père.

Gittens jeta un coup d'œil à Braxton puis se retourna vers le lac, étrangement phosphorescent.

— Je vous ai dit de venir seul.

— Vous m'avez également dit de réfléchir.

Sourire suffisant.

— Je croirais regarder dans une glace.

J'eus un choc en voyant papa. Il vacillait comme s'il risquait à tout moment de s'écrouler raide mort. Des cercles noirs lui creusaient les yeux et ses cheveux détrempés étaient hirsutes. Il avait les mains croisées sur son ventre.

— Enlevez-lui les menottes, dis-je à Gittens.

Gittens s'exécuta sans hésitation et mon père massa ses poignets épais.

— Papa, tu es ivre ?

Il détourna les yeux, gêné.

Je lançai à Gittens, ridicule :

— C'est vous qui l'avez mis dans cet état.

— Non, Ben. Il l'a fait tout seul. Je l'ai trouvé comme ça.

— Papa, qu'est-ce que tu lui as dit ?

Mon père fouilla le sable du regard en quête d'une réponse.

— Claude ? Tu lui as dit quelque chose ?

— Bien sûr que oui, fit Gittens d'un ton apaisant.

— Je ne m'adressais pas à vous ! (J'agrippai mon père par les biceps et le secouai.) Papa ?

— Ça va, intervint Gittens, Ben, calmez-vous. Je le savais déjà.

— Qu'est-ce que vous voulez dire, vous le saviez déjà ?

— Allons, Ben, réfléchissez ! J'avais un avantage : je savais que je n'avais pas tué Danziger. J'étais le seul à pouvoir en être sûr.

Je me sentis pris de vertige. J'examinai Gittens. Des grains de sable adhéraient à ses tennis et au revers de son treillis. La pluie perlait sur son manteau. Lorsqu'il bougea, les gouttes roulèrent sur ses manches.

— Ça va, Ben. restez calme, reprit Gittens.

Il ouvrit son manteau et sortit avec un mouvement de bascule une arme coincée dans sa ceinture.

Lorsqu'il se tourna vers moi, nous fûmes interrompus par un cri :

— Hé !

Braxton s'approcha en pointant une arme sur Gittens.

Gittens prit le pistolet d'un doigt et me le tendit.

— Ça va, Ben. Vous et moi n'avons pas besoin d'armes.

Je pris le lourd pistolet, le gros .38 noir que mon père avait porté pendant des années en qualité de chef de la police.

— L'arme du crime, dit simplement Gittens.

— C'est délirant.

— Si vous le dites, Ben. Nous laisserons les services balistiques confirmer.

Il me vint à l'esprit que je pourrais balancer l'arme dans le lac. Je la vis tournoyer dans l'air, contre le ciel lumineux, fendre l'eau, disparaître.

Gittens se tourna vers Braxton.

— Ça va, Harold. On discute, c'est tout.

Braxton baissa son arme – mon Beretta – et recula d'un pas.

— Longtemps, je n'ai pas réussi à comprendre pourquoi vous vous donniez tant de mal pour suivre cette affaire, pourquoi vous preniez tant de risques. Vous paraissiez trop intelligent pour tenter ainsi le diable. Au début j'ai cru que vous aviez dû tuer Danziger. C'était la seule explication. Mais cela ne tenait pas la route. Vous n'êtes pas un tueur. Et même dans le cas contraire, vous n'auriez pas été aussi négligent. Il m'a fallu du temps pour comprendre : vous protégiez quelqu'un.

— Braxton...

— Non. Harold est trop malin. En plus, il n'en avait pas besoin. Harold et Danziger avaient déjà conclu leur marché.

Dans ma main, le .38 était lourd et encore chaud du contact avec la ceinture de Gittens. J'enveloppai de mes doigts la crosse en plastique pour le plaisir sensuel de sa forme et de ses croisillons en relief.

— Papa, je crois que tu ferais mieux d'y aller. Martin et moi devons parler.

— Je suis désolé, Ben, me dit-il.

Il me regarda, puis me serra contre lui. Son nez contre mon oreille, j'entendis son souffle sortir de ses narines.

— Ça va, papa. (Je lui tapotai le dos pour lui signaler qu'il était temps de nous séparer. Mais il ne lâcha pas prise. Peut-être qu'il ne le pouvait pas.) D'accord, répétai-je.

Il m'enlaçait toujours. Par-dessus son épaule, je vis Braxton planté près de la Bronco qui nous observait.

Cette nuit de septembre – cela pouvait-il ne remonter qu'à six semaines ? on aurait dit une autre vie – mon père avait fait son apparition au poste de police avec une traînée de sang rouge sur sa chemise et son visage. Il paraissait en état de choc. Radoteur, incohérent. Il ne pouvait pas expliquer le sang et, le prenant à tort pour le sien, je le palpai en quête d'une blessure. C'était le sang de Danziger. Papa l'avait tué d'une seule balle de .38.

Devant moi au poste, il répétait la même question et la même réponse :

— Qu'est-ce que j'ai fait ? Je l'ai fait. Qu'est-ce que j'ai fait ? (Et puis :) Ben, qu'est-ce que nous allons faire ?

J'hésitai. Qu'allions-nous faire ?

Danziger. Lors de notre brève conversation, quelques heures avant sa mort, j'avais senti la douceur de Bob Danziger. Il m'avait même plu – sa décence manifeste – même quand il m'avait annoncé qu'il m'inculperait pour le suicide assisté d'Anne Truman.

*Pouvais-je lui dire quelque chose ?* voulait-il savoir. *Quelque chose qui lui permettrait d'atténuer les faits dans son dossier – un flic participant à une euthanasie. Un flic ! Aidez-moi, chef Truman, aidez-moi à comprendre. Je suis venu ici dans l'espoir que vous m'apprendriez quelque chose, que vous me feriez changer d'avis. Si vous n'étiez pas un flic, alors peut-être, peut-être...*

Je lui avais répondu que je n'avais rien à dire, qu'il avait perdu son temps. C'était un problème familial de toute façon.

*Vous savez,* m'avait dit Bob Danziger, *c'est un assassinat, vous comprenez ça ? L'intention est là, toute l'affaire était planifiée. J'ai essayé de le transformer en homicide par imprudence ou sans préméditation, mais je n'arrive pas à trouver un moyen. Les faits ne collent pas.* D'une main, il se frottait la peau sous les yeux. Il avait des taches de rousseur sur le dos de la main. *Parfois ce boulot est insupportable.*

Quelques heures plus tard, Danziger avait disparu.

Et je me retrouvai face à mon père, un filet de sang de Danziger coincé dans ses cheveux.

— Je ne pouvais pas les laisser te prendre, Ben. Pas toi en plus d'Annie. Je ne pouvais pas. Quand j'ai appris, j'ai juste...

Qu'est-ce qu'on fait ?

J'hésitai.

Qu'est-ce que j'allais faire ? Qu'est-ce qu'un fils, policier de surcroît, était censé faire ?

J'hésitai – puis, en une seconde, je pris ma décision.

— Où est l'arme, papa ?

— Je l'ai lâchée par terre.

— Où ?

— Dans le bungalow.

— Papa, il faut qu'on aille la récupérer. Tout de suite, tu m'entends ?

Je n'excuse pas mes actes et je n'excuse certainement pas ceux de mon père. Je ne me sentais tout simplement pas la force

– pas la volonté – d'effacer complètement ma famille. Ma mère était morte, et maintenant un dénommé Danziger venait de mourir à son tour. Je tentai de mettre un terme à la chaîne de souffrance.

Nous nous rendîmes au bungalow, récupérâmes l'arme de papa et verrouillâmes la porte.

Et l'attente commença.

Une heure, une journée, une semaine.

Je ne cessai de retourner dans le bungalow. J'examinais le corps. Je lus les dossiers de Danziger et découvris le mode opératoire du Mission Posse : une balle dans l'œil, exactement comme mon père avait tué Danziger. Une convergence décisive. J'arrangeai un peu la scène, pour que cela ressemble à un assassinat commis par un gang. Je brûlai le dossier concernant la mort de ma mère. Pour retarder la découverte du corps et détruire les papiers qui portaient à présent mes empreintes, une nuit, je plongeai la Honda de Danziger dans le lac.

Puis je fermai le bungalow et attendis. À peine une semaine après, papa se mettait à boire en douce. J'attendais toujours, incertain, j'avais besoin que quelqu'un d'autre trouve le corps pour que rien ne me relie à sa découverte ; en même temps j'espérais qu'on ne le trouverait jamais, j'espérais que sa décomposition détruirait inexorablement le lien de mon père – et le mien – avec lui. Quand je me sentis incapable d'attendre plus longtemps – quand ma paranoïa et la déchéance de papa parurent restreindre le temps dont nous disposions – je « découvris » le corps.

En ma qualité d'étudiant en histoire, je n'aurais pas dû être dupe. Tout historien vous le dira : il n'y a pas de fin à un enchaînement d'événements. Il n'y a pas de cause sans effet, pas d'incident sans conséquences. J'ai essayé de briser cette chaîne de souffrance, mais en vain. Je ne pouvais pas empêcher la douleur de mon père. Seulement la détourner vers les autres.

Les collines de l'autre côté du lac, tapissées de sapins, luisaient dans l'obscurité.

— Nous sommes allés dans un endroit comme ça une fois, dit Gittens, dans le New Hampshire, quand j'étais petit. Un bungalow près d'un lac, toute la famille. Je me souviens d'une petite fille dans un autre bungalow. Environ mon âge, une ravissante

petite blonde en maillot de bain bleu. Elle faisait de la gymnastique sur la plage. Elle avait une démarche élastique, comme si elle risquait à tout instant de se mettre à courir. (Il regarda l'eau.) Vous savez, je n'ai jamais adressé la parole à cette fille.

J'avais du mal à l'écouter. J'avais l'impression de m'effondrer – qu'une structure intérieure finissait par céder et s'écrouler. Ce n'était pas de la peur ; la peur semblait déjà hors de propos, depuis longtemps. Plutôt une sensation d'épuisement. D'acceptation. De capitulation.

Cela dut se lire sur mon visage, ou alors Gittens, avec son instinct pour repérer la faiblesse, le sentit.

— Restez calme, Ben. réfléchissez.

— Qu'est-ce que vous voulez, Gittens ?

Il me regarda, puis fourra une main sous mon manteau et me palpa, en quête d'un micro.

La pluie, jusque-là un brouillard en suspens dans l'air, se remit à tomber. À battre les arbres nus.

— Quel est votre prochain coup, Ben ?

Je ne réagis pas.

— Vous vous êtes gardé une porte de sortie ?

— Je ne vois pas de quoi vous parlez...

— Oh, ça va, Ben, arrêtez ! Vous êtes trop intelligent pour ça.

— Et quelle est votre porte de sortie ?

— J'en ai pas besoin.

— Non ? Franny Boyle va déclarer sous serment que vous avez tué Fasulo et Trudell.

— La crédibilité de Franny est inexistante. Lowery ne procédera pas à une inculpation avec Franny comme seul témoin. En outre, ce qu'a Franny, c'est du ouï-dire – des rumeurs murmurées à son oreille par des morts. Aucune n'est recevable. Vous avez oublié d'être bête, Ben. Allez, réfléchissez.

Mais j'avais l'esprit vide. Pas de sortie, pas d'avenir. Rien que le passé.

— Je peux vous aider, Ben, si vous le voulez bien. Les flics s'entraident. Laissez-moi vous aider.

— M'aider comment ?

— Ben, sans moi, il n'y a pas de preuve. C'est à moi que votre vieux a avoué, je suis le seul à savoir que cette arme dans

votre main est celle du crime. Si je la boucle, on n'a rien contre votre vieux. Ou vous.

— Qu'advient-il de l'affaire Danziger ? Ils vont avoir besoin d'un coupable.

— Braxton.

— Ils ne le goberont jamais. Danziger avait conclu un marché avec lui.

— Ils goberont ce que je leur vends. Surtout si vous me soutenez, si nous collaborons.

— Mais...

— Laissez Braxton payer, Ben, pour tout. Il l'a bien cherché. Il a déjà fait suffisamment de mal comme ça. Ce n'est que justice. Braxton ne fait pas partie des gentils, Ben. Nous sommes les gentils. Souvenez-vous-en. Laissez-moi lui parler. Il avouera les deux...

— Avouera ? Il n'a rien...

— Il avouera ! Il avouera, et puis il m'agressera comme il l'a fait avec vous la semaine dernière. Il s'emparera de mon arme et le coup partira.

— C'est un meurtre.

— Non, c'est la chose à faire. Il faut que nous fassions ce qui est nécessaire, Ben.

Je secouai la tête.

— Je ne peux pas.

— Vous n'avez rien à faire. Laissez-moi juste le sale boulot.

Je fus incapable de répondre.

— Ben, il n'y a pas d'autre moyen. Si je pars d'ici, votre vieux purge une condamnation à vie sans remise de peine. Ils vous feront payer aussi, pour obstruction. Laissez-moi vous aider. Vous n'avez pas les idées claires, là.

— Qu'est-ce que cela vous apporte, Gittens ?

Il haussa les épaules.

— Vous vous débarrassez de Braxton, continuai-je. C'est le seul qui reste qui puisse vous porter préjudice. Voilà pourquoi Danziger tenait tant à l'avoir. Vous avez tuyauté Braxton cette nuit-là. Il est le témoin qui peut vous situer derrière cette porte rouge.

D'un hochement de tête, Gittens demanda le .38 que je tenais. Je le lui tendis, l'esprit lent et embrumé.

— Ben, ce que je vous propose, c'est la seule porte de sortie. Prenez-la.

Je fixai le lac, avec sa phosphorescence lunaire et sa bordure sombre de collines.

— Prenez-la, insista Gittens.

Je fis non de la tête.

Gittens lâcha un soupir contrarié.

— Ne faites pas ça, Ben. C'est ce qu'on fait après échec et mat qui compte. Il faut que nous nous fassions confiance.

— C'est ce que vous avez dit à Artie Trudell ?

Il y eut un silence. La pluie martelait la surface du lac.

Il soupesa le .38 dans sa main, puis le glissa dans sa ceinture.

— C'est un sacré choix que vous faites, Ben. C'est de votre père qu'il est question.

Je regardai mon père, debout avec Braxton près de la Bronco. Le Chef. Ratatiné, trempé jusqu'aux os, tout petit.

Ce qui s'est passé ensuite, je ne me le rappelle pas clairement. Cela me revient par éclairs : mon bras qui s'abaisse, un souffle jaillissant de ma bouche, la vibration dans ma paume. En revanche les sons restent nets : le boom de la matraque de John Kelly sur le crâne de Gittens, un bruit creux comme le sabot d'un cheval sur les pavés ; puis le corps de Gittens tombant lourdement sur le sable.

La matraque rebondit du crâne de Gittens avec une telle force que je la lâchai. Elle tournoya au-dessus de mon épaule et atterrit par terre.

Il n'y eut pas de sang au début. Le corps gisait à plat ventre, immobile.

Levant les yeux, je vis Braxton et mon père accourir, puis me retournai vers le lac et l'éclat de l'eau me frappa de nouveau.

Le corps bougea. Ses jambes pédalèrent lentement sur le sable.

Braxton et mon père le fixaient.

— C'est la seule solution, leur dis-je.

Mon père me regarda. Les traits décomposés, la bouche entrouverte.

— C'est la seule solution.

J'entendis ma voix – si maître de soi, si calme – et j'en fus

surpris. J'étais tout sauf calme. Quelque chose venait de se déchaîner en moi, une sorte de folle énergie que je ne pouvais ni ne voulais maîtriser. Je cherchai la matraque du regard. Où était-elle ? Je l'avais entendue heurter le sable – je l'avais entendue !

Gittens grogna et tenta de se redresser sur les genoux.

Je cherchai de nouveau la matraque. Où était-elle, bordel ? Il me la fallait maintenant !

Gittens se traîna vers le lac avec un grognement indistinct. Il avait du sang criblé de grains de sable dans les cheveux.

— Qu'est-ce qu'on fait ? demandai-je à mon père.

Il ne répondit pas. Il me regarda en clignant les yeux, les sourcils froncés. Des plis creusaient sa peau autour de sa bouche, de tristes petites poches se formaient sous ses yeux et la pluie ruisselait sur son visage.

J'étais incapable de le regarder. Je me tournai vers Braxton :

— Alors ?

Braxton désigna du menton Gittens qui tentait de se mettre à quatre pattes.

— Vous voulez que je le fasse ?

Je lui dis que non.

Gittens se mit à ramper. Il avait les avant-bras dans l'eau maintenant.

— C'est ce qu'il faut faire, dit Braxton.

Je m'approchai de Gittens, lui passai les bras autour du torse et le lâchai dans l'eau peu profonde. Le froid le ranima. Il poussa des bras pour soulever sa tête et ses épaules. Le lac n'était profond que d'une trentaine de centimètres à cet endroit. La main droite sur le haut de son crâne, je l'aplatis dans l'onde. Il se libéra la tête et haleta, se débattant comme un fou. Son imperméable jaune luisait. Mes mains lui entourèrent le crâne, les doigts sur ses oreilles, les pouces pressant contre l'occiput, la petite corne osseuse à l'arrière du crâne, je lui maintins le visage sous la surface du lac. Un petit hululement jaillit en bulles de l'eau. Qui domina le bruit de ses efforts. Haut perché, comme les pleurs d'un bébé. Le pire son que j'aie jamais entendu.

# Épilogue

Près d'un an s'est écoulé depuis cette nuit près du lac. Un an depuis que j'ai décidé de mettre ces événements noir sur blanc, pour comprendre le comment et le pourquoi. Pour faire mes aveux.

Vous avez sans aucun doute envie de connaître la fin de l'histoire. Les détails. La vérité, toute la vérité, rien que la vérité, comme disent les juristes. Vous voulez des réponses. D'accord.

On a retrouvé le corps de Martin Gittens dans le port de Boston, submergé dans la boue devant Battery Point dans les Flats. Le rapport du coroner notait que ses poumons étaient pleins d'eau douce, non du liquide saumâtre du port. Mais personne ne parut trop se formaliser de cette incohérence, pas après que les rumeurs commencèrent à circuler – des rumeurs de la propre histoire de Gittens, de Fasulo et de Trudell et, oui, Bob Danziger. Une fois que tout le monde – procureurs, journalistes et bons citoyens – eut atteint l'accord tacite que Gittens avait commis tous ces meurtres, la propre noyade de l'inspecteur parut une affaire moins urgente. Justice rudimentaire et tout cela. Valait mieux ne pas y regarder de trop près. Cela reste, techniquement, une enquête ouverte. Un cas en attente.

On soupçonna brièvement Harold Braxton du meurtre de Gittens, jusqu'à ce qu'on révèle qu'il se trouvait en détention à Versailles, Maine, à l'époque. Si quelqu'un s'était soucié de vérifier la cellule à Versailles cette nuit-là, il l'aurait trouvée vide. Braxton et le chef Truman étaient tous les deux absents et ils ne donnèrent pas de nouvelles avant l'aube. Mais personne ne véri-

fia. Et personne ne remarqua la moquette détrempée à l'arrière de la Bronco, où nous installâmes le corps de Gittens sous une couverture pour son ultime retour à Boston. Quant au meurtre de Danziger, toutes les accusations contre Braxton furent abandonnées dans les deux semaines et, pour ce que j'en sais, Braxton s'est volatilisé, avec Ed Kurth lancé à sa poursuite telles les Furies.

Andrew Lowery est toujours le procureur général du comté du Sussex et sera sans aucun doute maire de Boston un jour. Et un excellent, en plus.

Quant à John Kelly, sa vieille matraque repose sur mon bureau alors que j'écris. Mais Kelly est mort. Heurté par-derrière par un chauffeur ivre alors qu'il faisait la queue à un péage sur l'autoroute du New Hampshire. Le chauffeur, dix-sept ans, avait trois grammes d'alcool dans le sang d'après l'alcootest. Il s'en est sorti indemne. Kelly a été enterré auprès de sa femme et de sa fille, Theresa Rose, éternellement âgée de dix ans.

J'ai accompagné Caroline aux funérailles par un froid matin bruineux. Un changement perceptible se peignait sur son visage ce jour-là, une perplexité à vif. C'était déconcertant de la voir aussi secouée, mais je comprenais. Elle ne s'était pas attendue à la mort de son père, ne l'avait pas cru capable de mourir. Je connaissais la sensation – la terreur égoïste qui imprègne le deuil – parce que j'avais vécu avec pendant près d'une année.

J'ai vu Caroline à de nombreuses reprises depuis. Je ne sais pas ce qui va en ressortir à part une note de téléphone astronomique et quelques kilomètres de plus au compteur de ma vieille Saab. Pour l'instant, cela me suffit de la rejoindre et d'être avec elle. Caroline cuisine ; j'emmène Charlie à des matchs des Red Sox. Je me suis pratiquement trouvé un foyer.

Au cours de l'une de ces visites, Caroline m'offrit un cadeau : un sac en plastique thermosoudé contenant le verre du Ritz-Carlton. Le verre était couvert de mes empreintes à la ninhydrine.

— Casse-le.

Je lui expliquai que je ne le pouvais pas. C'était le dernier objet que ma mère avait touché.

— Casse-le, répéta-t-elle.

Je n'en ai jamais rien fait.

Il est bien sûr des secrets que je n'ai pas partagés avec Caroline – des secrets de famille concernant le côté dingue des

Truman, et notre rôle dans la mort de Bob Danziger et de Martin Gittens. Je ne lui ai jamais confié que je sens encore le cuir chevelu de Gittens bouger sous mes doigts, que j'entends encore ce cri étouffé par l'eau qu'il a poussé. Je sais que je ne peux avoir Caroline tant que je garde mon secret ; en même temps je ne peux pas lui avouer la vérité et espérer d'elle qu'elle reste. Mais comme je ne suis pas encore prêt à la voir partir, je me tais.

En août, Caroline et Charlie sont enfin venus à Versailles et nous avons loué un bungalow au bord du lac. Caroline s'est amourachée du lac comme ma mère l'avait fait. Quand elle nageait, j'avais l'impression que le lac lui ouvrait les bras, l'accueillait en son sein. Et je revoyais le film tressautant de ma mère enceinte allongée sur sa bouée et disant à la caméra : « Bonjour, Ben... » À la fin de cette semaine-là, je me rappelle Caroline dans l'eau jusqu'aux genoux, les poings sur les hanches, admirant la vue. Des ronds concentriques dans l'eau, des collines, des nuages.

— C'est joli ici, dit-elle. Tout est si propre, si net.

— Nous avons besoin de procureurs ici aussi, tu sais.

— Oui, Ben, a-t-elle fait en riant. J'aurai l'impression de vivre sur Mars.

— C'est déjà un début.

Mon père ? La tache du meurtre de Danziger ne l'a pas quitté. Il a réussi à arrêter de boire, mais son cœur lui a causé des ennuis. Au printemps, il me demanda de lui confier un travail de bénévole au poste pour s'occuper. « Je réglerai la circulation, je remplirai des paperasses, n'importe quoi. » Je lui répondis non. D'un ton moralisateur, je lui dis que le meurtre n'était pas la fin de sa vie, mais qu'il le rendait inapte à un travail de police. Un moment de grande hypocrisie et finalement je cédai et l'autorisai à traîner au poste. Mais au bout de quelques jours il cessa de venir. En juin, il partit s'installer dans une ville voisine. L'exil du Chef suscita beaucoup de perplexité à Versailles. Les gens se dirent qu'il avait dû mourir un peu à la disparition de sa femme, comme il arrive souvent aux conjoints. Une erreur d'interprétation que je ne corrigeai pas. Je ne sais pas s'il est possible pour papa de trouver le pardon pour ce qu'il a fait. Mais je pense qu'il surmontera ses problèmes et poursuivra sa vie. C'est la manière Truman.

Et moi. Je suis toujours le chef de Versailles, bien que je ne sache pas combien de temps je vais encore y rester. La ville mérite mieux. En attendant, j'ai pris l'habitude de faire des rondes, comme John Kelly m'y avait encouragé, bien qu'on ne puisse arpenter que Central Street dans cette ville et ce n'est pas long. Je fais ça deux fois par jour, quotidiennement, en m'arrêtant pour bavarder à l'Owl, chez McCarron et au bazar. Un temps j'ai emporté la matraque de Kelly dans ces rondes. Je l'ai même fait tourner, du moins j'ai essayé. Si vous la portez correctement, disait Kelly – si vous vous tenez bien – vous n'aurez jamais à l'utiliser. C'est un peu de sagesse policière à laquelle j'avais envie de m'accrocher, mais je ne pouvais plus y croire. Pas avec le souvenir de la tête de Gittens entre mes mains, pas avec ses mouvements désordonnés entre mes jambes dans trente centimètres d'eau. Non, je ne prends plus la matraque. Je la laisse posée sur mon bureau ou rangée dans un tiroir. Peut-être que je la donnerai à Caroline. Ou à Charlie. Je ne veux pas l'avoir sous les yeux.

Voilà donc les détails, les « faits ». C'est ainsi que se termine l'histoire.

Mais l'histoire ne se termine jamais, n'est-ce pas ? L'histoire avec un H majuscule – cette vague de succession d'incidents, propulsés par des courants de hasard, de chance et de coïncidence – coule sans se soucier des débuts et des fins. La seule véritable fin est l'instant présent, le bouillonnement de la vague qui avance.

Revenons-en au présent. Alors que j'écris ces lignes, nous sommes en septembre. Les intérimaires de l'été sont tous partis reprendre leurs jobs d'hiver et le personnel du poste se résume à Dick et moi. Vidée de ses estivants, Versailles a retrouvé sa population de plusieurs centaines d'habitants. C'est de nouveau la saison des feuilles, mais ce n'est pas un problème. Les amateurs de feuillages multicolores sont des gens plus âgés que les touristes de l'été et ils sont généralement charmants, même les gens des plaines du Taxachusetts. C'est une période calme.

Je suis au poste, seul à mon bureau. C'est le crépuscule mais je n'ai pas encore allumé. La pénombre a quelque chose de confortable.

Dès que j'en aurai terminé ici, je descendrai au lac pour nager. C'est la meilleure époque de l'année, affirmait toujours

ma mère. Le soir, l'air est frais, mais l'eau reste chaude après un été au soleil. En fait, les températures de l'air et de l'eau sont suffisamment proches pour créer une illusion : quand on nage la nuit, il arrive qu'on ne sache plus faire la différence entre l'air et l'eau et dans le noir, on a une sensation de gravité zéro, d'apesanteur. En me rendant au lac, je passerai devant l'endroit où se dressait le bungalow de Bob Danziger. (Le bungalow a été rasé, non pour des raisons d'hygiène mais parce qu'on le jugeait impossible à louer. Je me gare parfois à cet endroit-là.) Je laisserai mes vêtements dans la Bronco et entrerai directement dans l'eau, je la laisserai m'envelopper, et je nagerai jusqu'au centre du lac, là où il est le plus profond.

## Note de l'auteur

Tous les Bostoniens vous le diront, il n'existe pas de quartier du nom de Mission Flats dans leur ville. Pas plus qu'un Versailles dans le Maine, à ma connaissance. Lorsqu'il est fait mention d'endroits réels, j'ai joyeusement modifié les détails chaque fois que c'était nécessaire, selon les besoins de la fiction. Pour le reste, l'avertissement habituel s'applique : les incidents et les personnages décrits ici ne sont que le produit de l'imagination de l'auteur.

La photocomposition de cet ouvrage
a été réalisée par
GRAPHIC HAINAUT
59163 Condé-sur-l'Escaut

**Transcontinental**
IMPRESSION
IMPRIMERIE GAGNÉ

IMPRIMÉ AU CANADA